D1387200

The A.C.E. Spelling Dictionary

Find words quickly
and
improve your spelling

The A.C.E. Spelling Dictionary
By David Moseley and Catherine Nicol

Acknowledgements

The authors would like to thank all those who took part in the field trials in England, Northern Ireland, Scotland and Wales. Special thanks are due to Ronald Beresford for his expert phonetic advice and to George Macbride for helping us to meet the needs of Scottish users.

Learning Development Aids
Duke Street
Wisbech
Cambs. PE13 2AE
England

The A.C.E. Spelling Dictionary
LD425
© David Moseley & Catherine Nicol

First Published 1986
Second Edition 1986
Third Edition 1987
Fourth Edition 1988
Fifth Edition 1989

All rights reserved. No part of this publication
may be reproduced without the prior permission of
the publisher.

ISBN 0 905 114 16 7

Printed in Great Britain by
Ebenezer Baylis & Son Ltd
The Trinity Press, Worcester and London

CONTENTS

INTRODUCTION

This spelling dictionary is designed for writers of all ages. It is intended for both school and home use. It is easy to use, even if you find spelling difficult. You will soon be able to find any word you need in just a few seconds. All you have to do is to look at the index, turn to the page you need and then scan down a single column.

The index gives the alphabet across the page and is the key to the different sections. Within each section the words are arranged in alphabetical order. Once you have understood how to use the index, you should never again have to ask someone else how to spell a word. Later, when you know where the different sections are, you will be able to do without the index and find words even more quickly.

Before starting to use the dictionary it is important to understand what you have to do. The first two sections of this introduction should be studied carefully; and you should practise looking up the words given as examples. Children may need an adult to help them at this stage. Perhaps the most important thing to understand is that you have to *listen* to the way you say a word. Try to think not of vowel letters but of vowel sounds.

English spelling does not obey simple rules. Although a proportion of words can be called 'regular', there are very many exceptions and uncommon patterns. The vowel sounds present the biggest problem. There are more than two hundred different vowel spellings associated with the eighteen basic English vowel sounds. This can cause delay and frustration when looking up words in an ordinary dictionary. The vowel sound classification used in this Aurally Coded English dictionary is, however, an efficient and powerful aid. You will be able to find words very quickly, as most columns are short. Every time you look down a column for a word you will see how different written symbols are used to represent the same spoken sound.

This ACE dictionary consists of three main parts, each including five or six sections. All the words in a section have the same or nearly the same vowel sound. Vowel sounds are made with the voice, with the mouth open.

The first five sections of 'short' vowel sounds are printed on white paper. These sounds, as a rule, are the ones taught at school:

PART 1   a   as in cat
          e   as in elephant
          i   as in pig
          o   as in dog
          u   as in duck   & oo   as in woodpecker

The 'alphabet-name' vowel sounds are printed on blue paper. These are 'long' vowel sounds:

PART 2   ae   as in snail
          ee   as in eagle
          ie   as in lion
          oe   as in goat
          ue   as in newt   & oo   as in smooth

The last six sections include spellings with the letter 'r' and two double sounds. These are printed on white paper and are also 'long' vowel sounds:

PART 3   ar   as in shark
          air   as in bear
          er   as in worm
          or   as in horse
          oi   as in oyster
          ou   as in owl

As this is a spelling dictionary, word meanings are given only if two or more words sound the same or nearly the same. However, using the ACE dictionary to look up spellings will make it easier for you to use other dictionaries for looking up meanings. It should also improve your spelling. You will think of long words as made up of smaller parts, often corresponding to spoken syllables. As you become more aware of the common patterns, unusual spellings will stand out from the others and hold your attention. It is a good idea to write down unusual spellings in a personal spelling book, noting the 'tricky' part or parts and using the 'look-cover-write-check' routine.

HOW TO USE THE SPELLING DICTIONARY

The 60 Second Guide

HOW TO USE THE DICTIONARY

To find a word in the dictionary you have to do two things:

(1) pick out the first strong or the first clear vowel sound
(2) decide on what you think is the first letter in the word

The index tells you where to find any one of 16,000 words. You will soon be able to link each vowel sound with its spelling symbol. The animal pictures and the word examples will help you to do this. A word will nearly always be where you think it is, even if you are wrong about the first letter. Sometimes you have to turn over to the next page and sometimes you will be asked to look on another page.

When you have turned to the right page, you only have to run down one of the columns. So, if you are looking for the word 'sub-mar-ine' on page 130 you look in the column of three-syllable words. The number of stars at the top of the column is the same as the number of syllables. Every syllable contains a vowel sound, and you can tell how many syllables are in a word if you say it slowly and tap at the same time. This rhyme may help:

> "One tap for 'fun'
> And two for 'be-gun'
> Three taps for 'sta-di-um'
> And four for 'gym-na-si-um'."

Longer words containing four or more syllables are to be found on the right hand side of each page. The longest word in the dictionary has eight syllables.

This is the full routine

TO LOOK UP   submarine

SAY 'sub . . .' ⟩	SAY 'u' ⟩	GO TO INDEX ⟩
Say the first syllable. Say it really slowly. Find the vowel sound.	Say the vowel sound on its own.	See pages x-xi or the separate sheet.

FIND u (as in duck) ⟩	FIND S ⟩	IT'S PAGE 130! ⟩
Find the spelling symbol for the vowel sound, at one side of the index page.	Scan through the alphabet across the page for the first letter in the word.	Find this with one finger, while pointing at the letter S.

P. 130 IS IN PART 1 ⟩	OPEN BOOK IN PART 1 ⟩	FIND PAGE 130 ⟩
This part contains words with 'short' vowel sounds, printed on white paper.	u is the last sound in Part 1.	All pages with even numbers are on the left hand side.

TAP OUT sub-ma-rine TAP-TAP-TAP ⟩	LOOK UNDER * * * ⟩	 DIRECT HIT!
Say the word slowly and tap out the syllables.	You won't have to turn to the next page this time!	

This is the basic routine:

TO LOOK UP   rhinoceros

SAY 'rhi . . .' ⟩

SAY 'ie' ⟩

GO TO INDEX ⟩

FIND ie (as in lion) ⟩

FIND R ⟩

IT'S PAGE 189! ⟩

PAGE 189 is in Part 2 ⟩

OPEN BOOK IN PART 2 ⟩

FIND PAGE 189 ⟩

TAP OUT rhi-no-ce-ros TAP-TAP-TAP-TAP ⟩

LOOK UNDER **** ⟩

GOT IT!

Now try it yourself!

Here are some more words for you to find, using the basic routine. Start by saying the word quite normally, not by 'sounding out'. The vowel sounds are given for you in these practice examples:

monster	(SHORT o)
friend	(SHORT e)
bicycle	(LONG ie)
noise	(LONG oi)
accident	(SHORT a)
fright	(LONG ie)
multiplication	(SHORT u)
fortune	(LONG or)
squirrel	(SHORT i)
nose	(LONG oe)
beautiful	(LONG ue)
name	(LONG ae)
farther	(LONG ar)
burglary	(LONG er)
hour	(LONG ou)
hairdresser	(LONG air)

Neutral vowel sounds

If you find it hard to tell which is the first strong vowel sound in a word, take the first one you can hear clearly, as long as it is in the first or second syllable. Suppose you want to look up 'supposed'. Here the strong vowel sound is the 'oe' sound in the second syllable, and the word is under 'S' on page 207. However, if you pick out the 'u' sound, you will find the word on page 132, after the other words in the 'neutral vowel' box. So, if you cannot see a word where you think it should be, see if it is in a neutral vowel box. You will soon notice that neutral vowels sound rather like a quiet grunt. They are never strong sounds.

Listen to the way you pronounce 'balloon', for example:

| SAY 'ba . . . .' > | SAY 'a' > | A NEUTRAL SOUND! > |

Start to say the word, at a normal speed.

You can hardly hear this sound in the word.

It's not like the a sound in cat.

So, to find 'balloon' in the dictionary, listen for the strong vowel sound (in the second syllable):

| SAY 'balloo . .' > | SAY 'oo' > | GO TO INDEX > |

In all of the following words the strong vowel sound is in the second syllable, but you will probably succeed in finding the words all the same if you try to identify the letters used for the neutral vowel sound. However, as neutral vowels all sound much the same it is easier to go by the strong vowel.

WORD	STRONG VOWEL	WORD	STRONG VOWEL
above	SHORT u	guitar	LONG ar
absurd	LONG er	infectious	SHORT e
advertisement	LONG er	laboratory	SHORT o
amazing	LONG ae	magician	SHORT i
apart	LONG ar	manouevre	LONG oo
appearance	LONG ee	observer	LONG er
appendicitis	SHORT e	occurred	LONG er
applause	LONG or	opponent	LONG oe
approach	LONG oe	particular	SHORT i
association	LONG oe	performer	LONG or
because	SHORT o	pollution	LONG oo
before	LONG or	position	SHORT i
circumference	SHORT u	potatoes	LONG ae
collection	SHORT e	prepared	LONG air
collision	SHORT i	production	SHORT u
conceited	LONG ee	remarkable	LONG ar
conclusion	LONG oo	remain	LONG ae
conductor	SHORT u	report	LONG or
confetti	SHORT e	request	SHORT e
describing	LONG ie	revenge	SHORT e
deserve	LONG er	reverse	LONG er
despair	LONG air	surrender	SHORT e
destroy	LONG oi	surroundings	LONG ou
discuss	SHORT u	survivor	LONG ie
disgusting	SHORT u	tonight	LONG ie
effect	SHORT e	towards	LONG or
emotional	LONG oe	trapeze	LONG ee
encouragement	SHORT u	tremendous	SHORT e
enough	SHORT u	velocity	SHORT o
exhaust	LONG or	vocabulary	SHORT a

GETTING THE MOST OUT OF THE DICTIONARY

Looking up words in order to spell them correctly is only one way of using the ACE Dictionary. Other ways of using it can be just as valuable and can help to increase your speed of word-recognition as well as your knowledge about words. You can do this by timing yourself as you look for words of a certain type. You might like to work with someone else and take turns in looking up words. The words can be chosen by topic, by use, by length, by stress pattern, by sound, by features of spelling or by grammatical function. It can also be fun to think of combinations of these – for example, to find as many long words as possible that can be used to express enjoyment of food, picking out only those where the stress is (greedily) placed on the first syllable.

The authors hope that many more ideas for actively exploring the dictionary will be thought of by those who use it. What is provided here is a more detailed account of some of the rules that have been followed by the authors, especially those that relate to alphabetical order and to the inclusion of different forms of the same word. You do not need to understand all of these before you start to use the dictionary, but you may need to refer to them at times and they may also suggest some useful activities.

Alphabetic grouping of words

Within each section, words are grouped by initial letter, taken in alphabetical order. A letter is omitted if there are no words beginning with it in that section.

Within each column of words, there are smaller sets, each beginning with the same two letters. This makes the columns easier to scan, and cuts down word search time. It does not take long to learn that 'sc' is near the top of a column of words beginning with S, that 'sm' is about half way down and that 'sw' is near the bottom.

Some words are entered in more than one place. This happens when the first sound in the word does not uniquely determine what is the first letter. For example, words beginning with a silent letter (like 'knife' and 'gnome') are entered according to initial sound as well as spelling. Words like 'ceiling' and 'chassis' are entered under both S and C. Words like 'kangaroo' and 'karate' are entered under C and well as under K. Smaller print is used for double-entered words when they begin with a different letter from the rest of the words in a column.

In certain cases, cross-reference pointers are used instead of double or multiple entries. A cross-reference is always provided from K to C within the same section, instead of repeating a long list of C words under K. Dropped H's, confusion between initial E and I and between F and TH as well as uncertainty about the spelling of words beginning with QU are also taken care of by the use of cross-reference pointers.

Meaning

In cases where two words sound the same (or nearly the same) but have different meanings, you need to check that you have found the right word. All such words have an asterisk (*) against them and their meanings are given in brackets. These words are called homonyms (words with the same sound but with different meanings). Some of them are also homographs (words with the same spelling but with different meanings).

If the meaning or meanings do not fit the word you are looking for, all you have to do is to try another similarly-sounding word with an asterisk against it.

Plurals

If the plural form of a noun is not shown, it is safe to assume that you simply add an 's'. So, if you find 'journey', you will be able to spell 'journeys'.

All 'es' and '-ies' plurals are shown, for example 'box(es)' and 'baby(-ies)'. Where, as in 'baby(-ies)' there is a dash before the ending, it means that part of the word has to be removed before the plural ending is added. The most common pattern is for a final 'y' to be removed before adding '-ies'. Irregular forms such as 'calves' are treated in a similar way: 'calf(-ves)'.

Present participles

These are given for the more common words and in all cases where a final consonant is doubled before 'ing' is added (for example, 'swim' and 'swimming').

When the present participle form (ending in 'ing') is not given, you can be sure that the spelling falls into one of two patterns:

(a) for words not ending in 'e', add 'ing'
(b) for words ending in 'e', remove the 'e' before adding 'ing'.

Past tenses

The past tense form is given for the more common words and whenever a final consonant is doubled before 'ed' is added (for example, 'skid' and 'skidded').

In all words where the final 'ed' has the sound 't' (as in 'ticked') the ending is given in brackets: tick(ed).

All irregular past tense forms are given in full. They are entered in the appropriate sections, but are also included, enclosed in square brackets, immediately below the corresponding present tense form:

bring   buy
[brought]   [bought]

Comparatives and superlatives

These are given in full for the more common words and whenever a final consonant is doubled (as in 'bigger' and 'biggest'). Where a final 'y' is changed to '-ier' or to '-iest' this is also always shown (for example, 'saucy(-ier, -iest)'.

If you cannot find a particular word with the ending 'er' or 'est', you can be sure that the spelling falls into one of two patterns:

(a) for words not ending in 'e', add 'er' or 'est'
(b) for words ending in 'e', remove the 'e' before adding 'er' or 'est'.

DIALECTS

The vowel sound sections are based on 'BBC' pronunciation, but regional differences have been taken into account. Particular care has been taken to make the dictionary suitable for use in Scotland. Trials have taken place throughout the British Isles and wherever systematic shifts in the pronunciation of vowels have been noted, words have been entered in more than one section. Wherever a dash appears next to a word it means that for some speakers the word is pronounced with the same vowel sound as the other words in the section.

In the 'a' section words pronounced in a 'BBC' accent with an 'ar' sound have a dash against them. These words are pronounced with an 'a' in Scotland, and in most cases in the north of England. In the 'o' section the words with a dash against them belong there only for Scottish speakers. In the short vowel 'u' and 'oo' section, two 'BBC' sounds have been put together, with a dash against the 'oo' sound words. In the north of England there may be no difference in pronunciation between the two groups. In the section containing words with the long 'oo' sound, the words with a dash against them belong there only for Scottish speakers. In parts of the Midlands the sounds 'air' and 'er' are pronounced in the same way. The 'air' words therefore also entered in the 'er' section, a feature which also makes sense for some of the words as pronounced in Scotland.

A major feature of Scottish speech is the rolled 'r' following a vowel. This has important implications for Scottish users of the dictionary, since the 'BBC' ar, air, er and or sounds are pronounced differently in Scotland. 'Thistle-sign' cross-reference pointers are used in the appropriate sections, but these will not be needed if users learn to refer to the third part of the book for words with vowels followed by an 'r'. This applies for all of the short vowels, and for the long vowels ae and oe. It does not, however, apply for the long vowels ee, ie and ue.

The following table is provided for the benefit of Scottish users:

WORDS WITH	SECTION	EXAMPLES
SHORT a followed by 'r'	ar	shark, article
SHORT e followed by 'r'	er	early, nervous
SHORT i followed by 'r'	er	bird, firmly
SHORT o followed by 'r'	or	horse, warning
SHORT u followed by 'r'	er	hurt, worm
LONG ae followed by 'r'	air	rare, airport
LONG ee followed by 'r'	ee	clear, steer
LONG ie followed by 'r'	ie	wire, tyre
LONG oe followed by 'r'	or	hoarse, bored
LONG ue/oo followed by 'r'	ue/oo	pure, poor

HOW THE WORDS WERE CHOSEN

Both British and American sources have been used in compiling the ACE Spelling Dictionary. Also, words have been added as a result of field trials in which users kept records of words they needed but were unable to find.

When work started in 1967 on the first version of the ACE Dictionary, the two main sources of vocabulary were 'Words Your Children Use' by Edwards and Gibbon and Schonell's Essential Spelling List. Later, words were added from the Thornike—Lorge list and from the adult reading vocabulary list of Kucera and Francis. However, the most recent and comprehensive source is the American Heritage Word Frequency Book. This contains no fewer than 86,741 words types (words and word forms) from books used in schools by children in the age-range 8 to 14. The complete range of school subjects is covered.

Unless they were judged to be unfamiliar to British users, all words (but not all word forms) occurring in the first 23,000 word types of the American Heritage list are included in the ACE Dictionary. This is equivalent to excluding words only if they are used less than once in every 2,000,000 words of text. As explained above, plurals, present participles, past tense forms, comparatives and superlatives have not always been included if they are straightforward to spell.

In order to meet the needs of British students, the authors have also included lists supplied by subject teachers for all areas of the curriculum. Particular care has been taken to cover scientific, technical and mathematical vocabulary. The Evans Technical Dictionary and a list of mathematical terms published by the Scottish Examination Board are among the sources used.

A list of the publications from which words have been taken is given below:

Carroll, J. B., Davies, P. and Richman, B. (1971) *The American Heritage Word Frequency Book*. Boston, Houghton Mifflin.

Edwards, R. P. A. and Gibbon, V. (1964) *Words Your Children Use*. London, Burke.

Evans Technical Dictionary. (1982) London, Evans.

Kucera, H. and Francis, W. N. (1967) *Computational Analysis of Present-Day American English*. Providence, Brown University Press.

Schonell, F. J. (1932) *The Essential Spelling List*. London, Macmillan.

Scottish Examination Board (1984). Scottish Certificate of Education, Standard Grade.

Arrangements in Mathematics for Foundation, General and Credit Levels in and after 1986.

INDEX

Permission to photocopy

© LDA

	N	O	P	Q	R	S	T	U	V	W	X	Y	Z		
a	21	--	22	24	24	25	28	--	29	30	--	30	30	**a**	ACTIVE CAT
e	45	45	46	47	48	50	52	53	53	54	54	55	55	**e**	HEALTHY ELEPHANT
i	81	81	82	83	84	87	90	91	91	92	--	--	93	**i**	BIG PIGLET
o	105	106	108	109	110	111	113	113	114	114	---	115	115	**o**	WATCHFUL DOG
u oo	127	127	128	---	129	130	133	134	136	136	---	136	---	**u oo**	DUCK AND WOODPECKER

	N	O	P	Q	R	S	T	U	V	W	X	Y	Z		
ae	146	147	147	148	148	149	151	---	151	152	---	152	---	**ae**	BABY SNAIL
ee	165	165	166	167	167	169	172	---	173	174	---	175	175	**ee**	BREEDING EAGLE
ie	187	187	188	189	189	190	192	---	193	193	194	---	194	**ie**	LIVELY LION
oe	202	203	204	206	206	207	208	---	208	209	---	209	209	**oe**	LONELY GOAT
ue oo	218	218	219	219	220	221	222	223	223	223	---	224	224	**ue oo**	SMOOTH NEWT

	N	O	P	Q	R	S	T	U	V	W	X	Y	Z		
ar	232	---	233	---	233	234	235	---	235	---	---	235	235	**ar**	BASKING SHARK
air	---	---	239	---	240	240	241	---	241	241	---	---	---	**air**	RARE BEAR
er	249	249	250	251	251	252	253	254	254	255	---	255	---	**er**	EARLY BIRD WITH WORM
or	263	264	265	266	266	267	268	---	268	269	---	269	---	**or**	WARLIKE HORSE
oi	273	273	274	274	274	275	275	---	275	---	---	---	---	**oi**	OYSTER-CATCHER
ou	281	281	282	---	282	283	283	---	284	284	---	---	---	**ou**	AN OWL SOUND

Permission to photocopy

© LDA

A

*

act

add
*adds (does add)
*adze (tool)

-aft

*-alms (gift to
   charity)
Alps

am

an
and
*ant (insect)

apt

as
ash(es)
-ask(ed)
ass(es)

at

-aunt (relative)

axe(d)

for H . . .
see page 16

* *

-aardvark
abbess(es)
abbey
abbot
absence
absent
abstract

accent
access(ed)
acid
acrid
acted
acting
action
active
actor
actress(es)
actual(ly)

adapt
added
addend
adder
addict
adding
adult
-advance(d)
advent
adverb
adverse

affix(es)
Afghan
-after

-aghast
agile

alas
album
alcove
algae
Allah
alley
alloy(ed)
ally(-ies)
  (allied)
-almond
alpha
-see next page

* * *

abacus(es)
abandon(ed)
abdomen
abnormal(ly)
absentee
absolute

accident
accurate
acetate
acrobat
actively
actual(ly)

adapter/adaptor
additive
addressee
adequate
adjective
admirable
admiral
-advancement
-advancing
-advantage(d)
advertise(d)
advocate

affluence
affluent
Africa
African
-afternoon
-afterwards

aggravate
agitate
agonise(d)
   ze
agony(-ies)

Alaska
albatross(es)
alchemy
alcohol
algebra
alibi
alkali
alkaline
allergy(-ies)
alphabet
Alsatian
altitude
-see next page

* * * * [* *]

abnormally
aboriginal
aborigines
absolutely

academic(ally)
academy(-ies)
accessory(-ies)
accidental(ly)
accuracy(-ies)
accurately
accusation
acquisition
acrobatic(ally)
activity(-ies)
actually

adaptable
adaptation
adjectival(ly)
admirable
admiration
adolescence
adolescent
advantageous
adverbial(ly)

Afghanistan

aggravation
agitation
agoraphobia
agoraphobic
agricultural(ly)
agriculture

alabaster
alcoholic
algebraic(ally)
Algeria
alimentary
allegretto
alligator
alphabetical(ly)
altimeter
aluminium
-see next page

for a-r
see page 225

In these words you can hear the vowel sound **a** as in **cat**

1

** **

amass(es)
amassed
amber
amble(d)
ambling
ambush(es)
ambushed
ampere
ample

anchor
anger(ed)
angle(d)
*angler (person who
    fishes with hook
    and line)
angling
angry(-ier,-iest)
anguish(ed)
ankle
annexe(d)
annual(ly)
anode
-answer(ed)
anthill
anthrax
*antics (strange
    behaviour)
antique
*antiques (very old
    objects)
antlers
anvil
anxious

aphid/aphis
apple

Arab
arid
arrow(ed)

ashtray
-asking
aspect
asphalt
aspirin
asset
aster
asthma
-see next page

*** ***

amalgam
amateur
ambition
ambitious
ambulance
amethyst
ammeter
amplify(-ies)
    (amplified)
amplitude
amputate

anagram
analogue
analyse(d)
        ze
ancestor
ancestry(-ies)
anchorage
andante
Anglican
angrier
angriest
angrily
*angular (with sharp
    corners)
animal
aniseed
annual(ly)
anodise(d
        ze
anorak
-answering
antarctic
anteater
antelope
antenna(e)
anthracite
anthropoid
antifreeze
antonym
anxiously

aperture
apparent
appetite
applicant
apprehend
aptitude
-see next page

**** **** [** **]

amalgamate
ambassador
ambidextrous
ambiguous
ammunition
amphibian
amphibious
amphitheatre
amplification
amplifier

anachronism
anaesthesia/
anesthesia
anaesthetic/
anesthetic
analogy(-ies)
analysis(-es)
analytic(ally)
anatomical(ly)
anatomy(-ies)
Anglo-Saxon
animation
anniversary(-ies)
annually
antagonise(d)
        ze
antagonism
Antarctica
antecedent
anthology(-ies)
anthropologist
anthropology
antibiotic
antibody(-ies)
anticipate
anticipation
antimony
antiquity(-ies)
antiseptic(ally)
antitoxin
anxiety(-ies)
-see next page

for H ...
see page 16

 for a-r
see page 225

In these words you can hear the vowel sound a as in cat

✻ ✻   ✻ ✻ ✻   ✻ ✻ ✻ ✻ [✻ ✻]

athlete	aquatic	apostolic(ally)
atlas(es)	aqueduct	apparatus
atoll		apparently
atom	Arabic	apparition
attach(es)	arable	application
attached	arrogance	apposition
attack(ed)	arrogant	apprehension
attic	arrowhead	
attract		aquamarine
	asbestos	
-Auntie/Aunty	aspirin	aristocracy(-ies)
	assassin	aristocrat
average(d)	assonance	arithmetically
	asterisk	
*axes (more than one	asteroid	asparagus
axe or axis)	astronaut	aspiration
*axis (fixed or		assassinate
imaginary line)	athletic(ally)	assassination
axle	Atlantic	
	atmosphere	athletically
azure	attitude	
	attracted	
impasse	attraction	
	attractive	
	attributes	
	avalanche	
	avant-garde	

for H . . .
see page 16

avenue
average(d)

axiom

for a-r
see page 225

In these words you can hear the vowel sound a as in cat

3

In these words the first letter 'a' and the 'ae' are neutral vowels.

'AMAZING' WORDS

abate
abbreviation
abeyance
abide
[abode]
ability(-ies)
ablaze
aboard
abode
abolish(es)
abolished
abominable
abominate
abortion
abound
about
above
abrasive
abreast
abroad
abrupt
abscond
absorb(ed)
absorber
absorption
abstain(ed)
absurd
abundance
abundant
abuse(d)
abysmal(ly)
abyss(es)
accelerate
acceleration
accelerator
accept(able)
acceptance
accepting
accessible
accessory(-ies)
acclaim(ed)
accommodate
accommodation
accompaniment
accompany(-ies)
   (accompanied)
accomplish(es)
accomplished
accomplishment
accord(ance)
according(ly)
accordion
account
accrue(d)
accumulate
accumulation
accumulator
accuse(d)
accustom(ed)
acetylene
achieve(d)
achievement
acknowledge(d)
acknowledgement/
acknowledgment

acknowledging
across
acquaint(ance)
acquire(d)
acute
addicted
addiction
addictive
additional(ly)
address(es)
addressed
adhere(d)
adhesive
adieu
adjacent
adjoining
adjourn(ed)
adjust(ed)
adjuster
adjustment
administer(ed)
administrate
administration
administrator
admire(d)
admission
admit(ted)
admittance
admitting
adopt
adorable
adore(d)
adorn(ed)
adrenalin
adsorption
adrift
advance(d)
advancement
advancing
advantage(d)
adventure
adventurous
adverbial(ly)
adversity(-ies)
advertisement
advice
advisable
advise(d)
adviser
advisory
Aegean
aesthetic(ally)
afar
affair
affect(ed)
affection
affectionate(ly)
affiliate
affirm(ed)
affix(es)
affixed
affliction
afford
afloat
afoot

afraid
again
against
agenda
aggression
aggressive
aggressor
aghast
agility
ago
agog
agree(d)
agreement
agreeable
ahead
ahoy!
ajar
alarm(ed)
Alaska
alert
alight
alignment
alike
alive
allegiance
allegro
allergic
alliance
alliteration
allot(ted)
allotting
allotment
allow(ed)
allowance
alluvial
alluvium
aloft
alone
along(side)
aloof
aloud
amalgam
amalgamate(d)
amaze(d)
amazing
amenable
amend(ment)
America(n)
amid(st)
amino
amiss
ammonia
ammonium
amoeba
among(st)
amount
amuse(d)
amusement
anaemia/anemia
anaemic/anemic
anaesthetist/
anesthetist
anemone
anneal(ed)
annihilate

announce(d)
announcement
announcer
annoy(ed)
annoyance
anoint
anon(ymous)
another
apart
apartheid
apartment
apostle
apologetic(ally)
apologise(d)
   ze
apology(-ies)
apostrophe
appal(led)
appalling
appeal(ed)
appear(ed)
appearance
append
appendicitis
appendix(-ces)
applaud
applause
appliance
apply(-ies)
   (applied)
appoint(ment)
appreciate
apprentice(d)
apprenticeship
approach(es)
approached
approaching
appropriate
approval
approve(d)
approximate(ly)
approximation
aquarium
Arabia
arena
arise
[arose]
[arisen]
arithmetic
aroma
around
arouse(d)
arrange(d)
arrangement
array(ed)
arrest
arrival
arrive(d)
ascend(ing)
ascension
ascent
ashamed
ashore
aside
asleep

assault
assemble(d)
assembly(-ies)
assent
assert(ion)
assertive
assess(es)
assessed
assessment
assign(ed)
assignment
assimilate
assimilation
assist(ance)
assistant(s)
associate
association
associative
assorted
assortment
assume(d)
assumption
assurance
assure(d)
astern
astigmatism
astonish(es)
astonished
astonishment
astounded
astounding
astray
astrology
astronomer
astronomy
asylum
atone(d)
atonement
atrocious
attain(ed)
attainment
attempt(ed)
attend(ed)
attendance
attendant(s)
attention
attentive
attribute
aurora
Australia
avail(ed)
availability
available
avenge(d)
avoid(ed)
await
awake(d)
[awoke]
awaken(ed)
award
aware
away
awhile
awoke(n)
awry

<table>
<tr><td>*</td><td>* *</td><td>* * *</td><td>* * * *</td></tr>
</table>

*	* *	* * *	* * * *
back(ed)	backbone	bachelor	bacteria
*bad (not good)	background	badminton	ballerina
*bade (did bid)	backwards	-Bahamas	
badge	badger(ed)	balcony(-ies)	botanical
bag(ged)	badly	balloted	
ban(ned)	baffle(d)	-banana	
*band (strip of	baffling	Bangladesh	
material /	baggage	banishment	
stripe / group)	bagging	banister	
bang(ed)	baggy(-ier,-iest)	baptism	
*banned (forbidden)	bagpipes	baritone	
*bands (more than	balance(d)	barrelling	
one band)	ballad	barricade	
bang(ed)	ballast	barrier	
bank(ed)	*ballet (dance)	barrister	
*banns (announcement	*ballot(ed) (voting)	-basketball	
in church of plan	-balmy	bathysphere	
to marry)	bamboo	battalion	
bash(es)	bandage(d)	battery(-ies)	
bashed	bandit	battlefield	
-bask(ed)	bandy(-ies)	battleship	
bat(ted)	(bandied)		
batch(es)	banger	blackberry(-ies)	
-bath(ed)	bangle	blanketed	
	banish(es)		
black(ed)	banished	brassière	
blank(ed)	banjo(es/s)		
-blast	banker		
	bankrupt		
-bra	banner		
brad	banning		
brag(ged)	banquet		
bran	bantam		
-branch(es)	baptise(d)		
-branched	ze		
brand	*baron (lord)		
-brass(es)	barrack(ed)		
brat	barracks		
	barrage(d)		
	barrel(led)		
	*barren (not fertile)		
	barrow(ed)		
	basalt		
	-basket		
	-bastard		

-see next page

for a-r
see page 226

* *

-bathroom
*baton (short stick)
*batted (did bat)
*batten (board)
 batter
*battered (did
    batter)
 batting
 battery(-ies)
 battle(d)
 battling

 began
-behalf

 blackbird
 blackboard
 blacken(ed)
 blackmail(ed)
 blacksmith
 bladder
 blanket(ed)

 bracket
 bradawl
 braggart
 bragging
 bramble
-branches
 brandish(es)
 brandished
 brandy(-ies)
 brassière

for a-r
see page 226

In these words the first letter 'a'
is a neutral vowel. It.. er... er...
sounds like the 'a' in 'astonish'.

baboon	basalt
Bahamas	bazaar
balloon(ed)	bazooka
banana	blancmange
barometer	Brazil

In these words you can hear the vowel sound a as in cat

C

*

cab
cadge(d)
-calf(-ves)
-calve(d) (produce
a calf)
-calm(ed)
camp(ed)
can(ned)
-can't
cap(ped)
cash(es)
cashed
-cask
*-cast (throw /
mould / decide
parts in a
play / squint)
-[cast]
*-caste (social
class)
cat
catch(es)
[caught]

champ(ed)
*-chance (lucky
event / risk)
-chanced
-chant
*-chants (does
chant / more
than one chant)
chap
chapped
chat(ted)

clad
clam(med)
clamp(ed)
clan
clang(ed)
clank(ed)
clap(ped)
clash(es)
clashed
-clasp(ed)
-class(es)
-classed
-see next page

for Qu ...
see page 24

* *

cabbage
cabin
cackle(d)
cackling
cactus(es/-i)
*caddie (person paid
to carry golf clubs)
*caddy(-ies) (caddie /
box to hold tea)
(caddied)
cadging
café
caffeine
callous
camber(ed)
camel
camera
campaign(ed)
camper
*campers (people in a
camp)
camphor
camping
*campus(es) (college
or university
grounds)
camshaft
canal
cancel(led)
cancer
*candid (frank)
*candied (sugar-
coated)
candle
candy
canning
*cannon (gun / stroke
in billiards)
cannoned
cannot
canny(-ier,-iest)
*canon (musical
round / rank in
church / laws /
list of works)
canteen
canter(ed)
*canvas (cloth)
*canvass(ed) (seek
opinions and/or
support)
*canyon (deep and
narrow valley)
-see next page

* * *

cabinet
cadmium
calcium
calculate
calendar
calibrate
calico
callipers
calorie
camera
camouflage
Canada
cancelling
candidate
candlelight
candlestick
cannibal
canopy(-ies)
capital
caramel
caravan
caribou
carolling
carrier
carrion
carrycot
carrying
casserole(d)
castanets
-castaway
casually
casualty(-ies)
catalogue(d)
catalyst
catapult
cataract
category(-ies)
catholic
Catholic
cavalier
cavalry
cavity(-ies)

ceramic
-see next page

* * * * [* * *]

cafeteria
calamity(-ies)
calculation
calculator
Cambodia
cantilever(ed)
capacitor
capacity(-ies)
capitalise(d)
        ze
Caribbean
caricature(d)
casually
casualty(-ies)
catastrophe
catastrophic(ally)
category(-ies)
caterpillar

championship
chandelier
characterise(d)
        ze
characteristic(ally)
charioteer
charitable
chrysanthemum

classically
classification

collapsible
comparative
comparison
compassionate
compatible
congratulate
congratulations
constabulary(-ies)
contaminate
contamination

 for a-r
see page 227

7

In these words you can hear the vowel sound a as in cat

*

crab
crack(ed)
-craft
crag
cram(med)
cramp(ed)
crank(ed)
crash(es)
crashed

* *

capping
capstan
capsule
captain(ed)
captive
captor
capture(d)
*carat (measure of
    purity of gold)
carol(led)
carriage
*carrot (vegetable)
carry(-ies)
    (carried)
cascade
cashew
cashier(ed)
*caster/castor
    (caster sugar /
    swivelling wheel)
-casting
-castle
*-castor (castor oil)
casual(ly)
catching
cathode
catholic
Catholic
catkin
cattle
catty(-ier,-iest)
cavern

chaffinch(es)
chalet
challenge(d)
champagne
chandler
channel(led)
chapel
chapter
-charade
chasm
chassis
*chatted (had a chat)
chatter
*chattered (talked
    quickly and too
    much / rattled)
chatty(-ier,-iest)
*-chorale (hymn tune)
-see next page

* * *

champion(ed)
-chancellor
channelling
-chapati
character
chariot
charity(-ies)
chatterbox(es)

clarinet
clarify(-ies)
    (clarified)
clarity
classical(ly)
classify(-ies)
    (classified)

combatted
combatting
-commander
-commandment
companion
compassion
contraction
contractor
contralto(s)
contraption

kangaroo
-karate

for Qu ...
see page 24

for a-r
see page 227

In these words you can hear the vowel sound a as in cat

* *

cladding
clamber(ed)
clamming
clammy
clamour(ed)
clanger
clanking
clapper
clapping
classic(ally)
-classmate
-classroom
clatter(ed)

collapse(d)
combat(ted)
-command
compact
contract
-contrast
*-corral (enclosure
   for cattle and
   horses)

cracker
crackle(d)
crackling
-craftsman
craggy
cramming
crankshaft
cranny(-ies)
crevasse

-khaki

-Koran

for Qu ...
see page 24

for a-r
see page 227

In these words the first letter 'a' is a neutral vowel.

cacao	canoe(d)	caress(es)	chameleon
cadet	capillary(-ies)	caressed	chapati
Canadian	capricious	catarrh	charade
canary(-ies)	career(ed)	cathedral	charisma

In these words you can hear the vowel sound a as in cat

*

dab(bed)
dad
-daft
*dam (water-
barrier / mother
of animal)
dammed
*damn (swear word /
condemn)
damned
damp(ed)
-dance(d)
dank
dash(es)
dashed

drab
*-draft (rough plan /
selected group)
drag(ged)
drank
*-draught (current of
air / depth of
ship in water /
piece in game)
-draughts

* *

dabbing
dabble(d)
dabbling
dachsund
daddy
dagger
dally(-ies)
(dallied)
damage(d)
damsel
damson
-dancer
-dancing
dandruff
dandy(-ies)
dangle(d)
dangling
dapple(d)
dashboard
dazzle(d)
dazzling

decamp(ed)
-demand
*despatch(es) (send
off)
despatched
detach(es)
detached
detract

*dispatch(es)
(despatch /
message)
dispatched
distract
divan

dragging
dragon
-drama
drastic(ally)
-draughty(-ier,-iest)

* * *

daffodil
dalmatian
damaging

-demanded

-disaster
-disastrous
dismantle(d)
dismantling
distraction
distractor

dragonfly(-ies)
dramatic(ally)
dramatise(d)
ze
drastically

* * * * [*]

dandelion

dilapidated
dissatisfy(-ies)
(dissatisfied)

dramatically
drastically

for a-r
see page 228

In these words you can hear the vowel sound a as in cat

elapse(d)

ecstatic(ally)

ecstatically

enact
encamp(ed)
-enchant
-entrance(d)

elaborate
elastic(ally)

elaborate
elaboration
elastically
elasticity

embankment
embarrass(es)
embarrassed

embarrassing
embarrassment

er- or -ir- ?

es- or is- ?

em- or im- ?

em- or im- ?

exact
expand
expanse
extract

enamel(led)
enamour(ed)
-enchanting
entangle(d)
entangling
-entrancing

enamelling

en- or in- ?

erratically

en- or in- ?

er- or -ir- ?

erratic(ally)

establishment

er- or ir- ?

et- or it- ?

establish(es)
established

evacuate
evacuation
evacuee
evaluate
evaluation
evaporate
evaporation

es- or is- ?

exactly
examine(d)
-example
expanded
expanding
expansion
expansive
extraction
extractor

exaggerate
exaggeration
examination
expandable
explanatory
extrapolate
extravagance
extravagant
extravaganza

for H ...
see page 16

for I ...
see page 17

for a-r
see page 228

In these words you can hear the vowel sound a as in cat

11

*	* *	* * *	* * * * [*]
fact	fabric	fabulous	fabricated
fad	factor		fabrication
fag(ged)	factory(-ies)	factorise(d)	factually
fan(ned)	factual(ly)	ze	fantastically
fangs	faddy	factory(-ies)	fascinating
-fast	fagging	factual(ly)	fascination
fat(ter,test)	faggots	faculty(-ies)	fashionable
fax(ed)	fallow	Fahrenheit	-father-in-law
	famine	fallacy(-ies)	
flag(ged)	famish(es)	family(-ies)	financially
flan	famished	fanciful	
flange(d)	fanbelt	fantastic(ally)	flabbergasted
flank(ed)	fancy(-ies)	fantasy(-ies)	
flap(ped)	fancied	fascinate	fractionally
flash(es)	fanning	fascism	frantically
flashed	fascist	-fastener	
-flask	fashion(ed)	fattening	philatelist
flat(ted,ter,test)	-fasten(ed)		
flax	-faster	*-fiancé (male engaged	
	-fastest	to be married)	
*franc (French coin)	*-father (male parent)	*-fiancée (female	
-France	-fathered	engaged to be	
*frank (plain and	fathom(ed)	married)	
honest)	fatten(ed)	financial(ly)	
franked	fattening		
	fatter	flanelling	
	fattest		
	fatty(-ier,-iest)	fractional(ly)	
		frantically	
	finance(d)		
	flabby(-ier,-iest)		
	flagging		
	flagpole		
	flannel(led)		
	flapper		
	flapping		
	flappy		
	flasher		
	flashing		
	*flatted (made flat)		
	flatten(ed)		
	flatter(ed)		

for th ...
see page 28

*flattered (did
flatter)
flattest
flatting
-see next page

for a-r
see page 229

In these words you can hear the vowel sound a as in cat

* *

forbade

fraction
fracture(d)
fragile
fragment
frantic(ally)

for th ...
see page 28

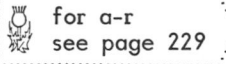 for a-r
see page 229

phantom

> In these words the first letter 'a'
> is a neutral vowel. It.. er... er...
> sounds like the 'a' in 'astonish'.
>
> facility(-ies)   fatigue(d)
> fallacious   flamingo(es/s)
> familiar

In these words you can hear the vowel sound a as in cat

*

gag(ged)
gang
gap(ped)
gas(es)
gassed
gash(es)
gashed
-gasp(ed)

glad(der,dest)
-glance(d)
gland
-glass(es)

gnash(es)
gnashed
gnat

grab(bed)
gram
grand
-grant
-graph(ed)
-grasp(ed)
-grass(es)
-grassed

* *

gadget
gagging
gallant
*galleon (ship)
galley
*gallon (measure)
gallop(ed)
gallows
gambit
*gamble(d) (risk)
gambler
*gambling (taking risks)
*gambol(led) (frisk)
gamma
gammon
gander
gangling
gangplank
gangster
gangway
gannet
gapping
garage(d)
garret
gasket
gassing
gather(ed)

-Ghana
-ghastly(-ier,-iest)

-giraffe

gladden(ed)
gladder
gladdest
glamour
-glasses
-see next page

* * *

galaxy(-ies)
gallery(-ies)
galvanise(d)
ze
*gambolling (frisking)
garrison

-Ghanaian

*glacier (mass of slow-moving ice)
glamorous
glandular

gradual(ly)
graduate
gramophone
grandchildren
grandfather
grandmother
grandparent
-grasshopper
gratitude
gravelling
gravity(-ies)

guarantee(d)

-gymkhana
gymnastics

* * * *

gasometer

gladiator

gradually
graduation
gravitation

....
 for a-r
see page 229
....

In these words you can hear the vowel sound **a** as in **cat**

✳ ✳

grabber
grabbing
gradual(ly)
grammar
grandad/granddad
grandeur
grandma
grandpa
grandstand
granite
granny(-ies)
-granted
graphite
grapple(d)
grappling
-grasslands
gravel(led)

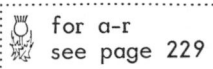 for a-r
see page 229

In these words the first letter 'a'
is a neutral vowel. It.. er... er...
sounds like the 'a' in 'astonish'.

galena   gazelle   graffiti
galoshes   gradation

*

hack(ed)
had
-half(-ves)
-halve(d)
ham(med)
hand
hang
[hung]
hanged
has
hash(ed)
hat
hatch(es)
hatched
hath
have
[had]

* *

habit
haddock
hadn't
halal
hallo
hammer(ed)
hamming
hammock
hamper(ed)
hamster
hamstring(ed)
[hamstrung]
handbag
handbrake(d)
handcuff(ed)
handed
handful
handle(d)
handling
*hand-made (made by hand)
*handmaid (servant)
*handsome (good-looking)
*hangar (building to house planes)
*hanger (means of hanging)
hanging
hanky(-ies)
*hansom (cab)
happen(ed)
happy(-ier,-iest)
harass(ed)
harrow(ed)
hasn't
hatchet
hatter
haven't
having
havoc
hazard

hello

* * *

habitat
Halloween
hamburger
handicap(ped)
handicraft
handiwork
handkerchief(s)
handlebar
handwriting
happening
happier
happiest
happily
happiness
harassment
haversack
Hawaii
Hawaiian
hazardous

* * * *

habitation
handicapping

for a-r
see page 230

In this word 'a' is a neutral vowel.

habitual(ly)

In these words you can hear the vowel sound a as in cat

*	* *	* * *	* * * * [*]
	impasse	il- or el- ?	il- or el- ?
	intact	imagine(d)	imaginary
			imagination
	in- or en- ?	im- or em- ?	imaginative
			immaculate
-Iran	inhabit(ed)		-impassable
-Iraq			implacable
		in- or en- ?	impractical
-Islam			
		-Iraqi	im- or em- ?
ix- or ex- ?			
		Islamic	inaccurate
			inadequate
		is- or es- ?	inflammable
			inflammatory
		Italian	inhabitant
		italic	inhabited
			inhabiting
		ix- or ex- ?	insanitary
			insanity
			intransitive
			in- or en- ?
			irrational(ly)
			ir- or er- ?
			is- or es- ?
			italicise(d)
			ze

for E . . .
see page 11

iv- or ev- ?

ix- or ex- ?

J

*

jab(bed)
jack(ed)
*jam (fruit boiled
with sugar /
crush / block)
jammed
*jamb (side post of
door or window)
jazz(ed)

* *

-giraffe

gymnast

jabber(ed)
jabbing
jackal
jackdaw
jacket
jack-knife
jagged
jamjar
jamming
jampot
jangle(d)
jangling
Japan
jasper

* * *

-gymkhana
gymnastics

jaguar
jamboree
Japanese
javelin

* * * *

January

for a-r
see page 230

In these words the first letter 'a'
sounds like the 'a' in 'astonish'.

Jacuzzi   Jamaica

K

*

knack

for C ...
see page 7

for Qu ...
see page 24

* *

-khaki

knapsack

-Koran

* * *

kangaroo
-karate

* * * *

In these words the first letter 'a'
sounds like the 'a' in 'astonish'.

kaleidoscope   karate

In these words you can hear the vowel sound a as in cat

*	* *	* * *	* * * *
lack(ed)	lacquer(ed)	Labrador	laminated
*lacks (does lack)	ladder(ed)	lacerate	laryngitis
lad	lagging	laminate	laterally
lag(ged)	lambing	Lancashire	lavatory(-ies)
lamb(ed)	lamp-post	landlady(-ies)	
lamp	lampshade	landowner	legality
-lance(d)	landed	lariat	
land	landing	lasagne	
lap(ped)	landlord	lateral(ly)	
Lapp	landmark	latitude	
lash(es)	landscape	lavatory(-ies)	
lashed	language	lavender	
lass(es)	languid	laxative	
-last	languor		
latch(es)	lanky(-ier,-iest)		
latched	lantern		
-laugh(ed)	Lapland		
*lax (slack)	lapping		
	larynx		
	lasso(ed)		
	-lasted		
	-lather(ed)		
	Latin		
	latter		
	lattice(d)		
	-laughter		
	-lava		
	lavish(ed)		
	-llama		

for a-r
see page 231

> In these words the first letter 'a'
> is a neutral vowel. It.. er... er...
> sounds like the 'a' in 'astonish'.
>
> | laboratory(-ies) | lament |
> |---|---|
> | laconic(ally) | lapel |
> | lagoon | lasagne |

*	* *	* * *	* * * * [* *]

*

ma'am
mad(der,dest)
mali
man(ned)
Manx
map(ped)
mash(ed)
-mask(ed)
mass(es)
massed
-mast
*mat (small rug)
match(es)
matched
*matt (not shiny)

* *

mackerel
*Madam (English)
*Madame (French)
madden(ed)
madder
maddest
madness
maggot
magic(ally)
magma
*magnate (wealthy
   businessman)
*magnet (iron which
   attracts iron)
malice
mallard
mallet
mammal
mammoth
manage(d)
mandrel
mangle(d)
mangling
mango(es/s)
manhood
mankind
*manner (way)
mannered
manning
*manor (large house
   with land)
mansion
*mantel (frame round
   fire)
*mantle (cloak)
manual(ly)
mapping
marriage
married
marrow
marry(-ies)
   (married)
mascot
massage(d)
masseur
masseuse
*massif (highlands)
*massive (huge)
-master(ed)
   -see next page

* * *

macabre
mackerel
mackintosh
Mademoiselle
magazine
magical(ly)
magistrate
magnetic(ally)
magnetise(d)
   ze
magnetite
magnify(-ies)
   (magnified)
magnitude
majesty(-ies)
malleable
management
manager
managing
mandolin
manganese
manicure(d)
manifest
manifold
*mannequin (model)
*mannikin (dwarf)
manslaughter
mantelpiece
manual(ly)
manuscript
marathon
marigold
mariner
maritime
mascara
masculine
masquerade
massacre(d)
-masterpiece
-mastery
mastodon
masturbate
matador
matinee
maximum

meander(ed)
mechanic(ally)
medallion

Mohammed
molasses

* * * * [* *]

macaroni
magically
magnesium
magnetically
magnetism
magnificent
maladjusted
malnutrition
manageable
manageress(es)
manifesto
mannerism
manometer
manually
manufacture(d)
manufacturer
manufacturing
marijuana
marionette
masturbation
mathematical(ly)
mathematician
mathematics

mechanical(ly)
menagerie
metabolism

miraculous

morality(-ies)

 for a-r
see page 232

In these words you can hear the vowel sound a as in cat

** **

matches
matching
*matted (twisted in
   a thick mass)
matter
*mattered (did
    matter)
matting
mattress(es)

meringue

-morale
-moustache(d)

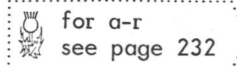
for a-r
see page 232

In these words the first letter 'a' is a neutral vowel.

'MAJESTIC' WORDS

machine(d)	mahogany	malaria	mama	maroon(ed)
machinery	majestic(ally)	Malaysia	manipulate	material(ly)
machinist	Majorca	malicious	manoeuvre(d)	mature(d)
magician	majority(-ies)	malignant	manure(d)	maturity

N

*	**	***	**** [*]
gnash(es)	knapsack	narrative	nationality(-ies)
gnashed		nasturtium	nationally
gnat	nagging	national(ly)	nationalism
	nana	natural(ly)	naturalist
knack	nanny(-ies)	naturalist	naturally
	napkin	navigate	navigable
nag(ged)	napping		navigation
nap(ped)	nappy(-ies)	nomadic	navigator
	narrow(ed)		
	-nasty		

In these words the first letter 'a'
sounds like the 'a' in 'astonish'.

    narrate   nasturtium
    narrator   nativity

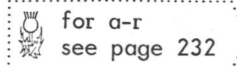
for a-r
see page 232

In these words you can hear the vowel sound a as in cat

*

pack
*packed (tightly
    filled)
*pact (agreement)
pad(ded)
pal
-palm(ed)
pan(ned)
pang
pant
pants
-pass(es)
*-passed (went by)
*-past (time that
    has passed /
    beyond)
pat(ted)
patch(es)
patched
-path

plaid
plait
plan(ned)
plank(ed)
-plant

pram
-prance(d)
prank

-psalm

* *

package(d)
packet
packing
padded
padding
paddle(d)
paddling
paddock
paddy
padlock(ed)
pageant
palace
*palate (taste)
*palette (board for
    mixing colours)
*pallet (mattress /
    tool)
pally(-ier,-iest)
pampas
pamper(ed)
pamphlet
pancake
*panda (animal)
*pander(ed) to
    (encourage by bad
    example or taste)
panel(led)
panic
panicked
panning
pansy(-ies)
panther
panties
pantry(-ies)
parish(-es)
parrot
parry(-ies)
    (parried)
passage
-passing
passion
passive
-passport
-password
pasta
*pastel (crayon /
    soft colour)
*pastille (sweet)
-pasture(d)
pasty(-ies)
-see next page

* * *

-Pakistan
Palestine
pancreas
panelling
panicking
pantograph
pantomime
parable
parachute
paradise
paradox(es)
paraffin
paragraph(ed)
parakeet
parallel(ed)
paralyse(d)
    ze
paranoid
parasite
parasol
paratroop
parody(-ies)
passageway
passenger
-passers-by
passionate
pasteurise(d)
    ze
-pastoral(ly)
patronage
patronise
    ze

pianist
piano(s)
-piranha

planetary
plantation
plasticine
platinum
platypus(es,-i)

practical(ly)
practising
protractor

-pyjamas

* * * * [* *]

-Pakistani
palaeontologist/
    paleontologist
palaeontology/
    paleontology
panorama
papier-mâché
parabola
parallelogram
paralysis(-es)
paralytic
paramecium
paraphernalia
parasitical(ly)
pastorally
pathological(ly)
patronising

philatelist

pianoforte

planetary

practically

for a-r
see page 233

In these words you can hear the vowel sound a as in cat

* *

patchwork
patchy(-ier,-iest)
patent
*patted (did pat)
patter
*pattered (did
    patter)
pattern(ed)
patting
patty(-ies)

perhaps

phantom

pianist
piano(s)

placard
placid
planet
plankton
planner
planning
-planted
-planter
-planting
plasma
-plaster(ed)
plastic
plateau
platen
platform
platter
-plaza

*practice (action)
*practise(d) (do or
    act / repeat for
    improvement)

for a-r
see page 233

In these words the first letter 'a' is a neutral vowel.
It... er.... er.... er.... sounds like the 'a' in 'astonish'.

'PATHETIC' WORDS

Pacific	papa	parenthesis(-es)	pathology(-ies)	patrolling
palatial(ly)	parade	pathetic(ally)	patrol(led)	pavilion

In these words you can hear the vowel sound a as in cat

23

*

quack(ed)

* *

quango(s)

* * *

* * * *

R

*

rack(ed)
-raft
rag(ged)
ram(med)
ramp
ran
-ranch(es)
rang
rank(ed)
*rap (knock)
*rapped (knocked)
*rapt (entranced)
rash(es)
-rasp(ed)
rat(ted)

*wrap (cover)
*wrapped (covered)

* *

rabbi
*rabbit (animal)
*racket (racquet /
    din / dishonest
    way of making
    money)
*racquet (bat with
    strings)
radish(es)
raffle(d)
-rafter
ragged
ragging
rally(-ies)
    (rallied)
ramble(d)
rambling
ramming
rampart
rancid
random
ransack(ed)
ransom(ed)
rapid
*rapping (knocking)
*rarebit (cheese
    on toast)
-rascal(ly)
rasher
-raspberry(-ies)
ratchet
-rather
ration(ed)
ratted
ratting
rattle(d)
rattling
ratty(-ier,-iest)

-see next page

* * *

rabbitted
rabbitting
radical(ly)
raffia
Ramadan
ramshackle
randomise(d)
            ze
rapidly
-raspberry(-ies)
rational(ly)
rattlesnake
ravenous

reaction
reactor
refraction
regatta

romantic(ally)

* * * * [*]

radically
Rastafarian
rationalise(d)
            ze
rationally
ravioli

reactionary(-ies)
reality(-ies)

romantically

for a-r
see page 233

In these words you can hear the vowel sound **a** as in **cat**

* *

react
refract
relax(es)
relaxed

romance(d)

wrangle(d)
wrangling
wrapper
*wrapping (covering)

for a-r
see page 233

In these words the 'a' is neutral.

raccoon/racoon
rapidity
ravine

S

*	* *	* * *	* * * * [*]
-psalm	chalet	ceramic	chandelier
	champagne		
*sac (pouch)	-charade	saccharine	sacrificial(ly)
*sack (large bag /	chassis	sacrifice(d)	salutary
plunder / dismiss		-safari	salutation
from a job)	sabbath	-Sahara	sanatorium
sack(ed)	sadden(ed)	-salami	sanctuary(-ies)
sad(der,dest)	sadder	salaried	sanitary
sag(ged)	saddest	salary(-ies)	sanitation
sand	saddle(d)	salutary	satisfaction
sang	sadly	salvation	satisfactory
sank	sagging	sanctify(-ies)	saturated
sash(es)	salad	(sanctified)	saturation
sat	salmon	sanctuary(-ies)	
	salvage(d)	sandpaper	Scandinavian
scab	-sample(d)	sandpiper	scantiest
scalp(ed)	-sampler	sanitary	
scamp	-sampling	sanity	-Somalia
scan	sanction	satellite	
*scanned (did scan)	sandal(led)	satisfy(-ies)	statically
*scant (hardly	sander	(satisfied)	statistician
enough)	sandstone	saturate	strangulation
scrap(ped)	sandwich(es)	Saturday	
scratch(es)	sandwiched	savanna	substantially
scratched	sapphire	saveloy	
-see next page	sapwood	saxophone	syllabically
	satchel		
	satin	scaffolding	
	satire		
	Saturn	-soprano(s)	
	savage(d)		
	Saxon	spatula	
	-see next page	-see next page	

for a-r
see page 234

In these words you can hear the vowel sound a as in cat

*

shack
-shaft
shag
shall
sham(med)
shank
shrank

slab(bed)
slack(ed)
slam(med)
slang
-slant
slap(ped)
slash(es)
slashed

smack(ed)
smash(es)
smashed

snack
snap(ped)
snatch(es)
snatched

spank(ed)
span
spanned
spat
splash(es)
splashed
sprang
sprat

stab(bed)
stack(ed)
-staff(ed)
stag
stamp(ed)
-stance
stand
[stood]
stank
strand
strap(ped)

swag
swam
swank(ed)

* *

scabbard
scabby
scaffold
scallop(ed)
scalpel
scamper(ed)
scanner
scanning
scanty(-ier,-iest)
scatter(ed)
scavenge(d)
scrabble
scrabbling
scraggy
scramble(d)
scrambling
scrapbook
scrapping
scrappy(-ier,-iest)
scrapyard
scratchy(-ier,-iest)

shabby(-ier,-iest)
shadow(ed)
shaggy(-ier,-iest)
shallow
shambles
shamming
shampoo(ed)
shamrock
shandy(-ies)
shanty(-ies)
shatter(ed)
shrapnel

slamming
slapping

smasher
smashing

snapping
snappy(-ier,-iest)

Spaniard
spaniel
Spanish
spanner
spanning
sparrow
spastic

-see next page

* * *

-staccato
stalactite
stalagmite
stamina
standardise(d)
ze
statically
statuesque
stratagem
strategy(-ies)
stratosphere

substantial(ly)
subtracting
subtraction
-sultana

syllabic(ally)

for a-r
see page 234

In these words you can hear the vowel sound **a** as in **cat**

* *

stabbing
stagger(ed)
stagnant
stallion
stammer(ed)
stampede
standard
standing
standpoint
standstill
stanza
static(ally)
statue
stature
straggle(d)
straggling
stranded
strangle(d)
strangling
strapping
-stratum(strata)

subtract
-surpass(ed)

for a-r
see page 234

swagger(ed)

In these words the first letter 'a'
is a neutral vowel. It.. er... er...
sounds like the 'a' in 'astonish'.

safari	saloon	statistics
Sahara	salute	statistically
salami	samosa	strategic(ally)
salinity	satirical(ly)	
saliva	spaghetti	

In these words you can hear the vowel sound a as in cat

*

tab
tack
*tacked (did tack)
*tacks (more than
  one tack)
*tact (skill in
  putting things
  to people)
tag(ged)
tan(ned)
tank
tap(ped)
-task
*tax(es) (money
  taken by
  government)
taxed

than
thank(ed)
that
thatch(es)
thatched
that's
*thrash(es) (beat)
thrashed
*thresh(es) (beat
  corn)
threshed

track
*track(ed) (did
  track)
*tract (pamphlet)
tram
tramp(ed)
-trance
trap(ped)
trash

twang(ed)

* *

tabby(-ies)
tableau
tablet
tackle(d)
tackling
tacky(-ier,-iest)
tactful(ly)
tactics
tactless
tadpole
tagging
talcum
talent
tally(-ies)
  (tallied)
tamper(ed)
tampon
tangent
tangle(d)
tangling
tango(s)
tangoed
tankard
tanker
tanner
tanning
tantrum
tappet
tapping
tariff
tarry(-ies)
  (tarried)
tassel(led)
tattered
tattoo(ed)
tavern
taxi(s)

thankful(ly)
that'd
that'll

tracksuit
traction
tractor
traffic
trafficked
tragic(ally)
trample(d)
trampling
-see next page

* * *

tabulate
tactfully
taffeta
tambourine
tangerine
tangible
tantalise(d)
     ze
tapestry(-ies)
taxation
taxpayer

thankfully

tobacco(s)
-tomato(es)

trafficker
trafficking
tragedy(-ies)
tragically
trampoline(d)
tranquilly
transaction
transcription
transferring
transformer
transfusion
transistor
transition
transitive
transitory
translation
translator
translucent
transmission
transmitted
transmitter
transmitting
transparent
transversal
transvestite
trapezoid
traveller
travelling

* * * * [* *]

tabulation
tabulator
tachometer
Tanzania
tapioca
tarantula
Tasmania

theatrical(ly)

tobacconist

trafficator
tragically
trampolining
tranquillity
tranquilliser
     zer
transatlantic
transferable
transformation
transistorised
     zed
transitional(ly)
transitory
transmutation
transparency(-ies)
transpiration
transportation
transubstantiation

tyrannical(ly)
tyrannosaurus

 for a-r
see page 235

In these words you can hear the vowel sound ⓐ as in cat

* *

tranquil(ly)
*transact (make a
deal)
transcribe(d)
*transect (cut
across)
transept
transfer(red)
transfix(es)
transfixed
transform(ed)
transit
translate
transmit(ted)
transpire(d)
transplant
transport
transpose(d)
transverse
trapper
trapping
trappings
travel(led)
traverse(d)

for a-r
see page 235

In these words the 'a' is neutral.

tattoo(ed)	trajectory(-ies)
trachea	trapeze
traditional(ly)	

V

*

van
valve(d)
-vase
-vast
vat

* *

vaccine
vacuum(ed)
valiant
valid
valley
value(d)
vampire
vandal
vanish(es)
vanished
vanquish(es)
vanquished
-vantage

* * *

vacillate
vaccinate
valentine
valiant
validate
valium
valuable
vandalise(d)
vanity(-ies)
vaseline
Vatican

verandah

-vibrato

* * * * [*]

vacillation
vaccination
validation
valuable
valuation
vandalism

vocabulary(-ies)

vulgarity(-ies)

for a-r
see page 235

In these words the
first 'a' is neutral.

vacate
vacation
validity
vanilla
variety(-ies)

In these words you can hear the vowel sound a as in cat

W

*	* *	* * *	* * * *
wag(ged)	wagging		
wax(ed)	waggle(d)		
	wagon		
whack(ed)	wagtail		
*wrap (cover)	wrangle(d)		
*wrapped (covered)	wrangling		
-wrath	wrapper		
	*wrapping (covering)		

Y

*	* *	* * *	* * * *
yank(ed)	yapping		
yap(ped)			

for a-r
see page 235

Z

*	* *	* * *	* * * *
		Zambia	
		-Zimbabwe	

In these words you can hear the vowel sound **a** as in **cat**

✢   ✢ ✢   ✢ ✢ ✢   ✢ ✢ ✢ ✢ [✢]

abreast   acceptance   accelerate
                     accepting   acceleration
*accept (take   accelerator
   something offered) adventure   acceptable
                                          accessory(-ies)
address(es)   aesthetic(ally)   acetylene
addressed
                     affected   adrenalin
*affect (alter)   affection   adventurous

again   agenda   aesthetically
against   aggression
                     aggressive   affectionate
ahead   aggressor   affectionately

amend   allegro   America
                     already   American
annexe(d)
any   amendment   anemone
                                          anybody
arrest   anyhow
                     anyone   appendicitis
ascend   anything   apprenticeship
*ascent (climb)   anyway
*assent (agree)   anywhere   authentically
assess(es)
assessed   appendix(-ces)
                     apprentice(d)
attempt
attend   ascension
                     assemble(d)
avenge(d)   assembly(-ies)
                     assessment

                     attempted
                     *attendance (those
                        present / rate of
                        attending)
                     attendant
                     *attendants (servants)
                     attended
                     attention
                     attentive   ┌·····················┐
                                          : 🌷 for e-r   :
                     authentic(ally)   : ⚱ see page 242   :
                                          └·····················┘

*

bed(ded)
beg(ged)
*bell (instrument)
*belle (beauty)
belt
bench(es)
bend
[bent]
best
bet(ted)
[bet]

bled
blend
bless(es)
blessed
[blest]

*bread (food)
*breadth (width)
breast
*breath (air passing
  in and out of
  lungs)
*bred (produced
  young / reared)

* *

beckon(ed)
bedding
bedrock
bedroom
bedside
bedtime
befell
befriend
beggar
begging
behead
beheld
Belgian
Belgium
bellow(ed)
belly(-ies)
bending
benzene
bereft
*beret (flat, round
  cap)
*berry(-ies) (fruit)
beset
[beset]
betted
better
betting
bevel(led)
beverage

blessed
blessing

breakfast
breastbone
breathless
brethren

*bury(-ies) (place
  deep down)
  (buried)

* * *

benefit(ed)
besetting
bevelling
beverage

breathalyse(d)
breathtaking

burial

* * * * [*]

beneficial(ly)
benefited
benefiting
benevolent

breathalyser

In these words the first letter 'e' is pronounced like the 'i' in 'pig'.

'BENEVOLENT' WORDS

became	behave(d)	beseech(es)
because	behaviour	beseeched
become	behead	[besought]
[became]	beheld	beset(ting)
[become]	behind	[beset]
becoming	behold	beside
befall	[beheld]	besides
[befell]	belief	besiege(d)
[befallen]	believe(d)	bestow(ed)
before(hand)	belong(ed)	betray(ed)
befriend	belonging	between
begin	beloved	betwixt
[began]	below	beware
[begun]	beneath	bewilder(ed)
beginner	benevolent	bewitch(es)
beginning	bereave(d)	bewitched
behalf	bereft	beyond

for e-r
see page 243

In these words you can hear the vowel sound e as in elephant

C

*

*cell (unit)
*cent (money / hundred)
*cents (money)

ce- or se- ?

*check(ed) (stop / test)
chef
*cheque (order to bank)
chess
chest

clef
cleft
cleanse(d)
clench(es)
clenched

crept
cress(es)
crest

kelp
kept
ketch(es)

for Qu ...
see page 47

* *

cadet
caress(es)
cassette

*cellar (underground storage room)
cello(s)
Celtic
cement
*censer (pan for burning incense)
*censor(judge of what may not be published)
census(es)
centaur
central(ly)
centre

ce- or se- ?

checking
chemist
cherish(es)
cherished
cherry(-ies)
chestnut

cleansing
clever

collect
commence(ed)
compel(led)
compress(es)
compressed
condemn(ed)
condense(d)
confess(es)
confessed
connect
consent
contempt
contend
content
contest
correct

credit(ed)
crescent
crevice
–see next page

* * *

celandine
celebrate
celery
celestial
cellophane
cellular
celluloid
cellulose
Celsius
cemetery(-ies)
censorship
centigrade
centipede
centrally
century(-ies)
cerebral
cerebrum

ce- or se- ?

chemical(ly)
chemistry

cleanliness

collecting
collection
collective
collector
compelling
complexion
compression
compressor
concentric
conception
concession
condenser
confession
confessor
confetti
conjecture(d)
connected
connecting
connection
connector
consensus
contestant
contention
convention
corrected
correction
correctly
–see next page

* * * * [* *]

celebrated
celebration
celebrity(-ies)
celestial
centenary(-ies)
centimetre
centrifugal(ly)
centurion
cerebellum
ceremonial(ly)
ceremony(-ies)

ce- or se- ?

chemically
cholesterol

commemorate
commemoration
competitive
competitor
confectioner
confectionery
confessional
congenital(ly)
consecutive
contemporary(-ies)
contemptible
contemptuous
conventional(ly)

crematorium

Czechoslovakia

for e-r
see page 244

33

In these words you can hear the vowel sound e as in elephant

** **

kennel
kestrel
ketchup
kettle

*** *** ***

credible
credited
creditor
crescendo(s)

In these words the first letter 'e'
is pronounced like the 'i' in 'pig'.

| celestial | cremate | crescendo(s) |
| cement | cremation | crevasse |

---

for e-r
see page 244

D

*	**	***	**** [** **]
dead	deaden(ed)	deafening	decimetre
deaf	deadly	debited	declaration
dealt	deafen(ed)	December	decorated
death	debit(ed)	deception	dedication
debt	debris	deceptive	definitely
deck(ed)	debtor	decimal	definition
den	debut/début	decorate	delegation
*dense (closely	*decade (ten years)	dedicate	delicacy(-ies)
packed / stupid)	deckchair	defective	democratic(ally)
dent	defect	defector	demonstration
*dents (more than	defence	defendant	dependable
one dent)	defend	defender	dependency(-ies)
depth	deflect	defensive	deprivation
desk	delta	deflection	derivation
	deluge(d)	definite	designated
dread(ed)	denim	delegate	desolation
dreamt	Denmark	delicate	desperation
dredge(d)	dental	democrat	destination
dregs	dentist	demonstrate	devastation
drench(es)	depend	density(-ies)	developer
drenched	depot	*dependant (person	developing
dress(es)	depress(es)	who depends)	development
dressed	depressed	*dependants (people	
	derrick	who depend)	digestible
dwell(ed)	descant	depended	directory(-ies)
[dwelt]	descend	*dependence (reliance)	
	*descent (way down)	*dependent (relying /	-see next page
	desert	hanging)	
	desperate	depression	
	detect	depressive	
	detest	deputy(-ies)	
	devil(led)	-see next page	
	-see next page		

for e-r
see page 245

In these words you can hear the vowel sound e as in elephant

✻ ✻   ✻ ✻ ✻   ✻ ✻ ✻ ✻ [✻]

digest   derelict   domestically
direct   descendant   domesticate
dispense(d)   descended
*dissent   designate   dyslexia
  (disagreement)   desolate
distress(es)   desperate
distressed   destiny(-ies)
                           destitute
                           detection
dreaded   detective
dreadful(ly)   detector
dredger   detention
dredging   *deterrence (prevention
dresser   by causing fear)
dressing   deterrent
                           *deterrents (more than
dwelling   one deterrent)
                           devastate
                           develop(ed)

                           digestion
                           dilemma
                           dimension
                           directed

In these words the first letter 'e'   direction
is pronounced like the 'i' in 'pig'.   directive
                                         directly
'DELIGHTFUL' WORDS   director
                                         discretion
                                         displeasure
                                         distressing

debate	deficient	depend(ed)
decamp(ed)	define(d)	dependable
decay(ed)	deflation	dependant
decease(d)	deflect(ion)	dependants
deceit	deform(ed)	dependence
deceive(d)	defy(-ies)	dependency(-ies)
December	(defied)	dependent
deception	degree	deport
deceptive	delay(ed)	deposit(ed)
decide	delete	depositing
deciduous	deliberate(ly)	depreciate
decipher(ed)	delicious	depreciation
decision	delight(ed)	depress(es)
decisive	delightful(ly)	depressed
declare(d)	delirious	depression
decline(d)	deliver(ed)	depressive
decree(d)	deliverance	deprive(d)
decry(-ies)	delivery(-ies)	derail(ed)
(decried)	demand(ed)	derivative
deduce(d)	democracy(-ies)	derive(d)
deduction	demobbed	descend(ed)
deductive	demolish(es)	descendant
defeated	demolished	descent
defect(or)	denial	describe(d)
defective	denomination	describing
defence	denominator	description
defend(ant)	denote	descriptive
defender	denounce(d)	desert(ed)
defensive	deny(-ies)	deserve(d)
defiance	(denied)	design(ed)
defiant	depart(ure)	designer
deficiency(-ies)	department	desirable

domestic(ally)

dreadfully

dyslexic

for e-r
see page 245

desire(d)	detain(ed)	deterrent
despair(ed)	detect(ion)	deterring
despatch(es)	detective	detest
despatched	detector	detract
despise(d)	detention	develop(ed)
despite	deter(red)	developer
dessert	detergent	developing
destroy(ed)	deteriorate	development
destroyer	deterioration	device
destruction	determination	devise(d)
destructive	determine(d)	devote(d)
detach(es)	determining	devotion
detached	deterrence	devour(ed)

*   * *   * * *   * * * * [* * * *]

ebb(ed)	any	aesthetic(ally)	aesthetically
edge(d)	echo(ed)	anyhow	anybody
egg(ed)	eddy(-ies)	anyone	
elf(-ves)	(eddied)	anything	eccentrically
elm	edging	anyway	economical(ly)
else	edit(ed)	anywhere	economics
			ecstatically
end	effect	eccentric(ally)	ecumenical(ly)
	effort	ecstasy(-ies)	
etch(es)		ecstatic(ally)	editorial(ly)
etched	eject	Ecuador	educated
		eczema	education
	elbow(ed)		educational(ly)
	elder	edible	Edwardian
	eldest	edited	
	elect	editor	effectively
	elsewhere	educate	effervescence
			effervescent
	ember	effective	
	emblem	effervesce(d)	electoral(ly)
	empire	effigy(-ies)	electorate
	empress(es)		electrical(ly)
	empty(-ies)	ejection	electricity
		ejector	electrocute
	em- or im-		electrolysis
		elderly	electrolyte
	ending	election	electrolytic(ally)
	endless	electors	electromagnetic(ally)
	engine	electric(ally)	electronic(ally)
	enter(ed)	electrode	elementary
	entrance	electron	elevated
	entry(-ies)	elegance	elevation
	envy(-ies)	elegant	eligible
	(envied)	element	elocution
	enzyme	elephant	
		elevate	el- or il- ?
	en- or in- ?	eleven(th)	
		eloquent	embryonic(ally)
	erect	-see next page	emigration
	errand		empirical(ly)
	error		
			em- or im- ?
	escort		-see next page
	esquire		
	essay		
	essence		
	-see next page		

See also E
on page 65

for H ...
see page 40

for I ...
see page 41

 for e-r
see page 245

In these words you can hear the vowel sound e as in elephant

* *

etching
ethics
ethnic(ally)

et- or it- ?

event
ever
every

excel(led)
*except (not
   including)
*excerpt (selected
   passage)
excess(es)
exempt
exhale(d)
exhort
exile
exit
expect
expel(led)
expense
expert
exploit
export
express(es)
expressed
extend
extent
extra
extract

See also E
on page 65

for H ...
see page 40

for I ...
see page 41

* * *

embedded
embellish(es)
embellished
embezzle(d)
embryo(s)
emerald
emery
emigrate
eminence
eminent
emperor
emphasis
emphasise(d)
      ze

em- or im- ?

endeavour(ed)
endocrine
enemy(-ies)
energy(-ies)
engineer(ed)
entering
enterprise
entertain(ed)
envelope
envious

en- or in- ?

epilogue
episode
epithet

equinox(es)

erection

escalate
escapade
Eskimo(s)
esplanade
essential(ly
estimate
estuary(-ies)

ethical(ly)
ethnical(ly)
etiquette
-see next page

* * * * [* * *]

energetic(ally)
engineering
entertainment
entertainer

en- or in- ?

epicyclic(ally)
epidemic(ally)
epilepsy(-ies)
epileptic(ally)

equatorial(ly)
equilibrium
escalator
especially
essentially
estimated
estimation

ethically
ethnically
etymological(ly)
etymology

eventually
everlasting
everybody

excavation
excellency(-ies)
exceptionally
exclamation
execution
executive
exemplary
exhibition
exhortation
-see next page

 for e-r
see page 245

In these words you can hear the vowel sound e as in elephant

37

In these words the first letter 'e' is pronounced like the 'i' in 'pig'.

'EFFECTIVE' WORDS

ecclesiastical(ly)
eclipse(d)
ecology
edition
effect(ively)
efficient
Egyptian
eject(ion)
ejector
elaborate
elaboration
elastic(ally)
elasticity
elect(ion)
elector(ate)
electoral(ly)
electrical(ly)
electricity
electrocute
electrode
electrolysis
electrolyte
electrolytic(ally)
electromagnetic(ally)
electron
electronic(ally)
eleven(th)
elicit(ed)
eliciting
eliminate
elimination
Elizabethan
ellipse
elliptical(ly)
elope(d)
elusive
emancipate
emancipation
embankment
embark(ed)
embarrass(es)
embarrassed
embarrassing
embarrassment
embedded
embedding
embellish(es)
embellished
embellish(es)
embellished
embezzle(d)
embroider(ed)
embroidery
emerge(d)
emergence
emergency(-ies)
emission
emit(ted)
emitter
emitting
emotional(ly)
emotive
empirical(ly)
employ(ed)
employee
employer
employment
emulsion(ed)
enable(d)
enabling
enact
enamel(led)
enamelling
enamour(ed)
encamp(ed)
encase(d)
enchant(ing)
encircle(d)
enclose(d)
enclosure
encounter(ed)
encourage(d)
encouragement
encyclopedia
endanger(ed)
endear(ed)
endearment
endeavour(ed)

endorse(d)
endow(ed)
endurance
endure(d)
enfold
enforce(d)
enforcement
engage(d)
engagement
engrave(d)
engraving
engulf(ed)
enjoy(ed)
enjoying
enjoyment
enlarge(d)
enlighten(ed)
enlist
enquire(d)
enquiry(-ies)
enormous
enough
enrage(d)
enrich(es)
enriched
enrol(led)
enrolment
enslave(d)
ensure(d)
entangle(d)
enthusiasm
enthusiastic(ally)
entire(ly)
entitle(d)
entrancing
entrust
enumerate
environment(ally)
envisage(d)
equality
equation
equator
equip(ped)
equipment
equipping
equivalence
equivalent
erase(d)
eraser
erect(ion)
erode
erosion
erotic(ally)
erratic(ally)
erupt(ed)
eruption
escape(d)
escarpment
especially
essential(ly)
establish(es)
established
establishment
estate
estrange(d)
eternal(ly)
evacuate
evacuation
evacuee
evade
evaluate
evaluation
evaporate
evaporation
evasion
event
eventual(ly)
evict
evolve(d)
exact(ly)
exaggerate
exaggeration
exalt(ed)
examination
examine(d)
example
exceed(ingly)
excel(led)

excelling
except(ionally)
excess(es)
excessive
exchange(d)
exchequer
excite(d)
excitedly
excitement
exciting
exclaim(ed)
exclamation
exclude
exclusion
exclusive(ly)
excretion
excuse(d)
excursion
exemplary
exempt
exert(ion)
exhaust(ed)
exhaustion
exhibit(ed)
exhibiting
exist(ed)
existence
exotic(ally)
expandable
expand(ed)
expanding
expansion
expansive
expect(ed)
expectant(ly)
expel(led)
expelling
expenditure
expense
expensive
experience(d)
experiment(ally)
explain(ed)
explaining
explanatory
explicit
explode
explore(d)
explorer
exploring
explosion
explosive
exponent
export
expose(d)
exposure
express(es)
expressed
expressing
expression
expressive
exquisite
extend(ed)
extending
extension
extensive
extent
exterior
exterminate
external(ly)
extinct(ion)
extinguish(ed)
extinguisher
extract(ion)
extractor
extraordinarily
extraordinary
extrapolate
extravagance
extravagant
extravaganza
extreme(ly)
extrusion
exuberance
exuberant

eventual(ly)
evergreen
everyone
everything
everywhere
evidence
evident

excavate
excellence
excellent
excelling
exception
excessive
exchequer
execute
exemption
*exercise (practice / use)
*exercise(d) (take exercise / use)
*exorcise(d) (cast out devil)
expectant
expected
expelling
expensive
expressing
expression
expressive
exquisite
extended
extending
extension
extensive
external(ly)

expectantly
expectation
expedition
expenditure
experiment
experimental(ly)
explanation
exploitation
exploration
exponential(ly)
exposition
externally

for e-r
see page 245

See also E
on page 65

for H ...
see page 40

for I ...
see page 41

In these words you can hear the vowel sound e as in elephant

*

fed
fell
*fell(ed) (cut down)
*felt (did feel /
    type of cloth)
fend
fence(d)
fetch(es)
fetched

fleck(ed)
fled
flesh(ed)
flex(es)
flexed

French
fresh
fret(ted)
friend

phlegm

* *

feather
feldspar
fellow
ferment
ferret(ed)
ferry(-ies)
    (ferried)
fester(ed)
festive
fetter(ed)

fledgeling/fledgling
Flemish

foretell
forget
forwent/forewent

freckles
Frenchman
fretsaw
fretted
fretting
friendly
friendship

pheasant

* * *

February
federal(ly)
fellowship
feminine
ferreted
ferreting
festival

fiesta

flexible
fluorescent

forgetful(ly)
forgetting

freshwater

phonetic(ally)

```
for th...
see page 52
```

* * * *

February
federally
federation
festivity(-ies)

flexibility

forgetfully

phonetically

```
for e-r
see page 246
```

In these words the
letter 'e' sounds
like the 'i' in 'pig'.

    ferocious
    ferocity

G

*

gem
get
[got]

glen

guess
*guessed (did guess)
*guest (person
    invited)

jest
jet(ted)

In this word the
'e' sounds like
'a' in 'astonish'.

    guerilla/guerrilla

* *

gazelle

general(ly)
generous
gentle
gently
gesture(d)
getting

ghetto(es/s)

jealous
jelly(-ies)
    (jellied)
jemmy(-ies)
jester
jetted
jetty(-ies)

* * *

general(ly)
generalise(d)
generate
generous
genetic(ally)
gentleman
gentlemen
genuine
gestation

jealousy(-ies)
jellyfish
jettison(ed)

In these words the first 'e'
has a short 'i' sound.

    genetic(ally)
    geranium

* * * * [* *]

generalisation
        zation
generalise(d)
        ze
generally
generation
generator
generosity
genetically
gesticulate

```
for e-r
see page 246
```

*	* *	* * *	* * * * [*]
head	head-dress(es)	haematite/hematite	hectically
health	headed	haemorrhage/	helically
hedge(d)	heading	hemorrhage(d)	helicopter
held	headlamp	headmaster	helter-skelter
hell	headland	headmistress(es)	hereditary
helm	headlight	headquarters	heredity
help(ed)	headline(d)	headwaters	heroism
hem(med)	headphones	healthier	hesitation
hemp	healthy(-ier,-iest)	healthiest	hexagonal(ly)
hen	heather	heavier	
hence	heaven	heaviest	hysterically
Herr	heavy(-ier,-iest)	heavily	
	heckle(d)	hectically	
	heckling	helical(ly)	
	hectare	helmeted	
	hectic(ally)	helpfully	
	hedgehog	hemisphere	
	hedgerow	heraldry	
	hedging	heritage	
	hefty(-ier,-iest)	*heroin (drug)	
	heifer	*heroine (female hero)	
	hello	hesitate	
	helmet(ed)	hexagon	
	helper		
	helpful(ly)	hysterics	
	helping		
	helpless		
	hemming		
	henceforth		
	herald		
	heron		
	herring		
	herself		
	himself		

for e-r
see page 247

> In this word the letter 'e'
> sounds like the 'i' in 'pig'.
>
> heroic(ally)

In these words you can hear the vowel sound **e** as in **elephant**

☆ ☆

if- or ef- ?

ij- or ej- ?

il- or el- ?

immense
impel(led)
impress(es)
impressed

im- or em- ?

incense(d)
indent
infect
inject
inspect
instead
intend
*intense (extreme)
intent
*intents (purposes)
invent
invest

ir- or er- ?

is- or es- ?

itself

iv- or ev- ?

ix- or ex- ?

☆ ☆ ☆

ic- or ec- ?

if- or ef- ?

ij- or ej- ?

il- or el- ?

impeller
impelling
impregnate
impression
impressive

im- or em- ?

incessant
indented
indenture(d)
infection
infectious
inherent
inherit(ed)
injection
inspection
inspector
intensive
intention
intestine
invention
inventive
inventor
investment
investor

in- or en- ?

is- or es- ?

iv- or ev- ?

ix- or ex- ?

☆ ☆ ☆ ☆ [☆ ☆]

ic- or ec- ?

if- or ef- ?

illegible

il- or el- ?

immensity
impeccable
imperative
impregnable
impressionism
impressionist

incredible
indefinitely
inedible
inevitable
inflexible
inheritance
inherited
inheriting
insecticide
insensitive
integrity
intelligence
intelligent
intensify(-ies)
   (Intensified)
intensity(-ies)
intentional(ly)
interrogate
interrogation
investigate
investigation
investigator

irregular
irregularity(-ies)

is- or es- ?

iv- or ev- ?

ix- or ex- ?

for E . . .
see page 36

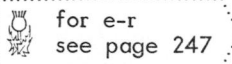

for e-r
see page 247

In these words you can hear the vowel sound e as in elephant

41

J

*	* *	* * *	* * * * [* *]
gem	general(ly)	general(ly)	generalisation
	generous	generalise(d)	zation
jest	gentle	ze	generalise(d)
jet(ted)	gently	generate	ze
	gesture(d)	generous	generally
		genetic(ally)	generation
	jealous	gentleman	generator
	jelly(-ies)	gentlemen	genetically
	(jellied)	genuine	gesticulate
	jemmy(-ies)	gestation	
	jester		
	jetted	**jealousy(-ies)**	
	jetty(-ies)	**jellyfish**	
		jettison(ed)	

for e-r
see page 248

K

*	* *	* * *	* * * *
kelp	kennel		
kept	kestrel		
ketch(es)	ketchup		
	kettle		
knelt			

for C ...
see page 33

for e-r
see page 248

for Qu ...
see page 47

In these words you can hear the vowel sound e as in elephant

L

*

*lead (metal)
*leant (did lean)
 leapt
*led (showed/shown
   the way)
 ledge
 left
 leg(ged)
 lend
*[lent] (did lend)
 Lent
 length
 lens(es)
 less
 let
 [let]
 let's

* *

lament
lapel

leather(ed)
lecture(d)
legend
leggings
leisure(d)
lemon
leopard
leper
*lessen(ed) (make
   less)
lesser
*lesson (period of
   instruction)
letter(ed)
letting
lettuce
level(led)
levy(-ies)
levied

* * *

Lebanese
Lebanon
lecturer
legendary
legislate
lemonade
leprechaun
leprosy
lesbian
letterbox(es)
lettering
levelling

lieutenant

* * * *

legendary
legislation
levitation

....
: for e-r
: see page 248
....

In these words the first letter 'e'
is pronounced like the 'i' in 'pig'.

legality   legitimate

In these words you can hear the vowel sound e as in **elephant**

43

* * * * * * * * * [* *]

*	* *	* * *	* * * * [* *]
meant	many	majestic(ally)	majestically
melt			
[molten]	meadow	measurement	mechanism
men	measure(d)	measuring	medically
mend	*medal (award /	medical(ly)	medication
mesh(es)	memento)	megaphone	medieval
meshed	*meddle(d) (interfere)	megaton	mediterranean
mess(es)	*meddler (person who	melody(-ies)	melancholy
messed	interferes)	membership	Melanesia
met	meddling	memento(es/s)	memorable
	medicine	memorable	memorandum
	*medlar (fruit)	memorise(d)	menstruation
	medley	ze	mentality(-ies)
	mellow(ed)	memory(-ies)	metabolism
	melon	meniscus(es/-i)	metallurgy
	melted	menstruate(d)	metamorphic
	melting	mentally	metamorphosis(-es)
	member	merrily	methylated
	membrane	merriment	metrically
	memoirs	mesmerise(d)	metropolitan
	menace(d)	ze	
	mental(ly)	messenger	molecular
	mention(ed)	metaphor	
	menu	metrical(ly)	
	merit(ed)	metronome	
	merry	Mexican	
	message	Mexico	
	messieux		
	messy(-ier,-iest)	momentum	
	*metal(led) (mineral		
	substance)		
	method		
	metric(ally)		
	*mettle (courage)		
	misdealt		
	misled		
	misspell(ed)		
	[misspelt]		
	misspend		
	[misspent]		

for e-r
see page 249

> In these words the first letter 'e'
> is pronounced like the 'i' in 'pig'.
>
> | mechanic(ally) | memento(es/s) | meridian |
> |---|---|---|
> | melodic(ally) | memorial | meticulous |
> | melodious | meniscus(es/-i) | mnemonic |

In these words you can hear the vowel sound e as in elephant

N

*	* *	* * *	* * * * [*]
knelt	necklace	nebula	necessarily
	nectar	nebulous	necessary
neck(ed)	neglect	necessary	necessity(-ies)
nest	nephew	negative	neglectfully
net(ted)	nestle(d)	neglectful(ly)	negligible
next	nestling	Netherlands	nevertheless
	netball		
	netted	November	
	netting		
	nettle(d)		
	network(ed)		
	never		

for e-r see page 249

> In these words the first letter 'e'
> is pronounced like the 'i' in 'pig'.
>
> | | |
> |---|---|
> | necessity(-ies) | neglectful(ly) |
> | negation | negotiate |

O

*	* *	* * *	* * * * [*]
	object	already	authentically
	obsess(es)		
	obsessed	authentic(ally)	objectionable
			obsessional(ly)
	offence	objection	
	offend	objective	
	oppress(es)	obsession	
	oppressed	obsessive	
		offensive	
		oppression	
		oppressive	
		oppressor	

for e-r see page 249

In these words you can hear the vowel sound e as in elephant

*	**	***	**** [** **]
peck(ed)	peasant	pathetic(ally)	parenthesis(-es)
peg(ged)	pebble		pathetically
pelt	*pedal (foot lever)	pedalling	
pen(ned)	pedalled	pedestal	pedestrian
pence	*peddle(d) (carry and	pedigree	penetration
pest	try to sell)	pelican	penicillin
pet(ted)	peddler	penalty(-ies)	*peninsula (land
	peddling	pendulum	almost surrounded
phlegm	pegboard	penetrate	by water)
	pegging	penniless	*peninsular (of/like a
pledge(d)	pellet	pensioner	peninsula)
	penance	pentagon	perceptually
press(es)	pencil(led)	peppermint	perennial(ly)
pressed	pendant	percentage	perishable
	penguin	perception	perpetually
	pennant	perceptive	pessimistic(ally)
	penning	perceptual(ly)	
	penny(-ies)	perfection	phonetically
	pension(ed)	perilous	
	pepper(ed)	periscope	pleasurable
	perfect	perpetual(ly)	plentifully
	peril	perplexing	
	perish(es)	perspective	potentially
	perished	pessimist	
	perplex(es)	petrify(-ies)	predatory
	perplexed	(petrified)	preferably
	pester(ed)	petticoat	preparation
	pestle		preposition
	petal(led)		prepositional(ly)
	*petrel (sea-bird)	phonetic(ally)	presentable
	*petrol (fuel)		presentation
	petting	plentiful(ly)	preservation
			presidential(ly)
		possession	professional(ly)
	pheasant	possessive	
		potential(ly)	
	pleasant		pterodactyl
	pleasure	*precedence (priority)	
	pledging	precedent	
	plenty	*precedents (previous	
		examples)	
	possess(es)	precipice	
	possessed	predator	
	-see next page	predatory	
		predicate	
		preferably	
		preference	
		pregnancy(-ies)	
		prejudice(d)	
		premature	
		premier	
		-see next page	

for e-r
see page 250

In these words you can hear the vowel sound e as in elephant

** **

precious
preference
pregnant
prelude
premier
*presence (being present)
present
*presents (gifts)
pressing
pressure(d)
prestige
pretence
pretend
prevent
profess(es)
professed
progress(es)
progressed
project
propel(led)
prospect
protect
protest

*** ***

presented
presenting
presently
president
pretended
prevalent
prevention
preventive
procession
profession
professor
progression
progressive
projectile
projection
projector
propelling
propeller
prospective
prospector
prospectus(es)
protected
protection
protective
protector

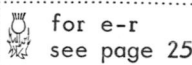 for e-r see page 250

In these words the first letter 'e' sounds like the 'i' in 'pig'.

'PHENOMENAL' WORDS

peculiar
pedestrian
peninsula
peninsular
perimeter
petition(ed)
petroleum
phenomena

phenomenal(ly)
phenomenon
precaution
precede(d)
preceding
precipitate
precipitation
precise(ly)

precision
precocious
predict(ion)
predictable
predominantly
prefer(red)
preferring
preliminary(-ies)

prepare(d)
preparing
prescribe(d)
prescription
present(ed)
presentable
presenting
preserve(d)

preside
presumably
presume(d)
pretence
pretend(ed)
prevail(ed)
prevent(ion)
preventive

 Q

*

quell(led)
quench(es)
quenched
quest

* *

quelling
question(ed)
quintet

* * *

questionnaire

* * * *

questionable

In these words you can hear the vowel sound e as in elephant

47

*	* *	* * *	* * * * [* *]
*read (looked at and understood)	ready(-ier,-iest)	readier	receptacle
realm	rebel(led)	readiest	recitation
*red (colour)	recess(es)	readily	recognition
rend	recessed	readiness	recollection
[rent]	reckon(ed)	rebelling	recommendation
rent	record	rebellion	recreation
*rest (repose / ones left over)	rector	rebellious	rectangular
*retch(es) (try to vomit)	redden(ed)	reception	referendum
retched	redder	receptive	regimental(ly)
	reddest	recession	registration
	reddish	recessive	regretfully
wreck(ed)	redskin	recipe	regularity(-ies)
wren	redwood	recognise(d) ze	regularly
wrench(es)	reference	recollect	regulation
wrenched	reflect	recommend	relatively
*wrest (seize)	refresh(es)	reconcile(d)	relativity(-ies)
*wretch(es) (unhappy creature)	refreshed	rectangle	relegation
	refuge	rectify(-ies) (rectified)	remembering
	reggae	rectory(-ies)	reminiscence
	regret(ted)	referee	reminiscent
	reject	reference(d)	repetition
	relent	reflected	repetitive
	relic	reflection	representation
	remnant	reflector	representative
	render(ed)	reflexive	represented
	rental	refreshment	representing
	repel(led)	refugee	reputation
	repent	regiment	resentfully
	reptile	register(ed)	reservation
	request	registrar	residential
	rescue	registry(-ies)	resignation
	*resent (feel angry at)	regretful(ly)	resolution
	resin	regretted	respectable
	respect	regretting	respectfully
	rested	regular	respectively
	resting	regulate	respiration
	restless	rejection	respiratory
	revenge(d)	relative	restoration
	reverence	relegate	revelation
	*reverend (deserving respect)	relentless	revolution
	*Reverend (title)	relevance	revolutionary(-ies)
	*reverent (feeling or showing reverence)	relevant	
		remedy(-ies) (remedied)	
	rosette	remember(ed)	
		remembrance	
	wreckage	Renaissance	
	wrestle(d)	-see next page	
	wrestler		
	wrestling		
	wretched		

for e-r
see page 251

48

In these words you can hear the vowel sound e as in elephant

In these words the first letter 'e' is pronounced like the 'i' in 'pig'.

'REFRESHING' WORDS

react(ion)
reactionary(-ies)
reactor
reagent
real
realise(d)
   ze
realism
realistic(ally)
reality(-ies)
really
rearm(ed)
rebel(led)
rebelling
rebellion
rebellious
rebound
recall(ed)
receding
receipt
receive(d)
receiver
receiving
receptacle
reception
receptive
recess(es)
recessed
recession
recessive
reciprocal(ly)
reciprocate
recital
recite
reclaim(ed)
recoil(ed)
record(ed)
recorder
recording
recover(ed)
recovery(-ies)
recruit
reduce(d)
reduction
refer(red)
referral
referring
refine(d)
refinery(-ies)
reflect(ed)
reflection
reflector
reflexive
reform(ed)
retract(ion)
refrain(ed)
refresh(es)
refreshed
refreshment
refrigerator
refund
refuse(d)
refusal
regain(ed)

regard(ed)
regardless
regatta
regret(ted)
regretful(ly)
regretting
rehearsal
rehearse(d)
reject(ion)
rejoice(d)
rejoin(ed)
relate(d)
relation(ship)
relax(es)
relaxed
release(d)
relent(less)
reliable
reliability(-ies)
reliance
relief
relieve(d)
religion
religious
reluctant(ly)
rely(-ies)
  (relied)
remain(ed)
remainder
remaining
remark(ed)
remarkable
remember(ed)
remembering
remembrance
remind(ed)
reminder
remote
removal
remove(d)
removing
Renaissance
renew(ed)
renown(ed)
repair(ed)
repay
[repaid]
repeal(ed)
repeat(ed)
repeating
repel(led)
repellent
repelling
repentance
repetitive
replace(d)
replacement
reply(-ies)
  (replted)
report(ed)
reporter
repose(d)
reproach(es)
reproached

republic(an)
repudiate
repulsive
request
require(d)
requirement
research(es)
researched
researcher
resemblance
resemble(d)
resembling
resent
resentful(ly)
resentment
reserve(d)
resign(ed)
resist(ance)
resistor
resolve(d)
resort
resource(d)
respect(able)
respectful(ly)
respective(ly)
respire(d)
respond
response
responsibility(-ies)
responsible
responsive
restore(d)
restrain(ed)
restrict(ion)
result(ed)
resultant
resulting
resume(d)
resuscitate
resuscitation
retain(ed)
retard(ed)
retire(d)
retirement
retort
retreat
return(ed)
returnable
returning
reveal(ed)
revenge(d)
reverberate
reverse(d)
reversal
reversible
review(ed)
revise(d)
revision
revive(d)
revolt
revolve(d)
revolver
revue
reward

* * *

repelling
repentance
repertoire
represent
-researcher
resemblance
resemble(d)
resembling
resentful(ly)
resentment
reservoir
*residence (house

repellent
repelling
repentance
repertoire
represent
resemblance
resemble(d)
resembling
resentful(ly)
resentment
reservoir
*residence (house)
resident
*residents (occupiers)
residue
resolute
respectful((y)
respective
restaurant
retention
retentive
retina
revenue
reverence
*reverend (deserving
  respect)
*Reverend (title)
*reverent (feeling or
  showing reverence)

for e-r
see page 251

In these words you can hear the vowel sound e as in elephant

✳

*cell (unit)
*cent (money / hundred)
*cents (money)

chef

said
says

*scent (perfume /
    smell)

sect
*sects (religious
    groups)
self
*sell (exchange
    for money)
[sold]
send
[sent]
*sense
    (understandable
    pattern)
sensed
*sent (made to go)
set
[set]
*sex(es) (male/
    female)
sexed

shed
[shed]
shelf(-ves)
shelved
shell(ed)
shred(ded)

sketch(es)
sketched

sledge(d)
slept
-see next page

✳ ✳

*cellar (underground
    storage room)
cement
*censer (pan for
    burning incense)
*censor (judge of what
    may not be published)
census(es)
central(ly)
centre(d)

sceptic
sceptre(d)
schedule(d)

second
section
sector
segment
seldom
select
selfish
*seller (person who
    sells)
senate
sending
señor
*sensor(detecting
    device)
sensual(ly)
sentence(d)
sepal
separate
session
setted
settee
setting
settle(d)
settler
settling
seven(th)
several
sexist
sextet
sexual(ly)
sexy(-ier,-iest)
-see next page

✳ ✳ ✳

celandine
celebrate
celery
celestial
cellophane
celluloid
cellulose
Celsius
cemetery(-ies)
centigrade
centipede
centrally
century(-ies)
cerebral
cerebrum

sceptical(ly)

secession
secondary(-ies)
second-hand
secretary(-ies)
secular
sedative
sediment
segregate
selected
selecting
selection
selective
selector
sellotape
semibreve
senator
señora
sensation
sensible
sensitive
sensual(ly)
sensuous
sentiment
sentinel
separate
September
serenade
settlement
-see next page

✳ ✳ ✳ ✳ [✳]

celebrated
celebration
celebrity(-ies)
celestial
centenary(-ies)
centimetre
centrifugal(ly)
centurion
ceremony(-ies)

secondary(-ies)
secretarial
secretary(-ies)
sedimentary
segregation
self-reliant
semicircle
semicircular
semicolon
semi-conductor
semi-detached
semiquaver
semolina
señorita
sensational(ly)
sensitivity(-ies)
sentimental(ly)
separated
separately
separation
seventieth
severity(-ies)
sexuality(-ies)
sexually

sincerity

specialisation
        zation
speciality(-ies)
specification
spectacular
speculation
spherically
-see next page

for e-r
see page 252

In these words you can hear the vowel sound e as in elephant

*	* *	* * *	* * * * [*]
smell(ed)	shedding	seventeen(th)	stegosaurus
[smelt]	shellfish	seventy(-ies)	
	shelter(ed)	several	successfully
speck	shepherd	severance	suggestible
sped	sheriff	sexism	susceptible
spell(ed)	shredded	sexual(ly)	
[spelt]	shredding		
spend		skeleton	symmetrical(ly)
[spent]	sledging		synthetically
spread	slender	spaghetti	
[spread]		specialise(d)	
	smelter	ze	
squelch(es)		specially	
squelched	special(ly)	specify(-ies)	
	speckle(d)	(specified)	
stealth	spectre	specimen	
stem(med)	spectrum(-a)	spectacle	
stench(es)	speller	spectacles	
*step (pace /	spelling	spectator	
stage)	spending	speculate	
*steppe (dry,	splendid	spherical(ly)	
treeless plain)	splendour		
stepped	spreading	steadily	
stet		steadiness	
strength	steady(-ies)	stealthier	
stress(es)	(steadied)	stealthiest	
stressed	stealthy(-ier,-iest)	stencilling	
stretch(es)	stellar	sterilise(d)	
stretched	stemming	ze	
	stencil(led)	stethoscope	
sweat	stepping	strenuous	
swell	strengthen(ed)		
[swollen]	stretcher	subjection	
swept	stretching	successful(ly)	
		succession	
	subject	successive	
	subtend	successor	
	success(es)	suggested	
	suggest	suggesting	
	suspect	suggestion	
	suspend	surrender(ed)	
	suspense	suspected	
		suspension	
	sweater		
	swelter	synthetic(ally)	

for e-r
see page 252

In these words the first letter 'e' sounds like the 'i' in 'pig'.

'SELECTED' WORDS

secession	secure(d)	selection	settee
seclude(d)	security(-ies)	selective	severe(ly)
secrete	select(ed)	selector	severity(-ies)
secretion	selecting	sequoia	specific(ally)

In these words you can hear the vowel sound e as in elephant

51

*

tell
[told]
tempt
ten(th)
tend
*tense (form of
    verb / stretched
    tight)
tensed
tent
*tents (more than
    one tent)
tenth
test
text

theft
them
then
thence
thread(ed)
threat

tread
[trod]
[trodden]
trench(es)
trend

twelfth
twelve

* *

technique
teddy(-ies)
telling
temper(ed)
tempest
template
temple
tempo(s)
tenant
tender(ed)
tendon
*tenner (ten pound
        note)
tennis
tenon(ed)
*tenor (male voice)
tension
tepid
terrace(d)
terrain
terror
tested
testing
testis(testes)
tether(ed)
textbook
textile
texture(d)

themselves
threaded
threaten(ed)
threshold

treadle
treasure(d)
treble(d)
trebling
trellis(ed)
tremble(d)
trembling
tremor
trendy(-ier,-iest)
trestle

twenty(-ies)

* * *

technical(ly)
telegraph(ed)
telephone(d)
telescope(d)
televise(d)
temperament
temperate
temperature
temporary
temptation
tendency(-ies)
tenderness
tenement
tentacle
tentative
terrible
terribly
terrier
terrify(-ies)
    (terrified)
territory(-ies)
terrorise(d)
        ze
tessellate
testicle
testify(-ies)
    (testified)
tetanus

therapy(-ies)

together
torrential(ly)

treacherous
treachery(-ies)
treasury(-ies)
tremendous

twentieth

* * * * [* *]

pterodactyl

technically
technological(ly)
technology(-ies)
telegraphy
telephonist
telephoto
television
temperamental(ly)
temperature
temporarily
temporary
terrarium
terrestrial(ly)
territorial(ly)
territory(-ies)
terrorism
tessellation
testimonial
testimony(-ies)

torrentially

> ☙ for e-r
> see page 253

In these words the first letter 'e'
is pronounced like the 'i' in 'pig'.

'TERRIFIC' WORDS
telegraphy   terrestrial(ly)
telephonist   terrific(ally)
tepee   tremendous

In these words you can hear the vowel sound ℮ as in elephant

*

* *

unless

* * *

* * * *

V

*	* *	* * *	* * * * [*]
Venn	vector	vegetable	vegetation
vent	velvet	venison	Venezuela
vest	vending	ventilate	ventilation
vet(ted)	vendor	ventricle	ventilator
vex(es)	vengeance	verify(-ies)	ventriloquist
vexed	venture(d)	(verified)	veterinary
	very	veteran	
	vessel		
	vestry(-ies)		
	veteran		
	vetted		
	vetting		

for e-r
see page 254

> In this word the letter 'e'
> sounds like the 'i' in 'pig'.
>
> velocity(-ies)

In these words you can hear the vowel sound e as in elephant

53

※

wealth
web(bed)
wed(ded)
[wed]
wedge(d)
weft
weld
well(ed)
Welsh
wench(es)
went
wept
west
*wet(ted,ter,test)
   (make wet / not
   dry)
[wet]

whelk
whelp(ed)
when
whence
*whet(ted) (sharpen)

wreck(ed)
wren
wrench(es)
wrenched
*wrest (seize)
*wretch(es) (unhappy
   creature)

※ ※

waistcoat

wealthy(-ier,-iest)
weapon
*weather (conditions
   outside / survive
   bad weather)
weathered
webbing
wedded
wedding
wedging
Wednesday
welcome(d)
welfare
Welshman
western
westward
*wetted (made wet)
wetter
wettest
*wetting (making wet)

*whether (if)
*whetted (sharpened)
*whetting (sharpening)

wreckage
wrestle(d)
wrestler
wrestling
wretched

※ ※ ※

Wednesday
wellington

whenever

※ ※ ※ ※

for e-r
see page 255

X

※

※ ※

※ ※ ※

※ ※ ※ ※ [※]

xenophobia
xenophobic

In these words you can hear the vowel sound e as in elephant

Y

*	* *	* * *	* * * *
yell(ed)	yelling	yesterday	
yelp(ed)	yellow		
yen			
yes	yourself		
yet	yourselves		

for e-r
see page 255

Z

*	* *	* * *	* * * * [*]
Zen	zealous		xenophobia
zest	zebra		xenophobic
	zenith		
	zephyr		

In these words you can hear the vowel sound e as in elephant

※

※ ※	※ ※ ※	※ ※ ※ ※ [※]
abyss(es)	abysmal(ly)	ability(-ies)
		abysmally
admit(ted)	addicted	
adrift	addiction	additional(ly)
	addictive	administer(ed)
affix(es)	addition	administrate
affixed	admission	administration
	admittance	administrator
amid	admitted	
amidst	admitting	affiliate
amiss		
	affliction	alliteration
assist		
	ambition	arithmetic
	ambitious	
		assimilate
	arisen	assimilation
		astigmatism
	*assistance (help)	
	assistant	auxiliary(-ies)
	*assistants (helpers)	
	attribute	

 for i-r
see page 242

In these words you can hear the vowel sound   i   as in   pig

*   * *   * * *   * * * *

*	* *	* * *	* * * *
*been (past form of 'be')	became	becoming	benevolent
	because	befallen	
	become	beforehand	binocular
bib	[became]	beginner	binoculars
bid	[become]	beginning	
[bade]	befall	behaviour	Bolivia
[bid]	[befell]	belonging	
[bidden]	[befallen]	beloved	
big	before	besetting	
bill	befriend	bewilder(ed)	
*billed (did bill)	begin		
*bin (container)	[began]	bishopric	
bit	[begun]		
bitch(es)	behalf	bricklayer	
bitched	behave(d)	brigadier	
	behead		
blink(ed)	beheld	busier	
	behind	busiest	
brick(ed)	behold	busily	
bridge(d)	[beheld]	businessman	
brim(med)	belief		
bring	believe(d)		
[brought]	belong(ed)		
brink	beloved		
brisk	below		
	beneath		
*build (construct)	bereave(d)		
[built]	[bereft]		
	beseech(es)		
	beseeched		
	[besought]		
	beset		
	[beset]		
	beside		
	besides		
	besiege(d)		
	besought		
	bestow(ed)		
	betray(ed)		
	between		
	betwixt		
	beware		
	bewitch(es)		
	bewitched		
	beyond		
	-see next page		

for i-r
see page 243

* *

bidden
bidding
bigger
biggest
bilious
billiards
billion
billow(ed)
biscuit
bishop
*bitten (past form
  of 'bite')
bitter
*bittern (bird)
*bizarre (peculiar)

blinkered
blinkers
blister(ed)
blizzard

Brazil
breeches
bridging
brigade
brilliance
brilliant
brimming
bringing
bristle(d)
bristling
*Britain (country)
British
*Briton (British
  person)
brittle

builder
building
business
busy(-ies)
  (busied)
busy(-ier,-iest)

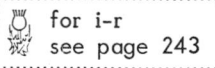
for i-r
see page 243

In these words you can hear the vowel sound i as in pig

*	* *	* * *	* * * * [*]
chick	cement	capricious	capillary(-ies)
chid			
chill(ed)	chicken(ed)	celestial	celebrity(-ies)
chimp	chidden	ceramic	celestial
chin	chiffchaff		certificate
chink	chilblain	charisma	
chintz	children	chickenpox	Christianity
chip(ped)	*Chile (country)	chimpanzee	chrysanthemum
	*chilli (hot spice)	chiselling	
cinch(es)	*chilly(-ier,-iest)	chivalrous	citizenship
	(cold)	chivalry	civilisation
click(ed)	chimney	chrysalis	zation
cliff	chipboard		
cling	chipmunk	cigarette	clinically
[clung]	chipping	*cilia (more than	
clink(ed)	chisel(led)	one cilium)	commissioner
clip(ped)	christen(ed)	cilium(-a)	coniferous
	Christian	cinema	considerable
crib(bed)	Christmas	cinnamon	considerate
cringe(d)		citizen	consideration
crisp	cigar	civilian	consistency(-ies)
	cinder	civilise(d)	conspicuous
crypt	cirrus	ze	conspiracy(-ies)
	cistern	civilly	constituency(-ies)
kick(ed)	citrus		constituent
kid(ded)	city(-ies)	clinical(ly)	contingency(-ies)
kids	civic	clitoris	continual(ly)
kill(ed)	civil		continuation
kiln		collision	continuous
kilt	clinic(ally)	commission(ed)	continuum
king	clipper	commitment	contributed
kink(ed)	clipping	committed	
kiss(ed)		committee	criminally
kit(ted)	commit(ted)	committing	critically
	conflict	condition(ed)	criticism
	conscript	conscription	
	consist	consider(ed)	cylindrical
	convict	consistent	
	convince(d)	consisting	kilometre
	-see next page	continual(ly)	kindergarten
		continue(d)	
		contribute	
		conviction	
		-see next page	

for Qu ...
see page 83

 for i-r
see page 244

In these words you can hear the vowel sound i as in pig

* *   * * *

create   created
cremate   creating
cribbing   creation
cricket   creative
crimson   cremation
crinkle(d)   crescendo(s)
crinkly   criminal(ly)
cripple(d)   crinoline
crisscross(ed)   critical(ly)
critic(ally)   criticise(d)
crystal   ze
                        crystalline
*cygnet (young swan)   crystallise(d)
*cymbals (discs to   ze
    clash)
                        cylinder
                        Cypriot
kidded
kidding
kidnap(ped)   kidnapper
kidney   kidnapping
killer   kilogram
killing   kimono(s)
kindle(d)
kindling
kingdom
kinky(-ier,-iest)
kipper
kissing
kitchen

for Qu ...
see page 83
kitted
kitten
kitting

for i-r
see page 244

In these words you can hear the vowel sound i as in pig

✻

did
dig(ged)
[dug]
dim(med)
din
ding
dip(ped)
disc/disk
dish(es)
ditch(es)
ditched

drift
drill(ed)
drink
[drank]
[drunk]
drip(ped)

✻ ✻

debate
*decade (ten years)
decamp(ed)
decay(ed)
*decayed (did decay)
decease(d)
deceit
deceive(d)
decide
declare(d)
decline(d)
decrease(d)
decree(d)
decry(-ies)
   (decried)
deduce(d)
defeat
defect
defence
defend
define(d)
deflect
deform(ed)
defy(-ies)
   (defied)
degree
delay(ed)
delete
delight
demand
demobbed
denote
denounce(d)
deny(-ies)
   (denied)
depart
depend
deport
depress(es)
depressed
deprive(d)
derail(ed)
derive(d)
-see next page

✻ ✻ ✻

December
deception
deceptive
decipher(ed)
decision
decisive
deduction
deductive
defeated
defective
defector
defendant
defender
defensive
defiance
defiant
deficient
deflection
deletion
deliberate
delicious
delighted
delightful(ly)
deliver(ed)
demanded
demolish(es)
demolished
denial
department
departure
*dependant (person
   who depends)
*dependants (people
   who depend)
depended
*dependence
   (reliance)
*dependent (relying /
   hanging)
deposit(ed)
depression
depressive
descendant
descended
describing
description
descriptive
deserted
designer
destroyer
destruction
destructive
-see next page

✻ ✻ ✻ ✻ [✻ ✻]

deciduous
deficiency(-ies)
deliberate
deliberately
delightfully
delirious
deliverance
delivery(-ies)
democracy(-ies)
denomination
denominator
dependable
dependency(-ies)
deposited
depositing
depreciate
depreciation
derivative
desirable
deteriorate
deterioration
determination
determining
developer
developing
development

dictatorial(ly)
dictionary(-ies)
differential
differently
difficulty(-ies)
digestible
digitally
dilapidated
diphtheria
diplodocus
diplomacy
diplomatic(ally)
directory(-ies)

-see next page

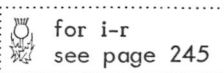
for i-r
see page 245

** ** **

descend
*descent (way down)
describe(d)
*desert (leave)
deserve(d)
design(ed)
desire(d)
despair(ed)
*despatch(es) (send
  off)
despatched
despise(d)
despite
*dessert (sweet dish)
destroy(ed)
detach(es)
detached
detain(ed)
detect
deter(red)
detest
detract
*device (gadget /
  plan)
*devise(d) (invent /
  work out)
devote
devour(ed)

dictate
diction
didn't
differ(ed)
difference
different
diffuse(d)
digest
digger
digging
digit
dimmer
dimming
dimple(d)
*dinghy(-ies) (small
  boat)
*dingy(-ier,-iest)
  (dull)
dinner
  -see next page

** ** **

detection
detective
detector
detention
detergent
determine(d)
*deterrence
  (preventing by
  causing fear)
deterrent
*deterrents (more
  than one deterrent)
deterring
develop(ed)
devoted
devotion

dictation
dictator
dictionary(-ies)
difference
different
differently
difficult
diffusion
digestion
digital(ly)
dignify(-ies)
  (dignified)
dignity(-ies)
dilemma
dimension
diminish(es)
diminished
diploma
directed
direction
directive
directly
director
disable(d)
disabling
disagree(d)
disappear(ed)
disappoint
disapprove(d)
disaster
disastrous
disbelief
disciple
discipline(d)
  -see next page

** ** ** ** [** **]

disciplinarian
discovery(-ies)
discriminate
discrimination
disgracefully
disintegrate
disloyally
disloyalty
disobedience
disobedient
disposition
disproportion
disqualify(-ies)
  (disqualified)
dissatisfaction
dissatisfy(-ies)
  (dissatisfied)
dissimilar
distinguishable
distribution
distributive
distributor
diversity
divisibility
divisible

dysentery
dyslexia

for i-r
see page 245

In these words you can hear the vowel sound i as in pig

⁎ ⁎   ⁎ ⁎ ⁎

diphthong	discomfort
dipper	discontent
dipping	discotheque
dipstick	discourage(d)
direct	discover(ed)
disarm(ed)	discretion
discard	discussing
discern(ed)	discussion
discharge(d)	disgraceful(ly)
disclose(d)	disgusting
disco(s)	dishearten(ed)
discount	dishonest
*discreet (careful	dishwasher
not to embarrass)	disinfect
*discrete (separate)	disloyally
*discus(es) (disc)	disloyalty
*discuss(es) (debate)	dismally
*discussed (debated)	dismantle(d)
disease(d)	dismissal
disgrace(d)	dismissing
disguise(d)	displacement
*disgust (strong	displeasure
dislike)	disobey(ed)
dishcloth	disorder(ed)
dishes	disposal
dislike(d)	disproven
disloyal(ly)	disregard
dismal(ly)	disruption
dismay(ed)	disruptive
dismiss(ed)	distilling
dismount	distinction
disown(ed)	distinctive
*dispatch(es)	distinguish(es)
(despatch /	distinguished
message)	distraction
dispatched	distractor
dispense(d)	distressing
disperse(d)	distribute
displace(d)	disturbance
display(ed)	divided
displease(d)	dividend
dispose(d)	dividers
disprove(d)	dividing
[disproven]	division
dispute	divisor
disrupt	
*dissent	dynasty(-ies)
(disagreement)	dysentery
dissolve(d)	dyslexic
-see next page	dystrophy(-ies)

for i-r
see page 245

※ ※

distance(d)
distant
distil(led)
distinct
distort
distract
distress(es)
distressed
district
distrust
disturb(ed)
disused
dither(ed)
divan
diverge(d)
diverse
divert
divide
divine(d)
divorce(d)
dizzy(-ier,-iest)

dribble(d)
dribbling
drifted
driftwood
drinker
drinking
dripping
driven
drizzle(d)
drizzling

dwindle(d)
dwindling

 for i-r
see page 245

In these words you can hear the vowel sound i as in pig

*	* *	* * *	* * * * [* * * *]
	éclair	eccentric(ally)	eccentrically
	eclipse(d)		ecclesiastical(ly)
		edition	ecology
	effect		economy(-ies)
		effective	
	eject	efficient	effectively
			efficiency
	elect	Egyptian	
	ellipse		elaborate
	elope(d)	eg- or ig- ?	elaboration
			elastically
	el- or il- ?	ejection	elasticity
		ejector	electoral(ly)
	embark(ed)		electorate
	embed(ded)	elaborate	electrical(ly)
	embrace(d)	elastic(ally)	electricity
	embroil(ed)	election	electrocute
	emerge(d)	electors	electrolysis
	emit(ted)	electric(ally)	electrolyte
	employ(ed)	electrode	electrolytic(ally)
		electron	electromagnetic(ally)
	em- or im- ?	eleven(th)	electronic(ally)
		*elicit(ed) (draw out)	elicited
	enact	*elusive (hard to find)	eliciting
	encamp(ed)		eliminate
	encase(d)	el- or il- ?	elimination
	enchant		Elizabethan
	enclose(d)	embankment	elliptical(ly)
	endear(ed)	embarrass(es)	
	endorse(d)	embarrassed	el- or il- ?
	endow(ed)	embedded	
	endure(d)	embedding	emancipate
	enfold	embellish(es)	emancipation
	enforce(d)	embellished	embarrassing
	engage(d)	embezzle(d)	embarrassment
	England	embroider(ed)	embroidery
	English	emergence	emergency(-ies)
	engrave(d)	emission	emotional(ly)
	engulf(ed)	emitted	empirical(ly)
	enjoy(ed)	emitter	
	enlarge(d)	emitting	em- or im- ?
	enlist	emotion	-see next page
	enough	emotive	
	enquire/inquire(d)	employee	
	enrage(d)	employer	
	enrich(es)	employment	
	enriched	emulsion(ed)	
	enrol(led)		
	-see next page	em- or im- ?	
		-see next page	

for H ...
see page 71

for I ...
see page 72

** **

enslave(d)
*ensure(d) (make
    certain)
entire
entrance(d)
entrust

en- or in- ?

equate
equip(ped)

erase(d)
erect
erode
erupt

escape(d)
escort
estate
esteem(ed)
estrange(d)

es- or is- ?

evade
event
evict
evolve(d)

exact
exalt
exceed
excel(led)
*except (not
    including)
excess(es)
exchange(d)
excite
exclaim(ed)
exclude
excuse(d)
exempt
exert
exhaust
exhort
exist
-see next page

*** *** ***

enable(d)
enabling
enamel(led)
enamour(ed)
enchanting
encircle(d)
enclosure
encounter(ed)
encourage(d)
endanger(ed)
endearment
endeavour(ed)
endurance
enforcement
engagement
Englishman
engraving
enjoying
enjoyment
enlighten(ed)
enormous
enquiry/inquiry(-ies)
enrolling
enrolment
entangle(d)
entirely
entitle(d)
entrancing
envisage(d)

en- or in- ?

equation
equator
equipment
equipping

eraser
erection
erosion
erotic(ally)
erratic(ally)
erupted
eruption

er- or ir- ?
-see next page

** ** ** ** [** ** **]

enamelling
encouragement
encyclopedia
enthusiasm
enthusiastic(ally)
enumerate
environment
environmental(ly)

en- or in- ?

equality
equivalence
equivalent

erotically
erratically

er- or ir- ?

especially
essentially
establishment

eternally

evacuate
evacuation
evacuee
evaluate
evaluation
evaporate
evaporation
eventually

exaggerate
exaggeration
examination
exceedingly
exceptionally
excitedly
exclamation
exclusively
-see next page

for H ...
see page 71

for I ...
see page 72

In these words you can hear the vowel sound i as in pig

** ::

expand
expanse
expect
expel(led)
expense
explain(ed)
explode
exploit
explore(d)
export
expose(d)
express(es)
expressed
extend
extent
extinct
extract
extreme

:: :: ::

escarpment
essential(ly)
establish(es)
established

es- or is- ?

eternal(ly)

et- or it- ?

evasion
eventual(ly)

exactly
exalted
examine(d)
example
excellent
excelling
exception
excessive
exchequer
excited
excitement
exciting
exclusion
exclusive
excretion
excursion
exemption
exertion
exhausted
exhaustion
exhibit(ed)
existed
existence
exotic(ally)
expanded
expanding
expansion
expansive
expectant
expected
expelling
expensive
explaining
explicit
explorer
exploring
explosion
explosive

-see next page

:: :: :: :: [:: :: ::]

executive
exemplary
exhibited
exhibiting
exotically
expandable
expectantly
expenditure
experience(d)
experiment
experimental(ly)
explanatory
exploratory
exterior
exterminate
externally
extinguisher
extraordinarily
extraordinary
extrapolate
extravagance
extravagant
extravaganza
exuberance
exuberant

for H ...
see page 71

for I ...
see page 72

In these words you can hear the vowel sound i as in pig

* * *

exponent
exposure
expressing
expression
expressive
exquisite
extended
extending
extension
extensive
external(ly)
extinction
extinguish(es)
extinguished
extraction
extractor
extremely
extrusion

for H . . .
see page 71

for I . . .
see page 72

F

*	* *	* * *	* * * * [* * *]
fib(bed)	fibbing	familiar	facility(-ies)
fifth	fiction		
fig	fiddle(d)	ferocious	ferocity
fill(ed)	fiddler		fertility
film(ed)	fiddling	*fiancé (man engaged	
filth	fidget(ed)	to be married)	figurative
fin(ned)	fifteen(th)	*fiancée (woman	financially
finch(es)	fifty(-ies)	engaged to be	
Finn	figure(d)	married)	phenomena
fiord/fjord	filler	fictional	phenomenal(ly)
fish(es)	fillet	fictitious	phenomenon
fished	filling	fidgeted	
fist	filly(-ies)	fidgeting	philatelist
fit(ted)	filter(ed)	fidgety	philosophical(ly)
fix(es)	filthy(-ier,-iest)	fiesta	philosophy(-ies)
fixed		fiftieth	physically
fizz(es)	-see next page		physiological(ly)
fizzed		-see next page	physiology
-see next page			

for th . . .
see page 90

for i-r
see page 246

In these words you can hear the vowel sound i as in pig

*

flick(ed)
flinch(es)
fling
[flung]
flint
flip(ped)
flit(ted)

fridge
frill(ed)
fringe(d)
frisk(ed)

for th ...
see page 90

* *

finance(d)
finger(ed)
finish(es)
finished
Finland
Finnish
fiord/fjord
fiscal
*fisher (man who fishes)
fishes
fishing
fission
*fissure(d) (crack)
fitness
fitted
fitting
fixture
fizzle(d)
fizzy(-ier,-iest)

flicker(ed)
flimsy(-ies)
flipper
flipping
flitted
flitting

forbid
[forbad(e)]
[forbidden]
forgive
[forgave]
[forgiven]

friction
frigate
frigid
fritter(ed)
frizzy(-ier,-iest)

fulfil(led)

physics
physique

* * *

filament
filthiest
filtration
financial(ly)
fingernail
fingerprint
fingertip
finishing
fisherman

flamingo(es/s)

forbidden
forbidding
forgiven
forgiveness

frivolous

fulfilling

physical(ly)
physician
physicist

for i-r
see page 246

*

gift
gig
*gild (paint with
   gold)
*[gilt] (gilded)
gills
gin
give
[gave]
[given]

glimpse(d)
glint

grid
*grill(ed) (cook by
   direct heat /
   bars for cooking /
   food so cooked)
*grille (protecting
   set of bars in
   door or window)
grim
grin(ned)
grip(ped)
grit(ted)

*guild (association)
*guilt (responsibility
   for doing wrong)

jib(bed)
jig(ged)

* *

giggle(d)
giggling
gilded
*gilder (person who
   gilds)
gimlet
ginger(ed)
gingham
gipsy/gypsy(-ies)
giraffe
given
giver
giving

glimmer(ed)
glisten(ed)
glitter(ed)

grenade
griddle
grinning
gripping
gristle
gritting
grizzle(d)
grizzling
grizzly

*guilder (Dutch coin)
guilty(-ier,-iest)
guinea
Guinea
guitar

gymnast
gymslip
gypsy/gipsy(-ies)

jibbing
jiffy
jigging
jigsaw
jingle(d)
jingling

* * *

genetic(ally)

gibberish
Gibraltar
gingerbread

glycerine

*gorilla (ape)

*guerilla/guerrilla
   (agent of political
   violence)
guillemot
guillotine(d)

gymkhana
gymnastics
gymnosperm

* * * * [* *]

genetically
geographical(ly)
geography(-ies)
geological(ly)
geology
geometrical(ly)
geometry(-ies)
geranium

gymnasium

for i-r
see page 246

In these words you can hear the vowel sound i as in pig

*

hid
hill
*him (that male
    individual)
hinge(d)
hint
hip
his
hiss(ed)
hit
[hit]
hitch(es)
hitched

*hymn (song with
    verses sung in
    church)

* *

hiccup(ped)
hidden
hillside
hilltop
himself
hinder(ed)
hindrance
Hindu
hissing
hither
hitting

hymnal

* * *

habitual(ly)

heroic(ally)

hiccupping
hickory
hideous
historic(ally)
history(-ies)
hitherto

hypnosis
hypnotic(ally)
hypnotise(d)
        ze
hysterics

* * * * [* *]

habitually

hereditary
heredity
heroically

higgledy-piggledy
hilarious
Himalayas
hippopotamus(es/-i)
historian
historical(ly)

hypnotically
hypnotism
hysterical(ly)

*

if

ill

imp

*in (not outside)
inch(ed)
ink
*inn (small hotel)

is

it
itch(es)
itched
*its (belonging to
it)
*it's (it is)

for E ...
see page 65

for H ...
see page 71

* *

ic- or ec- ?

if- or ef- ?

ignite
ignore(d)

ij- or ej- ?

illness(es)

il- or el- ?

image(d)
immense
immerse(d)
immune
impact
impel(led)
implore(d)
imply(-ies)
   (implied)
import
impose(d)
impress(es)
impressed
imprint
improve(d)
impulse
impure

im- or en- ?

incense(d)
*incite (encourage
   strong feeling or
   action)
incline(d)
include
income
increase(d)
indeed
indent
index(ed)
indoors
induce(d)
indulge(d)
-see next page

* * *

idiom
idiot

id- or ed- ?

if- or ef- ?

igneous
ignition
ignorance
ignorant

ig- or eg- ?

ij- or ej- ?

illegal(ly)
*illicit (illegal)
illusion
*illusive (deceptive)
illustrate

il- or el- ?

imagery
imagine(d)
imitate
immediate
immersion
immigrant
immigrate
immobile
immortal(ly)
immunise(d)
   ze
impatience
impatient
impeachment
impeller
impelling
imperfect
impetus(es)
implement
impolite
importance
important
impregnate
impression
impressive
imprison(ed)
-see next page

* * * * [* * *]

ic- or ec- ?

idiomatic(ally)
idiotic(ally)

iguanodon

illegally
illegible
illiterate
illogical(ly)
illuminate
illumination
illustration
illustrative
illustrator
illustrious

il- or el- ?

imaginary
imagination
imaginative
imitation
immaculate
immediate
immediately
immensity
immigration
immortality
immortally
immovable
immunisation
   zation
immunity
impassable
impeccable
imperative
imperial(ly)
impersonal
impersonate
impersonation
impertinent
implacable
implication
impossibility
impossible
-see next page

for i-r
see page 247

In these words you can hear the vowel sound i as in pig

*	* *	* * *	* * * * [* *]
	inert	impromptu(s)	impractical
	infant	improper	impregnable
	infect	improvement	impressionism
	infer(red)	improving	impressionist
	infirm	improvise(d)	impunity
	inflame(d)	ze	impurity(-ies)
	inflate	impudence	
	inflict	impudent	
	inform(ed)	impulsive	im- or em- ?
	ingot		
	inhale(d)		inability
	inject	im- or em- ?	inaccessible
	injure(d)		inaccurate
	inland	incessant	inadequate
	inlet	*incidence (rate of	inappropriate
	innate	happening)	inattentive
	inner	incident	inaugural
	innings	*incidents (events)	inauguration
	input	incision	incapable
	inquest	incisor	incidental(ly)
	inquire/enquire(d)	included	inclination
	insane	including	incognito
	inscribe(d)	inclusion	incompatible
	insect	inclusive	incomprehensible
	insert	incoming	incongruity(-ies)
	*inshore (near the	incomplete	incongruous
	shore)	incorrect	inconsistent
	inside	increasing	inconvenience
	*insight	indented	inconvenient
	(understanding)	indenture(d)	incorporate(d)
	insist	India	incubation
	inspect	Indian	incubator
	inspire(d)	indicate	increasingly
	instal(led)	indifferent	incredible
	*instance (example)	indignant	incubator
	instant	indigo	incubation
	*instants (moments)	indirect	incurable
	instead	indistinct	indefinitely
	instinct	induction	independence
	instruct	inductive	independent
	insult	indulgence	indicated
	*insure(d) (protect	indulgent	indication
	against loss)	industry(-ies)	indicator
	-see next page	inertia	indifferent
		infantry	indigestible
		infection	indigestion
		infectious	indignation
		inference	indispensable
		inferring	individuality
		infinite	individual(ly)
		inflation	indivisible
		influence(d)	-see next page
		-see next page	

for E . . .
see page 65

for H . . .
see page 71

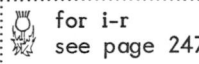 for i-r
see page 247

-see next page

73

In these words you can hear the vowel sound i as in pig

✻ ✻	✻ ✻ ✻	✻ ✻ ✻ ✻ [✻ ✻ ✻]
intact	informal(ly)	Indonesia
intake	informant	industrial(ly)
intend	infra-red	industrialisation
*intense (very strong)	infrequent	zation
intent	ingenious	industrialise(d)
*intents (purposes)	inhabit(ed)	ze
interest	inherent	industrious
into	inherit(ed)	inedible
intrigue(d)	inhuman	inefficiency
intrude	initial(led)	inefficient
invade	injection	inequality(-ies)
invent	injury(-ies)	inevitable
inverse	injustice	inexpensive
invert	innermost	inexperienced
invest	innkeeper	inferior
invite	*innocence (freedom	infinitesimal(ly)
invoice(d)	from guilt)	infinitive
involve(d)	innocent	infinity
inward	*innocents (people	infirmary(-ies)
	who have done	inflammable
in- or en- ?	no wrong)	inflammation
	inquiry/enquiry(-ies)	inflammatory
iq- or eq- ?	inscription	inflationary
	insisted	inflexible
Iran	insolence	influential(ly)
Iraq	insolent	influenza
	inspection	informally
ir- or er- ?	inspector	information
	installing	informative
Islam	instalment/	infuriate
isn't	installment	ingenious
issue(d)	instantly	ingenuity
isthmus	institute	ingredient
	instruction	inhabitant
is- or es- ?	instructor	inhabited
	instrument	inhabiting
itself	insulate	inheritance
	insulin	inherited
iv- or ev- ?	insulting	inheriting
	insurance	inhospitable
ix - or ex- ?	-see next page	initialling
		initiate
		initiative
		injurious
		innovation
		innumerable
		inoculate
		inorganic(ally)
		inquisition
		inquisitive
		-see next page

for E . . .
see page 65

for H . . .
see page 71

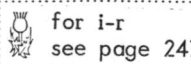
for i-r
see page 247

In these words you can hear the vowel sound i as in pig

* * *   * * * * [* *]

integer	insanitary
integral	insanity
integrate	insecticide
intensive	insensitive
intention	insignificant
intercept	inspiration
interested	installation
interesting	intantaneous
interfere(d)	institution
interlock(ed)	insufficient
interlude	insulation
internal(ly)	insulator
interpret(ed)	integration
interrupt	integrity
intersect	intellectual(ly)
intersperse(d)	intelligence
interval	intelligent
intervene(d)	intensify(-ies)
ir.terview(ed)	(intensified)
intestine	intensity(-ies)
intimate	intentional(ly)
intricate	interaction
intriguing	interception
introduce(d)	interchangeable
intruder	interested
intrusion	interesting
invaded	interference
invader	interior
invalid	intermission
invasion	intermittent
invention	internally
inventive	intermediate
inventor	international(ly)
inventory(-ies)	interpolate
inversion	interpretation
investment	interpreted
investor	interpreter
invited	interpreting
involvement	interrogate
	interrogation
in- or en- ?	interrogative
	interrupted
iq- or eq- ?	intersection
–see next page	intervention
	intestinal(ly)
	intolerable
	intonation
	intoxicate
	intoxication
	-see next page

for E ...
see page 65

for H ...
see page 71

In these words you can hear the vowel sound i as in pig

* * *   * * * * [* *]

Iraqi	intransitive
irrigate	intravenous
irritate	introduction
	introductory
ir- or er- ?	invariably
	inventory(-ies)
Islamic	invertebrate
	investigate
is- or es- ?	investigation
	investigator
Italian	invisible
italic	invitation
Italy	involuntary
it- or et- ?	in- or en- ?
ix- or ex- ?	iq- or eq- ?
	Iranian
	irrational(ly)
	irregular
	irregularity(-ies)
	irresistible
	irrigation
	irritability
	irritable
	irritation
	ir- or er- ?
	is- or es- ?
	italicise(d)
	ze
	it- or et- ?
	iv- or ev- ?
	ix- or ex- ?

for E ...
see page 65

for H ...
see page 71

for i-r
see page 247

In these words you can hear the vowel sound i as in pig

*	* *	* * *	* * * * [* *]
gin	ginger(ed)	genetic(ally)	genetically
	gipsy/gypsy(-ies)		geographically
jib(bed)	giraffe	gibberish	geography(-ies)
jig(ged)		Gibraltar	geological(ly)
	gymnast	gingerbread	geology
	gymslip		geometrical(ly)
	gypsy/gipsy(-ies)		geometry(-ies)
		gymnastics	geranium
	jibbing	gymnosperm	
	jiffy		gymnasium
	jigging		
	jigsaw		
	jingle(d)		
	jingling		

In these words you can hear the vowel sound i as in pig

*

kick(ed)
kid(ded)
kids
kill(ed)
kiln
kilt
kin
king
kink(ed)
kiss(ed)
kit(ted)

knit(ted)
[knit]

* *

kidded
kidding
kidnap(ped)
kidney
killer
killing
kindle(d)
kindling
kingdom
kinky(-ier,-iest)
kipper
kissing
kitchen
kitted
kitten
kitting

* * *

kidnapper
kidnapping
kilogram
kimono(s)

* * * *

kilometre
kindergarten

knickerbocker

for C ...
see page 59

knickers
knitted
knitting

for i-r
see page 248

for Qu
see page 83

In these words you can hear the vowel sound i as in pig

*	* *	* * *	* * * * [*]
lick(ed)	liberal(ly)	liberal(ly)	legitimate
lid	lichen	liberate	
lift	licorice	liberty(-ies)	liberally
limb	lifted	licorice	liberation
limp(ed)	lifting	limited	limitation
link(ed)	lily(-ies)	limiting	linguistically
*links (connections /	limit(ed)	linear	linoleum
golf course)	limpet	linguistic(ally)	literally
lip	linen	liniment	literary
lisp(ed)	linger(ed)	liquorice	literacy
list	linking	literal(ly)	literature
lit	lintel	literate	
live(d)	lipstick	literature	
	liquid	lithium	lyrically
lynch(es)	liquor	liverish	
*lynx(es) (animal)	liquorice	livery(-ies)	
	listed		
	listen(ed)	lyrical(ly)	
	listless		
	litmus		
	litter(ed)		
	little		
	liver		
	livid		
	living		
	lizard		
	lyric(ally)		

*	* *	* * *	* * * * [*]
midge	miaow	magician	manipulate
midst	mickey	malicious	
milk(ed)	midday	malignant	mechanical(ly)
mill(ed)	middle		melodically
*mince (cut into small pieces)	midget	meander(ed)	melodious
	midnight	mechanic(ally)	memorial
minced	midpoint	medallion	menagerie
mink	midway	melodic(ally)	meridian
mint	mildew(ed)	melodious	meticulous
*mints (more than one mint)	milkman	memento(es/s)	
	miller	meniscus(es/-i)	military
Miss	millet		millilitre
miss(es)	million	midsummer	millimetre
*miss(ed) (did miss)	mimic(ked)	militant	millionairess(es)
*mist (thin fog)	mineral	military	minority(-ies)
mitt	mingle(d)	militia	miraculous
mix(es)	mingling	milligram	miserable
mixed	minim	milliner	missionary(-ies)
	minnow	millionaire	misunderstand
myth	minstrel	mimicking	[misunderstood]
	minute	mimicry	
	mirage	mineral	mysterious
	mirror(ed)	miniature	mysticism
	mischief	minimal(ly)	mythology(-ies)
	misdeal	minimum	myxomatosis
	[misdealt]	minister(ed)	
	mislay	Minorca	
	[mislaid]	minuend	
	mislead	miracle	
	[misled]	mischievous	
	missile	miserable	
	missing	misery(-ies)	
	mission	misfortune	
	misspell(ed)	misgivings	
	[misspelt]	missionary(-ies)	
	misspend	mistaken	
	[misspent]	mistletoe	
	mistake		
	[mistook]	mnemonic	
	[mistaken]		
	mistress(es)	myriad	
	mistrust	mystery(-ies)	
	misuse(d)	mystical	
	mitten	mystify(-ies)	
	mixture	(mystified)	
		mythical	

Monsieur(Messieux)

Mr.
Mrs.

mystic(al)

for i-r
see page 249

In these words you can hear the vowel sound i as in pig

N

✻	✻ ✻	✻ ✻ ✻	✻ ✻ ✻ ✻
knit(ted) [knit]	knickers knitted knitting	mnemonic	knickerbocker
nib nil nip(ped) *nit (egg of louse / nitwit)	neglect	negation neglectful(ly)	nativity(-ies) necessity(-ies) neglectfully negotiate
nymph	nibble(d) nibbling nickel nickname nimble nipping nipple nitwit		

O

✻	✻ ✻	✻ ✻ ✻	✻ ✻ ✻ ✻ [✻ ✻]
	omit(ted)	official(ly)	auxiliary(-ies)
		omission omitted omitting	obliterate oblivion oblivious obsidian
		opinion	officially
			original(ly) originality originate

*	* *	* * *	* * * * [* * *]
pick(ed)	permit	Pacific	particular
pig(ged)	persist	pavilion	particularly
pill			
pin(ned)	physics	peculiar	peculiar
pinch(es)	physique	permission	pedestrian
pinched		permitted	peninsula
pink(ed)	pianist	permitting	peninsular
pip(ped)	piano(s)	persistence	perimeter
pit(ted)	picket	persistent	permissible
pitch(es)	picking	petition(ed)	petroleum
pitched	pickle(d)		
pith	pickling	physical(ly)	phenomena
	pickup	physician	phenomenal(ly)
prick(ed)	picnic	physicist	phenomenon
*prince (son of king)	*picture (painting,		philatelist
print	drawing or	pianist	philosophical(ly)
*prints (more than	photograph)	piano(s)	philosophy(-ies)
one print)	picture(d)	piccolo(s)	physically
	*pidgin (mixture of	picturesque	physiological(ly)
	two languages)	pinafore	physiology
	*pigeon (bird)	pinnacle	
	pigging	piranha	pianoforte
	piglet	piteous	pituitary
	pigment	pivoted	
	pigtail	pivoting	political(ly)
	pilchard		
	pilgrim	position(ed)	precipitate
	pillar		precipitation
	pillow(ed)	precaution	predictable
	pimple(d)	preceded	predominantly
	pincers	preceding	preliminary(-ies)
	pinion	precisely	preoccupation
	pinning	precision	presentable
	pipping	precocious	presumably
	*pistil (part of	prediction	principally
	flower)	preferring	proficiency
	*pistol (small hand	preparing	prohibited
	gun)	prescription	prohibiting
	piston	presented	prohibitive
	pitchblende	presenting	proliferate
	*pitcher (container	pretended	proliferation
	for liquids)	prettier	prolifically
	pitching	prettiest	provisional(ly)
	piteous	prevention	
	pitting	preventive	publicity
	pity(-ies)	primitive	
	(pitied)	-see next page	
	pivot(ed)		
	pixie		
	pizza		
	-see next page		

In these words you can hear the vowel sound i as in pig

* *

precede
precise
predict
prefer(red)
prepare(d)
prescribe(d)
present
preserve(d)
preside
presume(d)
pretence
pretend
pretty(-ier,-iest)
prevail(ed)
prevent
prickle(d)
prickly
primrose
princess(es)
printed
printer
printing
prism
prison
prisoner

pygmy(-ies)

* * *

*principal (chief)
principally
*principle (rule of action)
principled
prisoner
privacy
privilege(d)
prodigious
proficient
prohibit(ed)
prolific(ally)
provincial
provision
provisions

pyjamas
Pyrenees
pyramid
pyrites

Q

*

quick
quid
quill
quilt
quin
quince
quip(ped)
quit(ted)
[quit]
quiz(zed)

* *

quibble(d)
quibbling
quickly
quintet
quipping
quitted
quitting
quiver(ed)

* * *

quicksilver
quintuplet

* * * *

for i-r
see page 251

*	* *	* * *	* * * * [* *]
*real (genuine)	react	reaction	rapidity
	really	reactor	
rib(bed)	rebel(led)	reagent	reactionary(-ies)
rich(es)	rebound	realise(d)	realism
rid(ded)	recall(ed)	ze	realistic(ally)
[rid]	receipt	rebelling	reality(-ies)
ridge(d)	receive(d)	rebellion	receptacle
rift	recess(es)	rebellious	reciprocal(ly)
rig(ged)	recessed	receding	reciprocate
rim(med)	recite	receiver	recovery(-ies)
*ring(ed) (circle)	reclaim(ed)	receiving	refinery(-ies)
*ring (sound)	recoil(ed)	reception	refrigerator
[rang]	record	receptive	regretfully
[rung]	recruit	recession	relationship
ringed	reduce(d)	recessive	reliability(-ies)
rinse(d)	refer(red)	recital	reliable
rip(ped)	refine(d)	recorded	reluctantly
risk(ed)	reflect	recorder	remarkable
	reform(ed)	recording	remembering
*wring (twist)	refract	recover(ed)	repetitive
[wrung]	refrain(ed)	reduction	republican
wrist	refresh(es)	referral	repudiate
	refreshed	referring	resentfully
	refund	reflected	respectable
	refuse(d)	reflection	respectfully
	regain(ed)	reflector	respectively
	regard	reflexive	responsibility(-ies)
	regret(ted)	refraction	responsible
	rehearse(d)	refreshment	resuscitate
	reject	refusal	resuscitation
	rejoice(d)	regarded	returnable
	rejoin(ed)	regardless	reverberate
	relate	regatta	reversible
	relax(es)	regretful(ly)	
	relaxed	regretted	rhythmically
	release(d)	regretting	
	relent	rehearsal	ridiculous
	relief	rejection	ritually
	relieve(d)	related	
	rely(-ies)	relation	
	(relied)	relentless	
	remain(ed)	reliance	
	remark(ed)	religion	
	remind	religious	
	remote	reluctant	
	remove(d)	remainder	
	renew(ed)	remaining	
	renown(ed)	-see next page	
	repaid		
	repair(ed)		
	repay		
	[repaid]		
	-see next page		

In these words you can hear the vowel sound i as in pig

** **

*** ***

repeal(ed)
repeat
repel(led)
repent
replace(d)
reply(-ies)
  (replied)
report
repose(d)
reproach(es)
reproached
request
require(d)
research(es)
researched
*resent (feel
  angry at)
reserve(d)
resign(ed)
resist
resolve(d)
resort
resource(d)
respect
respire(d)
respond
response
restore(d)
restrain(ed)
restrict
result
resume(d)
retain(ed)
retard
retire(d)
retort
retreat
return(ed)
reveal(ed)
revenge(d)
reverse(d)
review(ed)
revise(d)
revive(d)
revolt
revolve(d)
reward

rhythm
rhythmic(ally)
-see next page

reminded
reminder
removal
removing
Renaissance
repeated
repeating
repellent
repelling
repentance
replacement
reported
reporter
republic
repulsive
requirement
researcher
resemblance
resemble(d)
resembling
resentful(ly)
resentment
resistance
resistor
resources
respectful(ly)
respective
resplendent
responsive
restriction
resultant
resulted
resulting
retarded
retention
retentive
retirement
returning
reversal
revision
revolver
rewritten

rhythmical(ly)

rickety
ridicule(d)
rigorous
ritual(ly)
riveted/rivetted
riveting/rivetting

* *

ribbing
ribbon
ridded
ridden
ridding
riddle(d)
riddling
*rigger (person
   who rigs)
rigging
rigid
*rigor (rigid state)
*rigour (severe
   conditions)
rimming
ringing
ripping
ripple(d)
rippling
risen
ritual(ly)
river
rivet(ed/ted)

wriggle(d)
wriggling
wrinkle(d)
wrinkling
written

In these words you can hear the vowel sound i as in pig

*	* *	* * *	* * * * [* *]
cinch(es)	cement	celestial	celestial
			certificate
schist	cigar	chivalrous	citizenship
scrimp	cirrus	chivalry	civilisation
scrip	cistern		zation
script	citrus	cigarette	
	city(-ies)	*cilia (more than one	cylindrical
shift	civic	cilium)	
shin(ned)	civil(ly)	cilium(-a)	salinity
ship(ped)		cinema	satirical(ly)
shrill	*cygnet (young swan)	cinnamon	
shrimp	*cymbals (discs to clash)	citizen	schizophrenia
shrink		civilian	schizophrenic(ally)
[shrank]	*Scilly (Isles)	civilise(d)	
[shrunk/shrunken]	scissors	ze	security(-ies)
	scribble(d)	civilly	severity(-ies)
sick	scripture		
sieve(d)		cylinder	significant
sift	seclude	Cypriot	similarity(-ies)
sill	secrete		similarly
silk	secure(d)	scriptural(ly)	simplicity
silt	select		simplification
sin(ned)	settee	secession	simulation
since	severe	secluded	simultaneous
sing		secretion	sincerity
[sang]	shilling	selected	sister-in-law
[sung]	shimmer(ed)	selecting	situated
sink	shingle	selection	situation
[sank]	shipment	selective	
[sunk/sunken]	shipping	selector	solicitor
sip(ped)	shipwreck(ed)	sequoia	sophisticated
sit	shiver(ed)	severely	
[sat]	shrivel(led)		specifically
six(th)		shipbuilding	spiritually
	sickness	shrivelling	
skid(ded)	signal(led)	–see next page	statistically
skill(ed)	*signet (seal / ring)		stimulation
skim(med)	*silly(-ier,-iest)		
skimp(ed)	(lacking sense)		subsidiary(-ies)
skin(ned)	silver(ed)		sufficiently
skip(ped)	simmer(ed)		–see next page
skit	simple		
	simpler		
slick	simply		
slid	–see next page		
slim(med)			
sling			
[slung]			
slink			
[slunk]			
slip(ped)			
slit			
[slit]			
–see next page			

for i-r
see page 252

✻ | ✻ ✻ | ✻ ✻ ✻ | ✻ ✻ ✻ ✻ [✻ ✻]

✻	✻ ✻	✻ ✻ ✻	✻ ✻ ✻ ✻ [✻ ✻]
smith	sincere	Sicily	syllabically
	sinew	signalling	symbolically
sniff(ed)	singer	signature	symbolism
snip(ped)	singing	signify(-ies)	symbiosis
	single(d)	(signified)	symbiotic(ally)
sphinx(es)	singly	silhouette	symmetrical(ly)
spill(ed)	sinning	silica	sympathetic(ally)
[spilt]	sipping	silicon	symphonically
spin	sissy(-ies)	*sillier (more silly)	synonymous
⌊span⌋	sister	silliest	synthesiser
⌊spun⌋	sitter	silverware	synthetically
spit	sitting	similar	systematic(ally)
[spat]	sixpence	simile	
[spit]	sixteen(th)	simplify(-ies)	
splint	sixty(-ies)	(simplified)	
split	sizzle(d)	simulate	
⌊split⌋	sizzling	sincerely	
sprig		Singapore	
spring	skidded	singular	
⌊sprang⌋	skidding	sinister	
⌊sprung⌋	skilful(ly)	sixtieth	
	skillet		
squib	skimming	skilfully	
squid	skinning		
squint	skinny(-ier,-iest)	slippery	
	skipper		
stick	skipping	snivelling	
[stuck]	skittle		
stiff		specific(ally)	
still(ed)	slimming	spiritual(ly)	
stilts	slipper(ed)		
sting	slippery	statistics	
[stung]	slipping	stimulant	
stink	slipstone	stimulate	
[stank]	slither(ed)	stimulus(-i)	
[stunk]	slitting	stinginess	
stint			
stitch(es)	smitten	submission	
stitched		submissive	
strict	sniffle(d)	submitted	
string	sniffling	submitting	
[strung]	snigger(ed)	subscription	
strip(ped)	snippet	sufficient	
-see next page	snivel(led)	suspicion	
	-see next page	suspicious	
		Switzerland	
		swivelling	
		-see next page	

for i-r
see page 252

In these words you can hear the vowel sound i as in pig

*

swift
swig
swill(ed)
swim
[swam]
[swum]
swing
[swung]
swish(ed)
Swiss
switch(ed)

* *

spilling
spinach
spindle
spinning
spinster
spitting
splinter(ed)
splitting
spirit
springboard
springtime
sprinkle(d)
sprinkling

squirrel

sticking
sticky(-ier,-iest)
stigma
stingy(-ier,-iest)
stirrup
stitches
stitching
stricken
stridden
stringent
stripper
stripping
striven

submit(ted)

swiftly
swimmer
swimming
swindle(d)
swindling
swinging
swivel(led)

symbol
*symbols (signs)
symptom
syringe(d)
syrup
system

* * *

sycamore
syllabic(ally)
syllable
symbolic(ally)
symbolise(d)
    ze
symmetry(-ies)
sympathy(-ies)
symphonic(ally)
symphony(-ies)
synchromesh
synchronise(d)
    ze
syndicate
synonym
synthesis(syntheses)
synthetic(ally)
Syria

for i-r
see page 252

*	* *	* * *	* * * * [* *]
thick	terrain	terrific(ally)	telegraphy
thin(ned)			telephonist
thing	thicket	timpani	terrestrial(ly)
think	thickness		terrifically
[thought]	thimble	tradition	
this	thinner	tremendous	theatrical(ly)
thrift	thinning	tributary(-ies)	theodolite
thrill(ed)	thistle	trickery	theological(ly)
	thither	Trinidad	theology(-ies)
tick(ed)	thrifty(-ier,-iest)		theoretical(ly)
till	thriven	typical(ly)	
tilt		tyrannise(d)	traditional(ly)
tin(ned)	ticket	ze	tributary(-ies)
tint	tickle(d)	tyranny(-ies)	trigonometric
tip(ped)	ticklish		trigonometry
tit	tiller		
	timber		typically
trick(ed)	timid		tyrannical(ly)
trim(med)	tinder		tyrannosaurus
trip(ped)	tingle(d)		
	tingling		
twig(ged)	tinkle(d)		
twin(ned)	tinkling		
twinge	tinning		
twist	tinsel		
twit	tipping		
twitch(es)	tiptoe(d)		
twitched	tissue		
	titter(ed)		
	tribute		
	trickle(d)		
	trickling		
	tricky(-ier,-iest)		
	trigger(ed)		
	trillion		
	trimming		
	trimmings		
	trinket		
	triple(d)		
	triplet		
	tripling		
	tripping		
	twiddle(d)		
	twiddling		
	twigging		
	twinkle(d)		
	twinkling		
	twinning		
	twisted		
	twisting		
	twitter(ed)		

for i-r
see page 253

In these words you can hear the vowel sound i as in pig

❊

❊ ❊

until

❊ ❊ ❊

❊ ❊ ❊ ❊

V

❊

❊ ❊

❊ ❊ ❊

❊ ❊ ❊ ❊ [❊]

vicar
vicious
victim
victor
victual
vigil
vigour
villa
village
*villain (wicked
    person)
*villein (free
    villager in
    medieval times)
vineyard
viscose
vision
visit(ed)
visual(ly)
vivid
vixen

vanilla

vermilion

vibrato
vicarage
victimise(d)
        ze
victory(-ies)
video
Vietnam
vigilance
vigilant
vigorous
villager
vinegar
viola
visible
visited
visiting
visitor
visual(ly)
visualise(d)
        ze
vitamin

validity

velocity(-ies)
vermiculite

vicinity
Victorian
victorious
Vietnamese
vigilante
visibility
visualise(d)
        ze
visually

for i-r
see page 254

*

whelk
*which (that /
    which one)
whiff(ed)
Whig
whim
whip(ped)
whisk(ed)
whiz(zed)

wick
width
wig(ged)
will(ed)
wilt
win
[won]
wince(d)
wind
wing(ed)
wink(ed)
wish(es)
wished
wisp
wit(ted)
*witch (woman said
    to use magic)
with

*wring (twist)
[wrung]
wrist
writ

* *

whimper(ed)
whinny(-ies)
    (whinnied)
whippet
whipping
whisker(ed)
whiskey
whisky(-ies)
whisper(ed)
whistle(d)
whistling
*whither (to which
    place)
Whitsun
whittle(d)
whittling
whizzing

wicked
wicker
wicket
widow(ed)
wigging
wiggle(d)
wiggling
wigwam
willing
willow
windmill
window
windpipe
windscreen
windward
windy(-ier,-iest)
winkle(d)
winkling
winner
winning
winter(ed)
wintry
wishing
wisdom
wistful(ly)
-see next page

* * *

whichever

wilderness(es)
window-sill
wintertime
wistfully
withdrawal

* * * *

witticism

for i-r
see page 255

In these words you can hear the vowel sound i as in pig

* *

witchcraft
withdraw
[withdrew]
withdrawal
withdrawn
*wither(ed) (become
  dry and shrivelled)
withhold
[withheld]
within
without
withstand
[withstood]
witness(ed)
witty(-ier,-iest)
wizened

women

wriggle(d)
wriggling
wrinkle(d)
wrinkling
written

for i-r
see page 255

Z

*

zinc
zip(ped)

* *

zigzag(ged)
zipper
zipping
zither

* * *

zigzagging
Zimbabwe

* * * *

*	* *	* * *	* * * * [* * * *]
*-all (every one)	-abroad	abolish(es)	abdominal
-alms	abscond	abolished	abominable
			abominate
*-awe (fear and wonder)	across	acknowledge(d)	
-awed	adopt	allotment	accommodate
-awl (boring tool)		allotted	accommodation
	agog	allotting	acknowledgement/
-ought		-almighty	acknowledgment
	allot(ted)	alongside	acknowledging
	almost	-already	
	aloft	-alternate	-alternating
	along		-alternative
	-alright	apostle	-alternator
	-also	-appalling	-altogether
	*-altar (holy table)		
	*-alter(ed) (change)	astonish(es)	anonymous
	-although	astonished	
	-always		apologetic(ally)
		-audible	apologise(d)
	anon	-audience	ze
		-auditory	apology(-ies)
	-appal(led)	-aurally	apostrophe
	-applaud	-aurora	approximate
	-applause	-Austria	approximately
		-authentic(ally)	approximation
	assault	-authoress(es)	
		-authorise(d)	astonishment
	-auburn	ze	astrology
	-auction(ed)	-autograph(ed)	astronomer
	*-auger (tool)		astronomy
	*-augur (suggest for the future)	-awfully	-auditory
	-August		Australia
	-august		-authentically
	-aural(ly)		-authority(-ies)
	-austere		-autobiography(-ies)
	-author		-autobiographical(ly)
	-autumn		-automatic(ally)
			-automation
	-awesome/awsome		-automobile
	-awful(ly)		-autonomic
	-awkward		-autonomous
			-auxiliary(-ies)

for H . . .
see page 102

for o-r
see page 256

In these words you can hear the vowel sound o as in dog

*   * *   * * *   * * * *

*-bald (lacking hair)
 -balk/baulk(ed)
*-ball (round object /
    dance)
*-balled (made into a
    ball)
*-balm (ointment)
 -baulk/balk(ed)
*-bawl (yell)
*-bawled (did yell)

 block(ed)
*blond (man with
    fair hair)
*blonde (woman with
    fair hair)
 blot(ted)

 bob(bed)
 bog(ged)
*bomb (explosive
    device)
 bombed
 bond
 boss(es)
 bossed
-bought
 box(es)
 boxed

-brawl(ed)
-broad
 bronze(d)
-brought
 broth

-balmy
-balsa
 balsam
-Baltic
-ballroom
-basalt
-bauxite

 because
-befall
 [befell]
-[befallen]
 belong(ed)
 beyond

 blancmange
 blockade
 blockboard
 blossom(ed)
 blotted
 blotter
 blotting

 bobbing
 body(-ies)
    (bodied)
 boggy(-ier,-iest)
 bombard
 bomber
 bonnet
 bonny(-ier,-iest)
 borrow(ed)
 bossy(-ier,-iest)
 bother(ed)
 bottle(d)
 bottling
 bottom(ed)
 boxer
 boxing

-broadcast
-[broadcast]
-broadside
 bronchial
 bronco

-befallen
 belonging

 bodily
 borrowing
 botany

-broadcasting
 broccoli
 bronchitis

barometer

binocular
binoculars

Bolivia
botanical

brontosaurus

In these words 'o' is a neutral vowel.
It sounds like the 'a' in 'astonish'.

Bolivia   botanical   brocade

for o-r
see page 257

*

-call(ed)
-calm(ed)
*-caught (got /
    trapped)
-caulk(ed)
-cause(d)
-caw(ed)

-chalk(ed)
chop(ped)

*-clause (words in
    sentence / part
    of written
    agreement)
-claw(ed)
*-claws (curved nails
    or limbs)

clock(ed)
clod
clot(ted)
cloth

cock(ed)
cod
cop(ped)
*cops (the police)
*copse (small wood)
cost
[cost]
cot
cough(ed)

-crawl(ed)
crock(ed)
croft
crop(ped)

cross(es)
crossed

for Qu ...
see page 109

* *

-calling
-cauldron
-causing
-caustic(ally)
-caution(ed)
-cautious

chocolate
chopper
chopping
chopsticks
chronic(ally)

clockwist
clotted
clotting

cobbler
cobweb(bed)
cocker
cockerel
cockle
Cockney
cockpit
cockroach(es)
cocktail
codfish
coffee
coffin
*collage (picture
    made by sticking
    items to a board)
collar(ed)
colleague
collect
*college (educational
    establishment)
collie
collier
column(ed)
combat(ted)
combine
comet
comic
comma
comment
commerce
common
commune
-see next page

* * *

cauliflower
-caustically

chloroform(ed)
chlorophyll
chronically

cochlea
cockerel
colliery(-ies)
colonise(d)
    ze
colony(-ies)
colonist
colossal(ly)
combatted
combatting
comedy(-ies)
comical(ly)
commentary(-ies)
commonplace
commonwealth
communal(ly)
communist
compensate
competence
competent
*complement
    (something that
    completes)
complicate
*compliment
    (expression of
    praise or
    politeness)
composite
comprehend
compromise
concentrate
concentric
concoction
conference
confidence
confident
confiscate
congregate
congruent
conical
conifer
conjugate
connoisseur
conqueror
-see next page

* * * * [* *]

-caustically

chronically
chronological(ly)

colossally
combination
comically
commentator
commodity(-ies)
communally
communism
commutative
commutator
comparable
compensation
competition
*complementary
    (making up a
    whole)
complication
*complimentary
    (expressing praise)
composition
compositor
comprehension
comprehensive
computation
concentration
concertina
condensation
confidential(ly)
confirmation
confrontation
conglomerate
conglomeration
congregation
conscientious
consecration
consequently
conservation
consolation
constellation
constitution
-see next page

for o-r
see page 258

In these words you can hear the vowel sound o as in dog

✳ ✳   ✳ ✳ ✳   ✳ ✳ ✳ ✳ [✳]

compact   consciousness   continental(ly)
complex(es)   consecrate   continuity(-ies)
compound   consequence   contraception
comrade   consequent   contraceptive
concave   consonant   contradiction
concept   constitute   contribution
concert   contemplate   controversial(ly)
concoct   continent   controversy(-ies)
concord   contradict   conversation
concrete   contrary   coronation
conduct   convalesce(d)   correlation
conflict   correspond   *correspondence
congress   corridor   (exchange of
*conker (horse   cosmetic(ally)   letters /
   chestnut)   cosmically   similarity)
conic   cosmonaut   correspondent
*conquer(ed) (defeat) cottoning   *correspondents (those
conquest   sending letters or
conscience   crockery   reports)
conscious   crocodile   corresponding
conscript   cosmetically
console   cosmically
constant
contact
content   kilometer
contents
contest
context
contour(ed)
contract
contrast
convent
converse
convert
convex
convict
convoy
copper
copy(-ies)
   (copied)
copping
*coral (substance
   formed from bones
   of sea creatures)
*corral (enclosure for
   horses and cattle)
cosmic(ally)
costly
costume(d)
cottage
cotter(ed)
cotton(ed)
-see next page

for Qu ...
see page 109

for o-r
see page 258

In these words you can hear the vowel sound o as in dog

* *

-crawling
cropping
crossbar
crossing
crossroads
crosswise
crossword
crotchet

for Qu ...
see page 109

for o-r
see page 258

In these words the first letter 'o' is a neutral vowel.
It... er.... er.... er.... sounds like the 'a' in 'astonish'.

'CORRECT' WORDS

cholesterol
chorale
cocoon(ed)
collapse(d)
collapsible
collect(ing)
collection
collective
collector
collide
collision
cologne
colonial(ly)
combat(ted)
combatting
combine(d)
combining
combustible
combustion
comedian
comedienne
command(er)
commandment
commemorate
commemoration
commence(d)
commercial(ly)
commission(ed)
commissioner
commit(ted)
commitment
committee
committing
commodity(-ies)
commotion
communal(ly)
commune(d)
communicate
communication
communion

community(-ies)
commutative
commute(r)
companion
compare(d)
comparing
comparison
compartment
compassion(ate)
compatible
compel(led)
compelling
compete
competitive
competitor
compile(d)
complain(ed)
complaint
complete(ly)
completion
complexion
component
compose(d)
composer
compress(es)
compressed
compression
compressor
comprise(d)
comprising
compulsory
compute(r)
computerise(d)
      ze
conceal(ed)
conceit(ed)
conceive(d)
concentric
conception
concern(ed)

concerning
concession
conclude
conclusion
concurrent
concuss(es)
concussed
concussing
concussion
condemn(ed)
condense(d)
condenser
condition(ed)
conditional(ly)
conduct(ion)
conductor
confectioner(y)
confer(red)
conferring
confess(es)
confessed
confession(al)
confessor
confetti
confide
confine(d)
confirm(ed)
conflict
conform(ed)
conformist
conformity
confront
confuse(d)
confusion
congenital(ly)
congratulate
congratulations
coniferous
conjecture(d)
conjunction

connect(ed)
connecting
connection
connector
conscription
consecutive
consensus
consent
conservative
conserve(d)
consider(ed)
considerable
considerate
consideration
consist(ing)
consistency(-ies)
consistent
console(d)
conspicuous
conspiracy(-ies)
conspire(d)
constabulary(-ies)
constituency(-ies)
constituent
construct(ed)
construction
constructive
consult
consume(d)
consumer
consumption
contagious
contain(ed)
container
contaminate
contamination
contemporary(-ies)
contempt(ible)
contemptuous
contend

content
contention
contest(ant)
contingency(-ies)
continual(ly)
continuation
continue(d)
continuous
continuum
contract(ion)
contractor
contralto(s)
contraption
contrary
contrast
contribute(d)
control(led)
controller
controlling
convenience
convenient
convention(ally)
converge(d)
convergent
converse(d)
conversion
convert(ible)
convey(ed)
conveyer
convict(ion)
convince(d)
convulse(d)
convulsion
convulsive
correct(ed)
correction
correctly
corrode
corrosion
corrupt(ion)

In these words you can hear the vowel sound o as in dog

*	* *	* * *	* * * * [*]
-daub(ed)	-daughter	demolish(es)	democracy(-ies)
-dawn(ed)	-dawdle	demolished	denomination
	-dawdling	deposit(ed)	denominator
dock(ed)			deposited
dodge(d)	demobbed	dishonest	depositing
dog(ged)			
doll(ed)	dissolve(d)	doctrinal(ly)	disqualify(-ies)
don(ned)		document	(disqualified)
dong(ed)	doctor(ed)	doggedly	
dot(ted)	doctrine	dominant	doctrinally
	dodgem	dominate	dolphinarium
*-draw (pull /	dodger	domino(es)	domination
sketch)	dodging		
[drew]	dodgy(-ier,-iest)		dromedary(-ies)
-[drawn]	dogging		
*-drawer (sliding	doghouse		
container)	dollar		
-drawl(ed)	dolphin		
drop(ped)	donkey		
	donning		
	dotted		
	dotting		

-draw (pull /
  sketch)
 [drew]
-[drawn]
*-drawer (sliding
   container)
-drawl(ed)
 drop(ped)

-drawbridge
-drawing
 droplet
 dropout
 dropping

> In these words 'o' is a neutral vowel.
> It sounds like the 'a' in 'astonish'.
>
> domain   domestic(ally)   domesticate

for o-r
see page 259

E

*	* *	* * *	* * * * [*]
	encore(d)	em- or im- ?	ecology
			economy(-ies)
	en- or in- ?	en- or in- ?	
			el- or il- ?
	evolve(d)	erotic(ally)	
			em- or im- ?
	exalt	exalted	
	-exhaust	-exhausted	en- or in- ?
		-exhaustion	
		exotic(ally)	equality
			erotically
			exotically

for I ...
see page 102

for o-r
see page 259

✲

-fall
 [fell]
-[fallen]
 false
 fault

-fawn(ed)

-flaunt
-flaw(ed)
 flock(ed)
 flog(ged)
 flop(ped)

 fog
 fond
 font
-fought
 fox(es)
 foxed

-fraud
 frock
 frog
 from
 frond
 frost
 froth(ed)

for th ...
see page 133

✲ ✲

-falcon
-fallen
-falling
-fallout
 falter(ed)
 faulty

 flogging
 flopping
 floppy(-ier,-iest)
 floral
 florist

 fodder
 foggy(-ier,-iest)
 foghorn
 follow(ed)
 folly(-ies)
 fondle(d)
 fondling
 forage(d)
 forehead
 foreign
 forest
 forgone/foregone
 forgot
 fossil
 foster(ed)
 foxglove

 frogman
 frolic(ked)

 phosphate

✲ ✲ ✲

foggiest

follower
following
foreigner
forestry
forgotten

frolicking

phosphorus

✲ ✲ ✲ ✲ [✲]

ferocity

phenomena
phenomenal(ly)
phenomenon
philosophy(-ies)
photographer
photography

 for o-r
see page 260

In these words you can hear the vowel sound o / as in dog

✻	✻ ✻	✻ ✻ ✻	✻ ✻ ✻ ✻
-gaunt	-gaudy(-ier,-iest)	galoshes	geography(-ies)
-gauze			geology
	globule	Gibraltar	geometry(-ies)
gloss(es)	glossy(-ies)		
glossed		globular	
	gobble(d)	glockenspiel	
-gnaw(ed)	*gobbling (greedily	glossary(-ies)	
	eating)		
god	goblet	godparents	
God	*goblin (evil spirit)	golliwog	
golf(ed)	goddess(es)	*gorilla (ape)	
gone	goggles	gossiping	
gong	golly		
gosh	gosling	grovelling	
got	gospel		
	gossip(ed)		
	Gothic		
	grotto(es/s)		
	grotty(-ier,-iest)		
	grovel(led)		
	grovelling		

for o-r
see page 261

In this word 'o' is a neutral vowel.
It sounds like the 'a' in 'astonish'.

gorilla

H

SHORT VOWEL ⓞ

*

*-hall (large room /
    passage)
halt
*-haul(ed) (drag /
    amount gained)
-hauled
-haunt
-hawk(ed)

hob
hog(ged)
honk(ed)
hop(ped)
hot

* *

-halter
-haughty(-ier,-iest)
-haunches

hobble(d)
hobbling
hobby(-ies)
hockey
hogging
Holland
holler(ed)
hollow(ed)
holly
honest
Hongkong
honour(ed)
hopper
hopping
hopscotch
horrid
horror
hostage
*hostel (place to stay
    in)
*hostile (unfriendly)
hotch-potch
hotter
hottest
hovel
hover(ed)

* * *

-haughtily

historic(ally)

holiday
hollyhock
homonym
honesty
honestly
honourable
horizon
horoscope
horrible
horrify(-ies)
    (horrified)
hospital
hovercraft

hypnotic(ally)

* * * * [*]

historical(ly)

holography
honorary
honourable
horizontal(ly)
horrifying
hospitable
hospitality
hostility(-ies)

hypnotically

for o-r
see page 261

⫿

*

for E ...
see page 99

* *

-instal(led)
involve(d)

iv- or ev- ?

* * *

impromptu(s)
improper

-installing
-instalment/
    installment
involvement

ir- or er- ?

ix- or ex- ?

for o-r
see page 262

* * * * [*]

ic- or ec- ?

illogical(ly)

impossible

-inaugural
inoculate

iq- or eq- ?

ir- or er- ?

ix- or ex- ?

102

In these words you can hear the vowel sound o as in dog

J

*
-jaunt
-jaw

job(bed)
jog(ged)
jolt
jot(ted)

* *
-jaunty(-ier,-iest)

jobbing
jockey(ed)
jodhpurs
jogging
jolly(-ies)
   (jollied)
jostle(d)
jostling
jotted
jotter
jotting

* * *
-Gibraltar

jocular

* * * *
geography(-ies)
geology
geometry(-ies)

for o-r
see page 262

K

*
knob
knock(ed)
*knot(ted) (tied
   fastening / hard
   part of wood /
   sea mile [per
   hour])

for C ...
see page 96

for Qu ...
see page 109

* *
knocker
knotted
knotting
knotty(-ier,-iest)
knowledge

In this word 'o' is a neutral vowel.
It sounds like the 'a' in 'astonish'.

Korea(n)

* * * *
kilometre

knowledgeable

for o-r
see page 262

*

-launch(es)
-launched
-law
-lawn

lob(bed)
*loch (Scottish word
    for 'lake')
*lock (fastening
    device)
locked
lodge(d)
loft
log(ged)
long(ed)
lop(ped)
loss(es)
lost
lot

* *

-launcher
-launder(ed)
-laundry(-ies)
 laurel
-lawyer

lobbing
lobby(-ies)
    (lobbied)
lobster
locker
locket
lodger
lodging
lofty(-ier,-iest)
logging
logic(ally)
longer
longest
lopping
lorry(-ies)
lotto
lozenge

* * *

laconic(ally)
-launderette

logical(ly)
lollipop
longitude

* * * * [* *]

laboratory(-ies)
laconically

logarithm
logically
longitudinal(ly)

for o-r
see page 263

In these words you can hear the vowel sound o as in dog

*

malt
-maul(ed)
-mauve

mob(bed)
mock(ed)
mop(ped)
mosque
moss(es)
moth

for o-r
see page 263

* *

Malta

mobbing
model(led)
modelling
moderate
modern
modest
module
mollusc
monarch
mongol
mongoose(s)
monsoon
monster
monstrous
mopping
*moral(ly) (concerning
    right and wrong)
*morale (confidence)
morrow
mossy(-ier,-iest)
mottled
motto(es/s)

* * *

melodic(ally)

mnemonic

moccasin
mockery(-ies)
modelling
moderate
modernise(d)
       ze
modesty
modify(-ies)
   (modified)
molasses
molecule
monastery(-ies)
monitor(ed)
monochrome
monotone
monoxide
monument
morally
moralise(d)
       ze
Morocco
mosquito(es)

* * * * [* * *]

mahogany
majority(-ies)

melodically

moderation
moderato
modification
modifier
molecular
monochromatic(ally)
monopolise(d)
       ze
monopoly(-ies)
monotonous
monumental(ly)
morality(-ies)

mythology(-ies)

In these words the
'o' may be neutral.

Mohammed   momentum
molasses   morale
molecular

N

*

-gnaw(ed)

knob
knock(ed)
*knot(ted) (tied fastening /
    hard part of wood /
    sea mile [per hour])

-naught/nought (zero)

nod(ded)
*not (used in
    denial, negation,
    refusal)
notch(es)
notched
-nought/naught (zero)

* *

knocker
knotted
knotting
knotty(-ier,-iest)
knowledge

-naughty(-ier,-iest)

nodding
nodule
nonsense
nostril
novel
novice
nozzle

* * *

mnemonic

-nautical(ly)
-naughtier
-naughtiest
-naughtiness

neurotic(ally)

nocturnal(ly)
nominal(ly)
nominate
novelty(-ies)

* * * *

knowledgeable

-nautically

neurotically

nocturnally
nominally
nonconformist
notwithstanding

for o-r
see page 263

In these words you can hear the vowel sound o as in dog

*

*-all (every one)
-alms

*-awe (fear and wonder)
-awed
*-awl (boring tool)

odd

of
off

on

-ought

ox(en)

for H ...
see page 102

* *

almost
-alright
also
*-altar (holy table)
*-alter(ed) (change)
-although
-always

-auburn
-auction(ed)
*-auger (tool)
*-augur (suggest for the
    future)
-August
-august
-aural(ly)
-austere
-author
-autumn

-awesome/awsome
-awful(ly)
-awkward

honest
honour(ed)

object
oblique
oblong

o'clock
octane
octave

oddment

offer(ed)
offering
office
offset
offshore
offside
offspring
offstage
often

olive
-see next page

* * *

-almighty
-already
-alternate

-audible
-audience
-auditory
-aurally
-aurora
-Austria
-authentic(ally)
-authoress(es)
-authorise(d)
            ze
-autograph(ed)

-awfully

honesty
honourable

obsolete
obstacle
obvious

occupant
occupy(-ies)
   (occupied)
octagon
October
octopus(es/-i)
oculist

oddity(-ies)

offering
offertory(-ies)
officer

ominous
omnibus

oncoming
onlooker
-see next page

* * * * [* * * *]

-alternating
-alternative
-alternator
-altogether

-auditory
Australia
-authentically
-authority(-ies)
-autobiography(-ies)
-autobiographical(ly)
-automatic(ally)
-automation
-automobile
-autonomic
-autonomous
-auxiliary(-ies)

honorary
honourable

obligation
observation
obsidian
obviously

occupation
occupier
octagonal

offertory(-ies)

operated
operatic(ally)
operating
operation
operator
opportunity(-ies)
opposition
optically
optimally
optimistic(ally)

-see next page

 for o-r
see page 264

In these words you can hear the vowel sound o as in dog

*	* *	* * *	* * * * [* *]
	omelette	opera	orienteering
		operate	
	onset	opossum	oxidisation
	onslaught	opposite	zation
	onward	optical(ly)	oxyacetylene
		optician	
	opera	optimal(ly)	
	optic(ally)	optimist	
	option	optional	
	orange	orator	
		oratory	
	osprey	origin	
	ostrich(es)		
		osmium	
	otter	osmosis	

for H ...
see page 102

oxen
oxide

oxidise(d)
ze
oxygen

for o-r
see page 264

In these words the first letter 'o' is a neutral vowel.
It... er.... er.... er.... sounds like the 'a' in 'astonish'.

'ORIGINAL' WORDS

obedience	obscene	obsessive	offence	oppress(es)
obedient	obscure(d)	obstruct(ion)	offend	oppressed
obey(ed)	obscurity(-ies)	obstructive	offensive	oppression
object(ion)	observant	obtain(ed)	official(ly)	oppressive
objectionable	observatory(-ies)	obtuse	omission	oppressor
objective	observe(d)	occasion(al)	omit(ted)	original(ly)
oblige(d)	observer	occasionally	omitting	originality
oblique	observing	occur(red)	opinion	originate
obliterate	obsess(es)	occurrence	opossum	
oblivion	obsessed	occurring	opponent	
oblivious	obsessional(ly)	o'clock	oppose(d)	

✷   ✷ ✷   ✷ ✷ ✷   ✷ ✷ ✷ ✷ [✷ ✷]

✷	✷ ✷	✷ ✷ ✷	✷ ✷ ✷ ✷ [✷ ✷]
-palm(ed)	-palfrey	peroxide	pathology
*-pause (brief gap / hesitate)	phosphate	phosphorus	phenomena
-paused			phenomenal(ly)
*-paw (foot of animal)	plotted	podgier	phenomenon
-pawed	plotting	podgiest	philosophy(-ies)
-pawn(ed)		policy(-ies)	photographer
*-paws (feet of animal)	pocket	politics	photography
	podded	pollinate	
plot(ted)	podding	pollution	politician
	podgy(-ier,-iest)	poltergeist	pollination
pod(ded)	polish(es)	polygon	Polynesia
pomp	polished	ponderous	polynomial
pond	polka	*populace (common people)	polyphonic(ally)
pop(ped)	pollen	*populous (full of people)	polyphony
pot(ted)	ponder(ed)	popular	polytechnic
	pontoon	populate	polyurethane
-prawn	popcorn	positive	popularity
prod(ded)	poplar	possible	pomegranate
prompt	poplin	possibly	population
prong(ed)	popping	postulate	possibility(-ies)
prop(ped)	poppy(-ies)	pottery(-ies)	
	porridge	poverty	predominantly
-psalm	possum		probability(-ies)
	posture(d)	-precaution	proclamation
	potted	probable	profitable
	potting	probably	propaganda
		prodigal	proposition
	problem	prodigy(-ies)	prosecution
	prodded	profited	prosperity
	prodding	profiting	provocation
	produce	progeny	provocative
	product	projectile	
	*profit(ed) (gain)	promenade	
	project	prominent	
	prolong(ed)	promising	
	promise(d)	propagate	
	proper	propelling	
	*prophet (inspired religious leader)	propellor	
	propose(d)	*prophecy(-ies) (statement about a future event)	
	propping	*prophesy(-ies) (make a statement about the future) (prophesied)	
	prospect		
	prosper(ed)		
	prostate	properly	
	prostrate	property(-ies)	
	proverb	-see next page	
	province		

for o-r
see page 265

In these words you can hear the vowel sound **o** as in **dog**

* * *

prosecute
prospective
prospector
prosperous
Protestant
prostitute
providence
provident

for o-r
see page 265

In these words the first letter 'o' is a neutral vowel.
It... er.... er.... er.... sounds like the 'a' in 'astonish'.

'PROFOUND' WORDS

phonetic(ally)	probation	professional(ly)	promote	prospectus(es)
photographer	procedure	professor	promotion	protect(ed)
photography	proceed(ing)	proficiency	pronounce(d)	protection
police(man)	procession	proficient	pronouncement	protective
polite(ly)	proclaim(ed)	profound	pronouncing	protector
political(ly)	procure(d)	profuse	pronunciation	protest
pollute	prodigious	profusion	propel(led)	protractor
pollution	produce(d)	progression	propelling	protrude
polyphony	producer	progressive	propeller	provide(d)
position(ed)	producing	prohibit(ed)	proportional(ly)	providing
possess(es)	production	prohibiting	proposal	provincial
possessed	productive	prohibitive	propose(d)	provision(s)
possession	profane	project(ion)	proprietor	provisional(ly)
possessive	profess(es)	projectile	propulsion	provocative
potato(es)	professed	projector	prospect(ive)	provoke(d)
potential(ly)	professing	prolific(ally)	prospector	

Ⓠ

* *

quadrant
quarrel(led)
quarry(-ies)
(quarried)

* * *

quadrangle
quadratic
quadruped
quadruple(d)
quadruplet
qualify(-ies)
(qualified)
quality(-ies)
quantity(-ies)
quarantine
quarrelling

* * * * [*]

quadrilateral
qualification

In these words you can hear the vowel sound o as in dog

*

-raw

rob(bed)
rock(ed)
rod(ded)
romp(ed)
rot(ted)

wrath

wrong(ed)

* *

-recall(ed)
resolve(d)
respond
response
revolt
revolve(d)

rhombus

robber
robbing
robin
rocker
rocket
rocky(-ier,-iest)
rodded
rodding
*rollick (act with
    enjoyment)
*rollock/rowlock
    (pivot for oar)
rosin(ed)
roster
rotted
rotten
rotting
*rowlock/rollock
    (pivot for oar)

* * *

rendezvous
responsive
revolver

robbery(-ies)
rockery(-ies)
rollicking

* * * * [* *]

responsibility(-ies)
responsible

for o-r
see page 266

In these words 'o' is a neutral vowel.
It sounds like the 'a' in 'astonish'.

romance
romantic(ally)

In these words you can hear the vowel sound o as in dog

*

-psalm

salt
-sauce
-saw
-saw(ed)
-[sawn]

-scald
scoff(ed)
scone
scotch(ed)
Scotch
-scrawl(ed)

-shawl
shock(ed)
shod
shone
shop(ped)
shot

slog(ged)
slop(ped)
slosh(es)
sloshed
slot(ted)

-small
smock(ed)
smog

sob(bed)
sock(ed)
sod
soft
solve(d)
song
-sought

-spawn(ed)
spot(ted)
-sprawl(ed)

-see next page

* *

-salty(-ier,-iest)
-saucer
-saucepan
-saucy(-ier,-iest)
-saunter(ed)
sausage

scholar
scoffing
Scotland
Scottish

shoddy(-ier,-iest)
shopper
shopping
shotgun

-slaughter(ed)
slogging
slopping
sloppy(-ier,-iest)
slotted
slotting

-smaller
-smallest
-smallpox
smocking

sobbing
soccer
socket
sodden
soften(ed)
softer
softly
software
soggy(-ier,-iest)
solder(ed)
solemn
solid
solvent
solving
sorrow(ed)
sorry(-ier,-iest)
sovereign

-see next page

* * *

-saucily

scholarship

shopkeeper

soldering
solenoid
solitary
solitude
soluble
solution
sombrero(s)
sovereignty(-ies)
soviet

-strawberry(-ies)

symbolic(ally)
symphonic(ally)

* * * * [*]

solubility

spontaneity
spontaneous

symbolically
symphonically
synonymous

for o-r
see page 267

In these words you can hear the vowel sound o as in dog

111

✻   ✻ ✻

squad   sponsor(ed)
squash(ed)   spotlight
squat(ted)   spotted
-squawk(ed)   spotting
                       sprocket
-stalk(ed)
-stall(ed)   squabble(d)
-staunch(es)   squabbling
-staunched   squadron
 stock(ed)   squalid
 stodge   squander(ed)
 stop(ped)   squatted
-straw   squatter
 strong   squatting

 swab(bed)   -stalling
 swamp(ed)   -stalwart
 swan   stockade
 swap(ped)   stocking(ed)
*swat (slap with a   stodgy(-ier,-iest)
    flat object)   stopping
*swot (study hard)   -strawberry(-ies)
                       stronger
                       strongest
                       strongly

                       swabbing
                       swallow(ed)
                       swapping
                      *swatted   (see
                      *swatting 'swat')
                      *swotted   (see
                      *swotting 'swot')

for o-r
see page 267

> In these words the first letter 'o'
> is a neutral vowel. It.. er... er...
> sounds like the 'a' in 'astonish'.
>
> society(-ies)   Somalia
> solicitor   sophisticated
> solution   soprano(s)

In these words you can hear the vowel sound o as in dog

*

-talk(ed)
-tall
*-taut (tight)
*-taught (instructed)
-taunt

-thaw(ed)
thongs
-thought
throb(bed)
throng(ed)

tongs
top(ped)
toss(ed)

trod
trot(ted)
trough(ed)

* *

-talking
-taller
-tallest

-thoughtful(ly)
throbbing
throttle(d)

toddle(d)
toffee
toggle
tomboy
tonic
tonsil
topic
topping
topple(d)
toppling
topsoil
torrent
toxic
toxin

trodden
trolley
trombone
tropic(ally)
trotted
trotting

* * *

-talkative

-thoughtfully

toboggan
tolerance
tolerate
tomahawk
tommy-gun
tomorrow
topical

tropical(ly)

* * * *

theodolite
thermometer

tonsillitis
topography
topology
topsy-turvy

tropically

for o-r
see page 268

In these words the first letter 'o'
is a neutral vowel. It.. er... er...
sounds like the 'a' in 'astonish'.

tobacco(s)   topography(-ies)
tobacconist   torrential(ly)
tomato(es)

U

*

* *

upon

* * *

* * * *

In these words you can hear the vowel sound o as in dog

V

*

*vault (gymnastic
  leap /
  underground room /
  arched roof)

*volt (unit of
  electrical force)

* *

volley(ed)
voltage
volume
vomit(ed)

* * *

volatile
volcano(es/s)
volcanic(ally)
voluntary
volunteer(ed)

* * * * [*]

velocity(-ies)

volcanically

> In this word 'o' is a neutral vowel.
> It sounds like the 'a' in 'astonish'.
>
> vocabulary(-ies)

W

*

waft
-walk(ed)
-wall(ed)
waltz(es)
waltzed
wand
want
was
*wash(es)
washed
wasp
watch(es)
watched
*watt (unit of
  electric power)
*watts (units of
  electric power)

*what (that or those
  which / which /
  how much / I do
  not understand)
*what's (what is)

wrath
wrong(ed)
-wrought

* *

wadding
waddle(d)
waddling
-walking
wallet
wallow(ed)
-walnut
-walrus
wander(ed)
wanted
wanting
warrant
warren
washer
*washers (people or
  machines that
  wash / insulating
  rings)
*washes (cleans with
  water)
washing
wasn't
watchdog
watchful(ly)
watching
watchman
watchword
-water(ed)

wobble(d)
wobbling
wobbly
wonky(-ier,-iest)

* * *

-wallpaper(ed)
warrior
washable
watchfully
-waterfall
-waterfowl
-watershed

whatever

* * * *

-walkie-talkie

> for o-r
> see page 269

In these words you can hear the vowel sound ○ as in dog

Y

*

yacht
-yawn(ed)

* *

yoghourt/
yoghurt/yogurt
yonder

* * *

* * * *

for o-r
see page 269

Z

*

* *

zombi/zombie

* * *

* * * *

zoology

In these words you can hear the vowel sound o as in dog

A

*	* *	* * *	* * * * [*]
	above	abundance	accompaniment
	abrupt	abundant	accompany(-ies)
			(accompanied)
	-adjourn(ed)	accomplish(es)	accomplishment
	adjust	accomplished	
	adult	accustom(ed)	
	-afoot	adjuster	
	among	adjustment	
	amongst		
		another	
	-assure(d)		
		assumption	
	-august	-assurance	

for u-r (ur/ir)
see page 242

B

*	* *	* * *	* * * *
blood	-because	becoming	brother-in-law
bluff(ed)	become	beloved	budgerigar
blunt	[became]		Bulgaria
blush(es)	[become]	brotherhood	
blushed	begun		
	beloved	buccaneer(ed)	
-book(ed)		bucketing	
	bloodshed	bucketful	
-brook(ed)	bloody(-ier,-iest)	-Buddhism	
brush(es)	blubber(ed)	budgerigar	
brushed	blunder(ed)	budgeting	
		buffalo(es)	
buck(ed)	-bookcase	-bulletin	
bud(ded)	-booklet	-bulldozer(ed)	
budge(d)	-bookshelf(-ves)	bumblebee	
buff(ed)	borough	bungalow	
bug(ged)	-bosom	buttercup	
bulb		butterfly(-ies)	
bulge(d)	brother	buttermilk	
bulk	Brussels		
-bull	-see next page		
-see next page			

for u-r (ur/ir)
see page 243

- or oo as in woodpecker

In these words you can hear the sound U as in duck

✻   ✻ ✻

bump(ed)	bubble(d)
bun	bubbling
bunch(es)	bucket(ed)
bunched	buckle(d)
bung(ed)	buckling
bunk(ed)	-Buddha
bus(es)	-Buddhist
*bussed (carried	budding
by bus)	budget(ed)
-bush(es)	budgie
-bushed	budging
*bust (upper part	buffer(ed)
of body /	buffet
break / arrest)	buffing
*but (except /	bugging
instead / yet)	buggy(-ies)
*butt (large cask /	bulbous
person made fun	bulky(-ier,-iest)
of / thick end of	-bulldog
tool or weapon /	-bullet
push with head)	-bullfrog
buzz(es)	-bullock
buzzed	-bully(-ies)
	- (bullied)
	-bulrush(es)
	bumper
	bundle(d)
	bundling
	bungle(d)
	bungling
	bunion
	bunker(ed)
	bunny(-ies)
	Bunsen
	burrow(ed)
	-bushel
	bustle(d)
	bustling
	-butcher(ed)
	butler
	*butted (pushed
	with head)
	*butter(ed) (spread
	with butter)
	button(ed)
	buttress(es)
	buttressed
	butty(-ies)
	buzzard
	buzzer

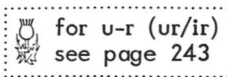

for u-r (ur/ir)
see page 243

- or oo as in woodpecker

In these words you can hear the sound U as in duck

117

*

chuck(ed)
chug(ged)
chum(med)
chump
chunk(ed)

club(bed)
cluck(ed)
clump(ed)
clung
clutch(ed)

come
[came]
[come]
-cook(ed)
-could

-crook
crumb
crunch(es)
crunched
crush(es)
crushed
crust
crutch(es)

cub
cuff(ed)
cup(ped)
-cure(d)
cut
[cut]

* *

chuckle(d)
chuckling
chugging
chumming
chutney

clubhouse
clumsy(-ier,-iest)
cluster(ed)
clutter(ed)

-colonel
colour(ed)
comfort
coming
compass(es)
concuss(es)
concussed
conduct
confront
conjure(d)
construct
consult
convulse(d)
-cooker
-cooking
corrupt
-couldn't
country(-ies)
couple(d)
coupling
courage
cousin
cover(ed)

-crooked
crumble(d)
crumbling
crumpet
crumple(d)
crumpling
-see next page

* * *

colander/cullender
colourful(ly)
colourless
combustion
comfortable
company(-ies)
concurrent
concussing
concussion
conduction
conductor
conjunction
conjurer/or
constable
constructed
construction
constructive
consumption
convulsion
convulsive
corruption
countrymen
countryside
coverage
covering

crustacean

cul-de-sac
culminate
cultivate
cultural(ly)
cumbersome
-curator
-curio
-curious
currency(-ies)
custody
customary
customer

* * * * [*]

circumference

colourfully
combustible
compulsory

crustacean

culminate
cultivation
culturally
-curiosity(-ies)
customary

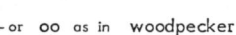 for u-r (ur/ir)
see page 244

- or oo as in woodpecker

In these words you can hear the sound u as in duck

☆ ☆

-cuckoo
 cuddle(d)
 cuddling
 culprit
 culture(d)
 cunning
 cupboard
 cupping
-curate
*currant (fruit)
*current (flowing
  stream / present)
 curry(-ies)
  (curried)
-cushion(ed)
 custard
 custom
 customs
 cutter
 cutting

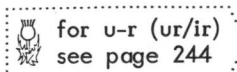

for u-r (ur/ir)
see page 244

> In this word the 'ou' is a neutral vowel.
>
> courageous

- or oo as in woodpecker

In these words you can hear the sound U as in duck

119

*

does
done
*dost (old form of
   'do', used with
   'thou')
doth
dove

drug(ged)
drum(med)
drunk

duck
*ducked (did duck)
*duct (tube or pipe)
dug
dull(ed)
dumb
dump(ed)
dunce
dusk
*dust (particles of
   earth or waste
   matter)
Dutch

* *

*discuss(es) (debate)
*discussed (debated)
*disgust (strong
   dislike)
disrupt
distrust

doesn't
double(d)
doubling
dozen

drugging
drummer
drumming

duchess(es)
duckling
duffel/duffle
dugout
dummy(-ies)
dumpling
dungeon
-during
dustbin
duster
dusty(-ier,-iest)

* * *

deduction
deductive
destruction
destructive

discomfort
discourage(d)
discover(ed)
discussing
discussion
disgusting
disruption
disruptive

dungarees

* * * *

discovery(-ies)

for u-r (ur/ir)
see page 245

E

*

for I ...
see page 123

* *

em- or im- ?

-endure(d)
engulf(ed)
enough
*-ensure(d) (make
   certain)
entrust

en- or in- ?

erupt

-Europe

* * *

emulsion(ed)

em- or im- ?

encourage(d)
-endurance

en- or in- ?

erupted
eruption

* * * *

encouragement

en- or in- ?

-European

for u-r
see page 245

-or oo as in woodpecker

In these words you can hear the sound U as in duck

F

*

flood
fluff(ed)
flung
flush(es)
flushed
flux(es)

-foot

front

fudge(d)
-full
fun
fund
fuss(es)
fussed

* *

flourish(es)
flourished
fluffy(-ier,-iest)
-fluoride
-fluorine
flurry(-ies)
   (flurried)
fluster(ed)
flutter(ed)

-football
-foothill
-foothold
-footpath
-footstep
-forsook

frontier
frustrate

fudging
-fulcrum
-fulfil(led)
-fully
fumble(d)
function(ed)
funfair
fungi
*fungous (spongy or
   in other ways
   like a fungus)
*fungus (type of
   plant)
funnel(led)
funny(-ier,-iest)
furrow(ed)
-fury(-ies)
fuzzy(-ier,-iest)

* * *

fluctuate
-fluorescent

frontier
frustrating
frustration

-fulfilling
functional(ly)
funnelling
funnier
funniest
-furious

* * * * [*]

fluctuation
-fluorescent

functionally
fundamental(ly)

for th ...
see page 133

 for u-r (ur/ir)
see page 246

- or oo as in woodpecker

In these words you can hear the sound u as in duck

G

SHORT VOWEL **U**   SHORT VOWEL **OO**

*

glove(d)
glum
glut

-good
-goods
-gourd

grub(bed)
grudge(d)
gruff
grunt

gulf
gull(ed)
gulp(ed)
gum(med)
gun(ned)
gush(es)
gushed
gust
gut(ted)
guts

* *

glutton

-goodbye
-goodness
-goodnight
-gooseberry(-ies)
govern(ed)

grubbing
grubby(-ier,-iest)
grudging
grumble(d)
grumbling
grumpy(-ier,-iest)

gudgeon
gullet
gulling
gulley/gully(-ies)
gumboil
gumming
gunner
gunning
guppy(-ies)
gusto
gusty(-ier,-iest)
gutter
gutting
guzzle(d)
guzzling

* * *

gluttony

-gooseberry(-ies)
governor
government

gunpowder
guttural(ly)
guttering

* * * *

gutturally

> 🦉 for u-r (ur/ir)
> see page 246

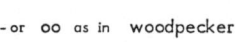 - or **oo** as in woodpecker

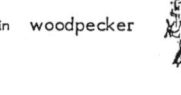

In these words you can hear the sound **u** as in duck

✢

-hood
-hook(ed)

hub
hug(ged)
hum(med)
hump(ed)
hunch(es)
hunched
hung
hunt
hush(es)
hushed
husk
hut
hutch(es)

✢ ✢

honey(ed)

hubbub
huddle(d)
huddling
hugging
hullo
humble(d)
humbling
humming
hundred
hundredth
hunger(ed)
hungry(-ier,-iest)
hunted
hunter
hunting
-hurrah!
-hurray!
hurry(-ies)
    (hurried)
husband
husky(-ies)
hustle(d)
hustling

✢ ✢ ✢

honeybee
honeycomb
honeydew
honeymoon

hummingbird
Hungary
hungrier
hurricane
hurrying

✢ ✢ ✢ ✢

Hungarian

🌼 for u-r
see page 247

I

✢

✢ ✢

indulge(d)
instruct
insult
*-insure(d) (protect
    against loss)

in- or en- ?

✢ ✢ ✢

impulsive

im- or em- ?

induction
inductive
indulgence
indulgent
injustice
instruction
instructor
insulting
-insurance

in- or en- ?

✢ ✢ ✢ ✢ [✢ ✢ ✢]

illustrious

-incurable
industrial(ly)
industrialisation
                zation
industrialise(d)
                ze
industrious
-infuriate
-injurious

in- or en- ?

⸛ for E . . .
see page 120

🌼 for u-r
see page 247

- or oo as in woodpecker

In these words you can hear the sound U as in duck

J

*	* *	* * *	* * * * [*]
judge(d)	judgement/judgment	justify(-ies)	-jurisdiction
jug(ged)	judging	(justified)	-jurisprudence
jump(ed)	juggle(d)		justification
junk	juggler		
just	juggling		
jut(ted)	jumble(d)		
	jumbling		
	jumper		
	jumping		
	junction		
	jungle		
	-juror		
	-jury(-ies)		
	justice		
	jutting		

K

*	* *	* * *	* * * *
	knuckle(d)		
	knuckling		

for C ...
see page 118

for u-r (ur/ir)
see page 248

- or oo as in woodpecker

In these words you can hear the sound U as in duck

✶	✶ ✶	✶ ✶ ✶	✶ ✶ ✶ ✶

✶

-look(ed)
love(d)

luck
lug(ged)
lugs
lull(ed)
lump(ed)
lunch(es)
lunched
lung
lunge(d)
-lure(d)
lush
lust

✶ ✶

London
-lookout
lover
lovely(-ier,-iest)

lucky(-ier,-iest)
luggage
lugging
*lumbar (lower back)
*lumber (junk /
   timber / move
   awkwardly)
lumbered
luncheon(ed)
luscious
lustre
lusty(-ier,-iest)

✶ ✶ ✶

lovable
loveliest

luckier
luckiest
luckily
lullaby(-ies)
lumbago
lumberjack
Luxembourg/Luxemburg
luxury(-ies)

✶ ✶ ✶ ✶

luxuriant
luxurious

 for u-r
see page 248

✶	✶ ✶	✶ ✶ ✶	✶ ✶ ✶ ✶ [✶]
monk	-manure(d)	mulberry(-ies)	-maturity
month	-mature(d)	multiple	mother-in-law
-moor(ed)		multiply(-ies)	mother-of-pearl
	-mistook	multiplied	multiplicand
much	mistrust	multitude	multiplication
muck(ed)		muscatel	multiplicative
muff(ed)	Monday	muscular	multiplier
musk	money(ed)		
mud	mongrel		
mug(ged)	monkey(ed)		
mum	-mooring		
mumps	-Moslem		
munch(es)	mother(ed)		
munched			
mung	muddle(d)		
mush	muddling		
must	muddy(-ier,iest)		
	mudguard		
	*muffin (teacake)		
	*muffing (missing a shot or catch)		
	muffle(d)		
	muffling		
	muggy		
	mulberry(-ies)		
	mumble(d)		
	mumbling		
	mummy(-ies)		
	*muscat (wine / grape)		
	*muscle (body tissue)		
	muscled		
	muscling		
	mushroom(ed)		
	*musket (gun)		
	-Muslim		
	*muslin (fine thin cotton)		
	*mussel (shellfish)		
	mustang		
	*mustard (plant with hot-tasting seeds)		
	muster		
	*mustered (called together)		
	mustn't		
	musty(-ier,-iest)		
	mutter(ed)		
	mutton		
	muzzle(d)		
	*muzzling (putting a muzzle on)		

> In this word the 'ou' is a neutral vowel.
>
> moustache

for u-r (ur/ir)
see page 249

- or oo as in woodpecker

In these words you can hear the sound **U** as in duck

✻

*none (not one)
-nook

nudge(d)
null
numb(ed)
*nun (woman in convent)
nut

✻ ✻

knuckle(d)
knuckling

nothing

nudging
nugget
number(ed)
nutmeg
nutty(-ier,-iest)
nuzzle(d)
nuzzling

✻ ✻ ✻

nonetheless

✻ ✻ ✻ ✻

for u-r
see page 249

O

✻

once
*one (1)

for H . . .
see page 123

✻ ✻

august

-obscure(d)
obstruct

oneself
onion

other

oven

✻ ✻ ✻

obstruction
obstructive

occurrence

otherwise

✻ ✻ ✻ ✻

-obscurity(-ies)

for u-r
see page 249

- or oo as in woodpecker

In these words you can hear the sound u as in duck

*

pluck(ed)
plug(ged)
*plum (fruit)
*plumb (lead weight
   on a cord / do
   work of plumber)
plumbed
plump(ed)
plunge(d)
plus(es)
plush

-poor

pub
puff(ed)
pug
-pull(ed)
pulp(ed)
pulse(d)
pump(ed)
pun(ned)
punch(es)
punched
punt
pup
-pure
-push(es)
-pushed
*-puss(es) (cat)
*pus (liquid from
   poisoned place)
*-put (place)
-[put]
*putt (hit golf
   ball gently /
   throw weight)

* *

plover
plugging
plumber
plumbing
plunder(ed)
plunging
-plural(ly)

-poorly

-procure(d)

public(ly)
publish(es)
published
-pudding
puddle(d)
puddling
puffin
-pulley
-pulpit
pulsar
pumice
pumpkin
pungent
punctual(ly)
puncture(d)
punish(es)
punished
punning
puppet
puppy(-ies)
-purely
-pushchair
-pussy(-ies)
putted
*-putting (placing)
*putting (doing
   putts)
putty(-ies)
  (puttied)
puzzle(d)
puzzling

* * *

percussion
percussive

-plurally

production
productive
propulsion

publicly
publican
publisher
-pullover
punctually
punctuate
punishment
-purify(-ies)
- (purified)
-purity

* * * * [*]

pronunciation

publication
publicity
pulmonary
punctually
punctuation
-purification

for u-r
see page 250

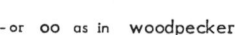

- or oo as in woodpecker

In these words you can hear the sound U as in duck

R

*

-rook
-room
*rough (uneven /
   harsh / crude)
roughed

 rub(bed)
ruck
*ruff (collar)
rug
rum
rump
run
[ran]
[run]
*rung (step of
   ladder / sounded)
runt
rush(es)
rushed
rust
rut(ted)

*wrung (twisted)

* *

refund
result

roughage
roughen(ed)
roughly

rubber
rubbing
rubbish
rubble
rucksack
rudder
ruddy
ruffle(d)
ruffling
Rugby
rugged
rugger
rumble(d)
rumbling
rumpus(es)
runner
running
runny(-ier,-iest)
runway
rupture(d)
rushing
Russia
Russian
rustic
rustle(d)
rustling
rusty(-ier,-iest)
rutted
rutting

* * *

recover(ed)
reduction
reluctant
republic
repulsive
resultant
resulted
resulting

-rookery(-ies)

ruffian

* * * * [*]

recovery(-ies)
reluctantly
republican
resuscitate
resuscitation

-Romania/Roumania/
  Rumania

for u-r
see page 251

- or oo as in woodpecker

In these words you can hear the sound U as in duck

129

*

scrub(bed)
scruff
*scull(ed) (row)
scrum
scum

-shook
-should
shove(d)
shrub
shrug(ged)
shrunk
shunt
shush(es)
shushed
shut
[shut]

*skull (bone of
   the head)
skunk

sludge
slug
slum(med)
slump(ed)
slunk
slush

smudge(d)
smug
smut

snuff(ed)
snug

*some (a certain
   number or amount)
*son (male child)
-soot

sponge(d)
spun
sprung
-see next page

* *

scrubbing
scuffle(d)
scuffling
sculptor
sculptress(es)
sculpture
scurry(-ies)
   (scurried)
scuttle(d)
scuttling

-secure(d)

-shouldn't
shovel(led)
shrugging
shudder(ed)
shuffle(d)
shuffling
shutter(ed)
shutting
shuttle(d)
shuttling

sluggish
slumber(ed)
slumming
slurry

smother(ed)
smudging
smuggle(d)
smuggler
smuggling

snuffing
snuffle(d)
snuffling

somehow
someone
something
sometime
sometimes
somewhat
somewhere
southern

splutter(ed)
spongy(-ier,-iest)
-sputnik
-see next page

* * *

scullery(-ies)

shrubbery(-ies)
shuttlecock

slovenly

somebody
somersault

structural(ly)
studying

submarine
subsequent
substitute
subtrahend
suddenly
suffering
suffocate
sulphuric
sultana
summarise(d)
     ze
*summary(-ies)
   (brief account)
summertime
*summery (like
   summer)
sumptuous
supplement

* * * * [*]

circumference

-security(-ies)

structurally

substitution
supplementary(-ies)

> for ur (ur/ir)
> see page 252

-or oo as in woodpecker

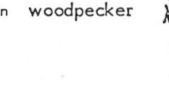

In these words you can hear the sound U as in duck

*

* *

-stood
struck
strung
strut(ted)
stub(bed)
stuck
stud(ded)
stuff(ed)
stump(ed)
stun(ned)
stung
stunk
stunt
strut(ted)

such
suck(ed)
suds
sulk(ed)
*sum(med) (total /
   exercise with
   numbers)
*sun (source of
   sunlight)
sunned
sung
sunk
-sure

swung

stomach(ed)
structure
struggle(d)
struggling
strutting
stubbing
stubble
stubborn
stubby(-ier,-iest)
studding
study(-ies)
   (studied)
stuffing
stumble(d)
stumbling
stunning
stutter(ed)

subject
subset
substance
subtle
suburb
subway
*succour (help)
*sucker (person or
   thing that sucks /
   shoot from stem or
   root / person who
   is easily tricked)
suckle(d)
suckling
suction
sudden
suffer(ed)
suffix(es)
-sugar(ed)
sulky(-ier,-iest)
sullen
sulphate
sulphur
sultan
summer
summing
summit
summon(ed)
sumptuous
-see next page

for ⋃-r (ur/ir)
see page 252

- or oo as in woodpecker

In these words you can hear the sound ⋃ as in duck

131

* *

sunbathe(d)
sunburn(ed/t)
*sundae (sweet dish)
*Sunday (day)
sunflower
sunken
sunlight
sunlit
sunning
sunny(-ier,-iest)
sunrise
sunset
sunshine
suntan(ned)
supper
supple
-surely
suspect

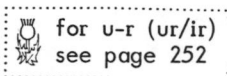

for u-r (ur/ir)
see page 252

In these words the first 'u'
sounds like 'a' in 'astonish'.

'SUCCESSFUL' WORDS

subdue(d)
subject(ion)
submerge(d)
submission
submissive
submit(ted)
submitting
subordinate
subscribe(d)
subscription
subside
subsidiary(-ies)
substantial(ly)
subtend
subtract(ing)
subtraction

suburban
succeed
success(es)
successful(ly)
succession
successive
successor
sufficient(ly)
suggest(ed)
suggestible
suggesting
suggestion
supply(-ies)
   (supplied)
support(ed)
supporter

supporting
suppose(d)
supposedly
surrender(ed)
surround(ed)
surroundings
susceptible
suspect(ed)
suspend
suspense
suspension
suspicion
suspicious
sustain(ed)

- or ○○ as in woodpecker

In these words you can hear the sound U as in duck

T

＊

thrush(es)
thrust
[thrust]

thud(ded)
thug
thumb(ed)
thump(ed)
thus

*ton (measure of weight)
tongue(d)
*tonne (1000 kilos)
-took
touch(es)
touched
tough
-tour(ed)

truck
trudge(d)
trunk
truss
*trussed (tied up firmly)
*trust (faith)

tub
tuck(ed)
tuft
tug(ged)
*tun (large barrel)
tusk

＊ ＊

thorough
thudded
thudding
thunder(ed)

touchdown
touching
touchy(-ier,-iest)
toughen(ed)
-tourist

trouble(d)
troubling
trudging
trumpet(ed)
truncheon
trundle(d)
trundling
trussing
trustee

tubby(-ier,-iest)
tugging
tumble(d)
tumbling
tummy(-ies)
tundra
tungsten
tunnel(led)
turret
tussle(d)
tussling

＊ ＊ ＊

thoroughbred
thoroughly
thunderous
thunderstorm

-tournament

troublesome
trumpeted
trumpeting
trustworthy

tunnelling

＊ ＊ ＊ ＊

for u-r (ur/ir)
see page 253

for u-r (ur/ir) see page 253

-or oo as in woodpecker

*

up(ped)

us

* *

onion
other
oven

udder

ugly(-ier,-iest)

Ulster

umpire(d)

unbend
[unbent]
unbind
[unbound]
unbolt
uncle
unclean
under
undo
[undid]
[undone]
undress(es)
undressed
unearth(ed)
unfair
unfit(ted)
unfold
unharmed
unheard
unhurt
unjust
unkind
unknown
unlatch(es)
unlatched
unless
unlike
unload
unlock(ed)
unpack(ed)
unroll(ed)
unsafe
unscrew(ed)
unseen
unsolved

-see next page

* * *

otherwise

ugliest

ultimate

umbrella

unable
unabridged
unaided
unaware
unbeaten
unbroken
unbuckle(d)
unbutton(ed)
uncanny(-ier,-iest)
uncertain
uncommon
unconscious
uncover(ed)
undamaged
undaunted
undefined
underclothes
underfoot
undergo
[underwent]
[undergone]
underground
undergrowth
underline(d)
underneath
underscore(d)
undersell
[undersold]
understand
[understood]
undertake
[undertook]
[undertaken]
underwear
underworld
underwrite
[underwrote]
[underwritten]
undisturbed
undoing
unduly
-see next page

* * * * [* *]

ultimately
ultrasonic(ally)
ultraviolet

unbearable
unbelievable
uncannier
uncanniest
uncertainty(-ies)
uncomfortable
unconsciously
unconventional(ly)
uncooperative
undecided
undercurrent
underdeveloped
undergraduate
underlying
understanding
understudy(-ies)
   (understudied)
undertaken
undertaker
underwater
underwritten
undesirable
undoubtedly
uneasiness
unemployment
unexpected
unfamiliar
unfortunately
ungratefully
unhappily
-see next page

for H . . .
see page 123

 for u-r
see page 254

- or oo as in woodpecker

In these words you can hear the sound u as in duck

* *

untie(d)
until
unto
untold
untouched
untrained
untrue
unused
unveil(ed)
unwell
unwind
[unwound]
unwise
unwrap(ped)

uphill
upkeep
upland
upon
upper
upright
uproar
uproot
upset
[upset]
upside
upstairs
upstream
upturn(ed)
upward

usher(ed)

utmost
utter(ed)

* * *

uneasy(-ier,-iest)
unending
unequal(led)
uneven
unexplored
unfasten(ed)
unfinished
unfitting
unfriendly(-ier,-iest)
unfurnished
ungrateful(ly)
unguarded
unhappy(-ier,-iest)
unhealthy
uninjured
unlikely
unlucky(-ier,-iest)
unnatural
unnoticed
unpainted
unpleasant
unravel(led)
unravelling
unscramble(d)
unscrambling
unselfish
unsettled
unstable
unsteady
untangle(d)
untangling
untidy(-ier,-iest)
untying
unwanted
unwelcome
unwilling
unworthy
unwrapping
unusual(ly)

upbringing
upheaval
upholster(ed)
uprising
upsetting
upside down

usherette
utterance

utterly

* * * * [* *]

unimportant
uninhabited
unlimited
unmistakable
unnecessarily
unnecessary
unpopular
unpredictable
unprotected
unquestionably
unravelling
unreasonable
unrelated
unreliable
unsanitary
unsociable
unsuccessful(ly)
unsuitable
unusually

upholstery

In these words the 'u' may be pronounced as a neutral vowel.

unless   until   upon

for H . . .
see page 123

 for u-r
see page 254

- or oo as in woodpecker

In these words you can hear the sound U as in duck

135

V

*

* *

vulgar
vulture

* * *

vulnerable

* * * * [* *]

vulgarity(-ies)
vulnerable
vulnerability

 for u-r
see page 254

W

*

once
*one (1)

-wolf(wolves)
-wolfed
*won (gained)
*-wood (timber / area
    with many trees)
-wool
*-would (was willing
    to / used to /
    was going to)

*wrung (twisted)

* *

oneself

-woman
wonder(ed)
wondrous
-wooden
-woodland
-woodwork
-woollen
-woolly
worry(-ies)
  (worried)
-worsted
-wouldn't

* * *

wonderful(ly)
wondering
-woodcutter
-woodpecker

* * * *

wonderfully

 for u-r
see page 254

Y

*

young
*-your (belonging
    to you)
*-you're (you are)
-yours

* *

youngster
-yourself
-yourselves

* * *

* * * *

- or oo as in woodpecker

In these words you can hear the sound u as in duck

*

ace(d)
ache(d)

age(d)

*aid (help)
*aide (helper)
*ail(ed) grow weak
aim(ed)
ain't

*ale (beer)

ape(d)

*ate (did eat)

eh

*eight (8)
eighth

* *

abate
ablaze
able
abstain

acclaim(ed)
acorn
acre
acquaint

afraid

again
against
aged
agent
ageing/aging

ailment

amaze(d)
amen

ancient
angel
anus

apex
April
apron

arrange(d)
array(ed)

ashamed
Asia
Asian
astray

attain(ed)

avail(ed)

awake(d)
[awoke]
[awoken]
await
away

eighteen(th)
eighty(-ies)

élite

* * *

abeyance
abrasive

acquaintance
acreage

adjacent

agency(-ies)

alien

amazement
amazing
amiable

apricot

arrangement

attainment

awaken(ed)

eightieth

* * * * [* *]

alienation

amiable

Arabia
Australia

availability
available
aviation
aviator

for H . . .
see page 144

for ae-r
see page 236

In these words you can hear the vowel sound ae as in snail

*

babe
bake(d)
*bail (bar on
    cricket stumps /
    payment for
    release / bail
    out)
bailed
bait
*baize (cloth)
*bale (bundle /
    bale out)
baled
*base (foot / central
    establishment /
    worthless)
*based (established)
*bass (low sound)
*baste (cover with
    melted fat /
    tack together)
bathe(d)
bay(ed)
*bays (more than
    one bay)

beige

blade
blame(d)
blaze(d)

brace(d)
*braid (plait /
    edging cloth)
braille
brain(ed)
*braise/braize (fish)
*brake (means of
    slowing or
    stopping)
brave(d)
bray
*brayed (did bray)
*braze(d) (join with
    hard solder)
*break (smash in
    pieces /
    interrupt /
    suddenly change)
[broke]
[broken]

* *

baby(-ies)
babied
bacon
baker
baking
baseball
basement
basic(ally)
basin
basis
bathing

became
behave(d)
betray(ed)

blazer

bracelet
braces
brazen
brazier
breakdown
breakers
breaking
breakthrough
brigade
brocade

* * *

bakery(-ies)
basically
bayonet(ed/ted)

behaviour

bravery
brazier

* * * *

babysitting
basically
bayonet(t)ed

for ae-r
see page 236

In these words you can hear the vowel sound ae as in snail

C

*

cage(d)
cake(d)
came
cane(d)
cape
case(d)
cave(d)

chain(ed)
change(d)
chase
*chased (did chase)
*chaste (pure)

claim(ed)
clay

crane(d)
crate
crave(d)
craze(d)

* *

cable(d)
cabling
canine
casing

chamber
changing
chaos
chasing

complain(ed)
complaint
contain(ed)
convey(ed)

cradle(d)
cradling
crater(ed)
crayon(ed)
crazy(-ier,-iest)
create
cremate

* * *

capable

changeable
chaotic(ally)

contagious
container
conveyer
courageous

crayoning
craziest
crazily
created
creating
creation
creative
cremation
crustacean

* * * * [*]

Canadian
capability(-ies)

chaotically

for Qu ...
see page 148

for ae-r
see page 236

*

dale
dame
Dane
date
day
*days (more than
    one day)
*daze (state of not
    thinking clearly)
dazed

deign

drain(ed)
drake
drape(d)

* *

dahlia
daily
dainty(-ier,-iest)
daisy(-ies)
danger
Danish
data
daybreak
daydream(ed)
daylight
daytime

debate
debris
début/debut
*decade (ten years)
decay(ed)
*decayed (did decay)
deflate
delay(ed)
derail(ed)
detain(ed)

dictate
disgrace(d)
dismay(ed)
displace(d)
display(ed)

domain

drainage
draper

* * *

dahlia
daintily
dangerous

deflation

dictation
dictator
disable(d)
disabling
disgraceful(ly)
displacement

drapery(-ies)

* * * *

disablement
disgracefully

for ae-r
see page 237

In these words you can hear the vowel sound ae as in snail

* * * * * * * * * * * *

eh

eight
eighth

éclair

eighteen(th)
eighty(-ies)

élite

embrace(d)

encase(d)
engage(d)
engrave(d)
enrage(d)
enslave(d)

en- or in- ?

equate

erase(d)

escape(d)
estate
estrange(d)

evade

exchange(d)
exclaim(ed)
exhale(d)
explain(ed)

eightieth

em- or im- ?

enable(d)
enabling
endanger(ed)
engagement
engraving

en- or in- ?

equation
equator

eraser

evasion

explaining

en- or in- ?

er- or ir- ?

for H ...
see page 144

for I ...
see page 144

for ae-r
see page 237

*

face(d)
fade
fail(ed)
*faint (weak)
faith
fake(d)
fame(d)
*fate (destiny)

feign(ed)
*feint (mock attack)
*fete (festival)

flake(d)
flame(d)

frail
frame(d)
fray(ed)
freight

phase(d)
phrase(d)

* *

fable(d)
faded
failure
faithful(ly)
famous
fatal(ly)
favour(ed)
favourite

flavour(ed)

forgave
forsake
[forsook]
[forsaken]

fragrance
fragrant
framework
freighter
frustrate

* * *

faithfully
fallacious
fatally
favourable
favourite

filtration

formation
forsaken

frustrating
frustration

* * * *

favourable
favourably

for th . . .
see page 151

for ae-r
see page 238

In these words you can hear the vowel sound ae as in snail

*

gain(ed)
*gait (way of
   walking)
gale
game
gaol/jail
gaoled/jailed
gape(d)
*gate (entrance)
gauge(d)
gave
gay
gaze(d)

glaze(d)

grace(d)
*grade (standard)
grain(ed)
grape
*grate (grid / rub
   hard)
grave
gray/grey
graze(d)
*great (big /
   important)
grey/gray
*greyed (turned
   grey)

* *

gaily
gaoler/jailer
gaseous
gateway

glacial

graceful(ly)
gracious
gradient
grapefruit
grateful(ly)
*grater (gadget for
   grating)
grating
graveyard
gravy(-ies)
*greater (more great)
greatest
greatly
grenade
greyhound

* * *

gaiety(-ies)

*glacier (mass of
   slow-moving ice)
*glazier (workman
   who fits glass
   in windows)

gracefully
gradation
gradient
gratefully

* * * *

geranium

gymnasium

for ae-r
see page 238

In these words you can hear the vowel sound ae as in snail

*

* *

* * *

* * * *

*hail (hard frozen
    rain / call name
    or greetings /
    come from)
 hailed
*hale (very healthy)
 haste
 hate
*hay (dried grass)
 haze

*hey! (ho!)

halo(ed)
hasten(ed)
hasty(-ier,-iest)
hated
hatred
haven
haystack
hazel
hazy(-ier,-iest)

hurray!

halfpenny(-ies)
hastily

herbaceous

for ae-r
see page 238

I

*

* *

* * *

* * * * [*]

ic- or ec- ?

el- or el- ?

em- or im- ?

inflame(d)
inflate
inhale(d)
innate
insane
invade

in- or en- ?

ir- or er- ?

is- or es- ?

ix- or ex- ?

impatience
impatient

inflation
invaded
invader
invasion

in- or en- ?

iq- or eq- ?

ir- or er- ?

iv- or ev- ?

ix- or ex- ?

incapable
inflationary

Iranian

for E ...
see page 141

for ae-r
see page 239

In these words you can hear the vowel sound ae as in snail

J

*

jade
jail/gaol
jailed/gaoled
jay

* *

jaded
jailer/gaoler

* * *

Jamaica

* * * *

geranium

gymnasium

K

*

*knave (rascal)

for C ...
see page 139

for Qu ...
see page 148

L

*

lace(d)
laid
*lain (rested)
lake
lame(d)
*lane (narrow road)
late
lathe
lay
[laid]
*lays (poems)
*laze (take it easy)

* *

label(led)
labour(ed)
ladies
ladle(d)
ladling
lady(-ies)
Laos
*laser (apparatus
    making light beams
    that can cut)
lately
later
latest
latex
lay-by
*layer (thickness of
    laid material /
    one that lays)
laying
layout
lazy(-ier,-iest)

* * *

labelling
labourer
ladybird
*lazier (more lazy)
laziest
laziness

lumbago

for ae-r
see page 239

In these words you can hear the vowel sound ɑe as in snail

*

mace
*made (formed)
*maid (girl)
*mail (post /
   armour)
mailed
maim(ed)
*main (chief /
   strength)
*maize (corn)
make
[made]
*male (masculine)
*mane (hair, as on
   neck of horse or
   lion)
mate
may
*maze (puzzle with
   many paths)

* *

maiden
mainland
mainly
mainsail
maintain(ed)
maker
make-up
makeshift
making
major
manger
mania
maple
mason
matron
maybe

mislay
[mislaid]
mistake
[mistook]
[mistaken]

* * *

maintenance
majorette
Malaya
mania
maniac
masonry
mayonnaise

mistaken

* * * *

Malaysia

for ae-r
see page 239

N

*

*knave (rascal)

nail(ed)
name(d)
*nave (part of
   church)
*nay (no)

*née (born with
   the name:-)
*neigh (noise made
   by horses)
neighed

* *

naked
naming
narrate
nasal(ly)
nation
native
nature
*naval (concerning
   warships)
*navel (tummy-button)
navy(-ies)

neighbour

* * *

narration
narrator
nationwide
nasally

negation
neighbourhood
neighbouring
neighbourly

* * * *

In these words you can hear the vowel sound ɑℯ as in snail

obey(ed)   occasion   Australia
obtain(ed)
                                                   occasional(ly)

P

*   * *   * * *   * * * * [* *]

pace   pagan   painfully   palatially
*paced (did pace)   painful(ly)   painstaking   palaeontologist/
page(d)   painted   palatial(ly)   paleontologist
paid   painter   patiently   patriotic(ally)
*pail (bucket)   painting   patriot
*pain (suffering)   papal
paint   papal   persuasion
*pale (whitish)   paper(ed)   persuasive
*pane (sheet of   parade
   glass)   pastry(-ies)   playfully
*paste (mixture of   patent
   powder and liquid)   *patience (ability to   potato(es)
pave(d)   wait for results)
pay   patient   probation
[paid]   *patients (people under
                 medical treatment)
phase(d)   patron
phrase(d)   pavement
                 paying
                 payload
*place(d) (position)   payment
plague(d)
*plaice (fish)   persuade
*plain (area of
   level land /   phrasing
   simple)
*plane (aeroplane /   placement
   flat surface /   placing
   smoothing tool)   *plaintiff (person who
plate   takes legal action)
play(ed)   *plaintive (sad-sounding)
                 player
*praise(d)   playful(ly)
   (glorify /   playing
   high approval)   playground
*pray (ask for help)   playmate
*prays (asks for   playtime
   help)   playwright
*prey (victim)
                 portray(ed)

                 prevail(ed)
                 proclaim(ed)
                 profane

for ae-r
see page 239

In these words you can hear the vowel sound ae as in snail

147

*

race(d)
rage(d)
raid
rail(ed)
*rain (water falling
   from clouds)
rained
*raise(d) (lift up)
rake(d)
range(d)
rate
rave(d)
ray
*rays (beams)

*reign (rule)
*rein (strap to
   control an animal)

* *

quail(ed)
quaint
quake(d)

rabies
racial(ly)
racing
racist
*radar (radio
   detection)
*raider (person who
   raids)
railing
railway
rainbow
raincoat
raindrop
rainfall
raining
rainy(-ier,-iest)
raises
raisin
raising
raven
rayon
razor

reclaim(ed)
refrain(ed)
regain(ed)
regime
reindeer
relate
remain(ed)
repay
[repaid]
replace(d)
restrain(ed)
retain(ed)

* * *

Quaker
quaver(ed)

racially
radial(ly)
radiant
radiate
radio(ed)
radium
radius(-ii)
rainier
rainiest
rapier
racism
rateable
ratio(s)

reagent
related
relation
remainder
remaining
Renaissance
replacement

rotation

* * * * [*]

radially
radiation
radiator
radioactive

relationship

Romania/Roumania/
Rumania

for ae-r
see page 240

In these words you can hear the vowel sound ae as in snail

※

safe
sage
*sail (travel by
    boat / sheet fixed
    to mast)
sailed
saint
sake
*sale (selling)
same
sane
save(d)
say
[said]

scale(d)
scrape(d)

shade
*shake (move quickly
    in different
    directions)
[shook]
[shaken]
shale
shame(d)
shape(d)
shave(d)
*sheik (Arab ruler)

skate
skein

slain
slate
slave(d)
*slay (kill)
[slew]
[slain]
*sleigh (sledge)

snake
snail

space(d)
*spade (tool)
Spain
*spayed (operated
    on to remove
    ovaries)
sprain(ed)
spray(ed)
-see next page

※ ※

sable
sabre
sacred
safeguard
safely
safer
safety
sago
sailing
sailor
salesman
saline
Satan
*saver (person or
    thing that saves)
saving
savings
saviour
*savour (enjoy a
    taste or smell)
saying

scalene
scaly
scraper

séance

shaded
shaker
shaking
shameful(ly)
shaver
shaving

skateboard
skater
skating

spacecraft
spaceship
spacesuit
spacious
-see next page

※ ※ ※

savoury(-ies)

shakily
shamefully

slavery

stabilise(d)
    ze
stadium
*stationary (still)
*stationery (writing
    materials)
stratosphere

※ ※ ※ ※

stabiliser
    zer
*stationary (still)
*stationery (writing
    materials)

for ae-r
see page 240

 149

In these words you can hear the vowel sound ae as in snail

*

**

stage(d)	stable(d)
*staid (serious and dull)	stabling
stain(ed)	stagecoach
stain(ed)	stainless
*stake (stick / bet / prize)	stamen
	staple(d)
staked	stapling
stale	stated
state	statement
stave(d)	statesman
[stove]	station(ed)
stay	status
*stayed (did stay)	staying
*steak (meat)	straighten(ed)
*straight (without curves)	strangely
	stranger
strain(ed)	stratus
*strait (channel)	
straits	survey(ed)
strange	sustain(ed)
stray(ed)	

*suede/suede (soft undressed leather)

sway
*swayed (did sway)

for ae-r
see page 240

In these words you can hear the vowel sound ae as in snail

T

*

*tail (part at the
    back)
tailed
take
[took]
[taken]
*tale (story)
tame(d)
tape(d)
taste

they
they'd
they'll
they've

trace(d)
trade
trail(ed)
train(ed)
*trait
  (characteristic)
*tray (board with
    raised edges, for
    carrying things)

* *

table(d)
tabling
taken
taking
takings
tailor(ed)
*taper(ed) (become
    thinner towards
    one end / waxed
    spill or wick)
*tapir (animal)
tasted
tasteful(ly)
tasty(-ier,-iest)

terrain

today

tracing
traded
trademark
trader
trading
trailer
trainer
training
traitor

* * *

tablecloth
tablespoon
takeaway
tastefully

for ae-r
see page 241

V

*

vague
*vain (conceited)
*vale (valley)
*vane (blade)
vaned

*veil(ed) (cover)
*vein (blood vessel /
    mood / streak)

* *

vacate
vacant
vapour

* * *

*vacation (holiday /
    process of leaving)
*vocation (calling /
    occupation)

* * * * [*]

vocational(ly)

for ae-r
see page 241

In these words you can hear the vowel sound ae as in snail

* | * * | * * * | * * * *

*wade (walk in water)   wafer   weightlessness

wage(d)   wager(ed)

waif   waistcoat

*wail(ed) (cry)   *waited (did wait)

*waist (narrow part   waiter

   of body)   waiting

*wait (stay)   waitress(es)

*waive (no longer   waken(ed)

   enforce)   wasted

wake(d)   wasteland

[woke]   wavelength

[woken]   waver(ed)

Wales   waving

wane(d)   wavy(-ier,-iest)

*waste (rubbish)   waylay

*wave (hand signal /   [waylaid]

   surge)

waved   weighbridge

*way (path)   weighing

                  *weighted (having

*weigh (find the   added weight)

   weight of)   weightless

*weighed (found the

   weight of)

*weight (heaviness /

   value)

*whale (sea-mammal)

*whey (watery part

   of sour milk)

for ae-r see page 241

* | * * | * * * | * * * *

yea

In these words you can hear the vowel sound ae as in snail

*	* *	* * *	* * * * [*]
	achieve(d)	achievement	abbreviation
	adhere(d)	adhesive	aesthetically
	agree(d)	Aegean	agreeable
	anneal(ed)	aesthetic(ally)	amenable
		agreement	anaemia/anemia
	appeal(ed)	allegiance	anaesthetist/
	appear(ed)		anesthetist
	asleep	amino	
		amoeba	appreciate
	austere		
		anaemic/anemic	
		appearance	
		arena	

In these words you can hear the vowel sound ee as in eagle

*   * *   * * *   * * * *

*be (to be / exist)
*beach(es) (shore)
 beached
 bead
 beak(ed)
 beam(ed)
*bean (vegetable)
 beard
 beast
*beat (batter /
    defeat)
 [beat]
 [beaten]
*bee (insect)
*beech (tree)
 beef(ed)
*been (from 'to be')
*beer (drink)
*beet (plant with
    sweet root)

*bier (frame to bear
    coffin)

 bleach(es)
 bleached
 bleak
 bleat
 bleed
 [bled]
 bleep(ed)

*breach(es) (gap /
    act of breaking)
 breached
 breathe(d)
*breech(es) (bottom
    part of gun)
 breed
 [bred]
 breeze(d)
 brief(ed)

beacon
beagle
beagling
beaker
beanstalk
beaten
*beater (person or
    thing that beats)
beating
beaver(ed)
beehive
beeswax
beetle
beetroot
being
belief
believe(d)
beneath
bereave(d)
[bereft]
beseech(es)
beseeched
[besought]
besiege(d)
*beta (Greek letter b)
between

breathing
briefcase
briefly

In these words the first letter 'e'
is pronounced like the 'i' in 'pig'.

'BENEVOLENT' WORDS

became	beginning	beseech(es)
because	behalf	beseeched
become	behave(d)	[besought]
[became]	behaviour	beset(ting)
[become]	behead	[beset]
becoming	beheld	besides
befall	behind	bestow(ed)
[befell]	behold	betray(ed)
[befallen]	[beheld]	betwixt
before(hand)	belong(ed)	beware
befriend	belonging	bewilder(ed)
begin	beloved	bewitch(es)
[began]	below	bewitched
[begun]	benevolent	beyond
beginner	bereft	

In these words you can hear the vowel sound ee as in eagle

*

cease(d)
*cede (give up)

*cheap (at low cost)
cheat
cheek(ed)
*cheep (chirp)
cheeped
cheer(ed)
cheese(d)
chief

clean(ed)
clear(ed)
cleat
cleave(d)
[cleft]
[clove]
[cloven]

*creak (noise)
creaked
cream(ed)
crease(d)
creed
*creek (inlet /
    stream)
creep
[crept]

keel(ed)
keen
keep
[kept]
*key (lever for lock or
    other mechanism /
    important / musical
    scale)
keyed

*quay (wharf)

for Qu ...
see page 167

** **

career(ed)

cedar
*ceiling (inner roof
    of room)

ce- or ci- ?

cheaper
*cheater (person who
    cheats)
cheeky(-ier,-iest)
cheerful(ly)
*cheetah (animal)
chiefly
chieftain

cleaner
cleaning
clearance
clearing
clearly
cleavage

compete
complete
conceal(ed)
conceit
conceive(d)

creature
creeper

keeper
keeping
keyhole
Kenya

kiosk

*** ***

cathedral

*cereal (food from
    grain / plant
    producing grain)

ce- or ci- ?

cheerfully

completion
completely
conceited

creosote

Korea
Korean

**** ****

chameleon

comedian
comedienne
convenience
convenient

In these words the first letter 'e'
is pronounced like the 'i' in 'pig'.

'CREATIVE' WORDS

celestial   creative
cement   cremate
create(d)   cremation
creating   crescendo(s)
creation   crevasse

*

deal
[dealt]
*dean (presiding
    officer)
*dear (beloved /
    expensive)
deed
deem(ed)
*dene (small valley)
deep
*deer(deer) (animal)

dream(ed)
[dreamt]

* *

dealer
decease(d)
deceit
deceive(d)
decent
decode
decrease(d)
decree(d)
deepen(ed)
deeper
deeply
defeat
defect
deflate
degree
delete
demon
detail(ed)
detour

de- or di- ?

diesel
disease(d)
*discreet (careful
    not to embarrass)
*discrete (separate)
displease(d)

dreaming
dreary(-ier,-iest)

* * *

decoding
defeated
deflation
deletion
deviate

* * * * [* *]

decompression
depreciate
depreciation
deteriorate
deterioration
deviation

In these words the first letter 'e'
is pronounced like the 'i' in 'pig'.

'DELIGHTFUL' WORDS

debate
decamp(ed)
decay(ed)
December
deception
deceptive
decide
deciduous
decipher(ed)
decision
decisive
declare(d)
decline(d)
decry(-ies)
    (decried)
deduce(d)
deduction
deductive
defect(or)
defective
defence
defend(ant)
defender
defensive
defiance
defiant
deficiency(-ies)
deficient
define(d)
deflation
deflect(ion)
deform(ed)
defy(-ies)
    (defied)
delay(ed)
deliberate(ly)
delicious
delight(ed)
delightful(ly)
delirious
deliver(ed)
deliverance

delivery(-ies)
demand(ed)
demobbed
democracy(-ies)
demolish(es)
demolished
denial
denomination
denominator
denote
denounce(d)
deny(-ies)
    (denied)
depart(ure)
department
depend(ed)
dependable
dependant
dependants
dependence
dependency(-ies)
dependent
deport
deposit(ed)
depositing
depress(es)
depressed
depression
depressive
deprive(d)
derail(ed)
derivative
derive(d)
descend(ed)
descendant
descent
describe(d)
describing
description
descriptive
desert(ed)
deserve(d)

design(ed)
designer
desirable
desire(d)
despair(ed)
despatch(es)
despatched
despise(d)
despite
dessert
destroy(ed)
destroyer
destruction
destructive
detach(es)
detached
detain(ed)
detect(ion)
detective
detector
detention
deter(red)
detergent
determination
determine(d)
determining
deterrence
deterrent
deterring
detest
detract
develop(ed)
developer
developing
development
device
devise(d)
devote(d)
devotion
devour(ed)

In these words you can hear the vowel sound ee as in eagle

*

each
ear
ease(d)
east
eat
[ate]
[eaten]
eaves

eel

eke(d)

eve

for H ...
see page 160

for I ...
see page 161

See also E
on page 65

See also I
on page 72

* *

eager
eagle
eardrum
earmark(ed)
earring
earshot
easel
Easter
eastern
eastward
easy(-ier,-iest)
eaten
eating

*eerie (weird)

Egypt

either

equal(led)

era

even
evening
evil(ly)

exceed
extreme

*eyrie/y(-ies) (nest
of bird of prey)

* * *

aesthetic(ally)

eagerly
easier
easiest
easily

em- or im- ?

endearment

en- or in- ?

equalise(d)
    ze
equalling
equally

evenly

excretion
extremely

oedipal
Oedipus

* * * * [* * *]

aesthetically

easygoing

ecclesiastical(ly)
ecological(ly)
economical(ly)
economics
economy(-ies)
ecumenical(ly)

em- or im- ?

en- or in- ?

equatorial
equiangular
equidistant
equilateral
equilibrium

Ethiopia

evolution

exceedingly
experience(d)
exterior

eliminate	endearment	establish(es)
elimination	enormous	established
Elizabethan	enough	establishment
ellipse	enumerate	estate
elliptical(ly)	equality	estrange(d)
elope(d)	equation	eternal(ly)
elusive	equator	evacuate
emancipation	equip(ped)	evacuation
emerge(d)	equipment	evacuee
emergence	equipping	evade
emergency(-ies)	equivalence	evaluate
emission	equivalent	evaluation
emit(ted)	erase(d)	evaporate
emitter	eraser	evaporation
emitting	erect(ion)	evasion
emotional(ly)	erode	event
emotive	erosion	eventual(ly)
emulsion(ed)	erotic(ally)	evict
enable(d)	erratic(ally)	evolve(d)
enabling	erupt(ed)	exceed(ingly)
enact	eruption	experience(d)
enamel(led)	escape(d)	exterior
enamelling	escarpment	extreme(ly)
enamour(ed)	especially	
endear(ed)	essential(ly)	

In these words the first 'e' sounds like 'i'.

'EFFECTIVE' WORDS

ecclesiastical(ly)	elector(ate)
eclipse(d)	electoral(ly)
ecology	electrical(ly)
edition	electricity
effect(ive)	electrocute
effectively	electrode
efficient	electrolysis
Egyptian	electrolyte
eject(ion)	electrolytic(ally)
ejector	electromagnetic(ally)
elaborate	electron
elaboration	electronic(ally)
elastic(ally)	eleven(th)
elasticity	elicit(ed)
elect(ion)	eliciting

In these words you can hear the vowel sound ee as in eagle

*   * *   * * *   * * * *

fear(ed)
feast
*feat (act)
fee
feed
[fed]
feel
[felt]
*feet (more than
   one foot)

field
fiend
fierce
fiord/fjord

*flea (insect)
*flee (run away)
[fled]
fleece(d)
fleet

free(d)
*freeze (chill /
   change from
   liquid to solid /
   hold steady)
[froze]
[frozen]
*frieze (decorated
   band / type of
   cloth)

faeces
fatigue(d)

fearful(ly)
feature(d)
feeble
feeding
feeler
feeling
female
fever(ed)

fielder
fiercely
fiord/fjord

fleecy(-ier,-iest)

foresee
[foresaw]
[foreseen]
freedom
freely
freestyle
freezer
freezing
frequent

fearfully

fiesta

frequency(-ies)
frequently

for th . . .
see page 172

> In these words the first letter 'e'
> is pronounced like the 'i' in 'pig'.
>
> ferocious   ferocity

In these words you can hear the vowel sound ee as in eagle

*   * *   * * *   * * * *

*jeans (trousers)
jeep
jeer(ed)

gear(ed)
geese
gene
*genes (more than
   one gene)

gleam(ed)
glee

*grease (oily
   substance)
greased
*Greece (country)
greed
Greek
green
greet
grief
grieve(d)

Jesus

genie
geyser

greasy(-ier,-iest)
greedy(-ier,-iest)
greenhouse
Greenland
greeted
greeting
grievance

galena

genius(es)

graffiti
greedily
Greenlander

In these words the first letter 'e'
is pronounced like the 'i' in 'pig'.

genetic(ally)   geology
geographical(ly)   geometrical(ly)
geography(-ies)   geometry(-ies)
geological(ly)   geranium

*　　　　　*　*　　　　　*　*　*　　　　　*　*　*　*

he	hearing	haematite/hematite	
*heal(ed) (cure / get better)	heated		
heap(ed)	heathen	helium	
*hear (receive by ear)	heating	heretofore	
[heard]	Hebrew		
*hears (does hear)	hero(es)		
heat			
heath			
heave			
[hove]			
heaved			
*he'd (he had / he would)			
*heed (notice / take seriously)			
*heel (part of foot / shoe)			
heeled			
*he'll (he will)			
*here (in this place)			
*here's (here is)			
he's			

In this word the letter 'e' sounds like the 'i' in 'pig'.

heroic(ally)

In these words you can hear the vowel sound ee as in eagle

*	* *	* * *	* * * * [*]
	ic- or ec- ?	ic- or ec- ?	ic- or ec- ?
	if- or ef- ?	id- or ed- ?	illegally
	ij- or ej- ?	if- or ef- ?	il- or el- ?
	il- or el- ?	ig- or eg- ?	immediate
	im- or em- ?	ij- or ej- ?	immedictely
			imperial(ly)
	increase(d)	illegal(ly)	
	indeed		im- or em- ?
	intrigue(d)	il- or el- ?	
			increasingly
	in- or en- ?	immediate	inferior
		impeachment	ingenious
	iq- or eq- ?		ingredient
		im- or em- ?	interior
	ir- or er- ?		
		increasing	in- or en- ?
	is- or es- ?	infrequent	
		ingenious	iq- or eq- ?
	iv- or ev- ?	intriguing	
			is- or es- ?
	ix- or ex- ?	in- or en- ?	
			iv- or ev- ?
		iq- or eq- ?	
			ix- or ex- ?
		ir- or er- ?	
		is- or es- ?	
		it- or ev- ?	
		ix- or ex- ?	

for E ...
see page 157

See also E
on page 65

See also I
on page 72

In these words you can hear the vowel sound ee as in eagle

*   * *   * * *   * * * *

gene   genie   genius(es)
*genes (more than one
    gene)   Jesus

*jeans (trousers)
 jeep
 jeer(ed)

K

*   * *   * * *   * * * *

keel(ed)   keeper   Korea
keen   keeping   Korean
keep   Kenya
[kept]   keyboard
*key (lever for lock   keyhole
    or other
    mechanism /   kiosk
    important /
    musical scale)
keyed

*knead (press with
    hands)
 knee
 kneel(ed)
 [knelt]

*quay (wharf)

for C ...
see page 155

for Qu ...
see page 167

In these words you can hear the vowel sound ee as in eagle

L

*

*lea (meadow)
*lead (show the way by going first / leash)
[led]
leaf
league
*leak (unwanted escape)
leaked
lean(ed)
[leant]
leap(ed)
[leapt]
lease
*leased (rented)
leash(es)
leashed
*least (smallest amount)
leave
[left]
leaves
*lee (shelter / sheltered side)
*leek (vegetable)
leer(ed)

*lied (German song)

* *

*leader (leading person or thing)
leading
leaflet
leaning
*leaver (person who leaves)
leaving
leeward
legion
legal(ly)
*lever (tool)
levered

*lieder (German songs)
litre

* * *

leadership
legally
lenient
leverage

Lima-bean

> In these words the first letter 'e' is pronounced like the 'i' in 'pig'.
>
> legality   legitimate

* * * *

*	**	***	**** [****]
me	machine(d)	machinist	machinery
meal	marine		material(ly)
*mean (intend /		meaningful(ly)	
miserly / poor)	meagre	media	meaningfully
[meant]	mealtime	median	mediation
*meat (flesh of	meaning	mediate	mediator
animal)	meantime	medium	meteorite
meek	meanwhile	meteor	meteorological(ly)
*meet (be in	measles	meteorite	meteorology
contact /	merely		
encounter)	meeting		mysterious
[met]	*meter (measuring		
mere	machine)		
	metered		
*mien (bearing /	methane		
look of person)	*metre (unit of		
	length / verse		
	rhythm)		
	misdeal		
	[misdealt]		
	mislead		
	[misled]		

In these words the first letter 'e' is pronounced like the 'i' in 'pig'.

meander(ed)	memorial
mechanic(ally)	meniscus(es/-i)
melodic(ally)	meridian
melodious	meticulous
memento(es/s)	mnemonic

In these words you can hear the vowel sound ee as in eagle

N

*

*knead (press with hands)
knee
kneel(ed)
[knelt]

near(ed)
neat
*need (require)

niche
niece

* *

nearby
nearer
nearest
nearly
neatly
needed
needle(d)
needling
negro(es)
neon
neither

* * *

* * * * [*]

Neapolitan

> In these words the first letter 'e'
> is pronounced like the 'i' in 'pig'.
>
> necessity(-ies)   neglectful(ly)
> negation   negotiate

O

*

* *

austere

oblique
obscene

* * *

oedipal
Oedipus

* * * *

obedience
obedient

＊

＊ ＊

＊ ＊ ＊

＊ ＊ ＊ ＊ [＊ ＊]

*pea (vegetable)
*peace (period
  without war)
 peach(es)
*peak (highest
  point)
 peak(ed)
*peal (ringing)
*pealed (rang)
 peat
*pee (urinate)
*peel (rind / skin)
*peeled (removed
  the rind or skin)
 peen(ed)
 peep(ed)
*peer(ed) (look
  hard / person of
  equal rank / lord)

*piece (part)
 pieced
*pier (upright
  support /
  structure
  extending into
  the sea)
 pierce(d)
*pique (hurt pride)

 plea
 plead
*pleas (requests)
*please (used when
  asking / give
  pleasure)
 pleased
 pleat

 police(d)

 preach(es)
 preached
 preen(ed)
 priest

peaceful(ly)
peacetime
peacock
peahen
peanuts
penis(es)
people(d)
perceive(d)

pianist
piano(s)
pierrot

pleasing

police(d)
policeman

preacher
precede
precinct
prefect
prefix(es)
prefixed
preview
priestess(es)
proceed

peaceable
peacefully
period

policeman

preceded
preceding
premature
premium
previous
procedure
proceeding

periodic
periodical(ly)

pianoforte

predecessor
prehistoric(ally)
previously

In these words the first letter 'e'
is pronounced like the 'i' in 'pig'.

'PHENOMENAL' WORDS

peculiar
pedestrian
peninsula
peninsular
perimeter
petition(ed)
petroleum
phenomena
phenomenal(ly)
phenomenon
precaution
precipitate
precipitation
precise(ly)
precision
precocious
predict(ion)
predictable
predominantly

prefer(red)
preferring
preliminary(-ies)
prepare(d)
preparing
prescribe(d)
prescription
present(ed)
presentable
presenting
preserve(d)
preside
presumably
presume(d)
pretence
pretend(ed)
prevail(ed)
prevent(ion)
preventive

In these words you can hear the vowel sound ee as in eagle

*quay (wharf)
queen(ed)
queer

queasy(-ier,-iest)
query(-ies)

R

reach(es)
reached
*read (look at and
   understand)
[read]
*real (genuine)
ream(ed)
reap(ed)
rear(ed)
*reed (plant /
   vibrating strip)
reef(ed)
*reek(ed) (stink)
*reel(ed) (spool /
   wind / stagger)

*wreak(ed) (bring about)
 wreath(ed)

ravine

reaches
reaching
react
reader
reading
really
reamer
rearm(ed)
reason(ed)
rebate
rebound
rebuild
[rebuilt]
receipt
receive(d)
*recent (not long
   past)
recess(es)
recessed
reclaim(ed)
recoil(ed)
redo
[redid]
[redone]
refill(ed)
reflex(es)
refund
regain(ed)
region
regroup(ed)
-see next page

reaction
reactor
reagent
realise(d)
   ze
reappear(ed)
rearrange(d)
reasoning
reassure(d)
receding
receiver
receiving
recently
reconstruct
regional(ly)
regrouping
reinforce(d)
renaming
repeated
repeating
replacement
reproduce(d)
reunion
rewritten

rheostat

reactionary(-ies)
realism
realistic(ally)
reality(-ies)
reasonable
rechargeable
reconstitute
regionally
rehabilitation
reinforcement
relaxation
reproduction
reunion

* *

reject
*relaid (laid again)
relay
[relaid]
*relayed (sent on as
    received)
release(d)
relief
relieve(d)
remake
[remade]
rename(d)
repay
[repaid]
repeal(ed)
repeat
replace(d)
research(es)
researched
reset
[reset]
retail(ed)
retell
[retold]
retreat
reveal(ed)
rewrite
[rewrote]
[rewritten]

In these words the first letter 'e' is pronounced like the 'i' in 'pig'.

'REFRESHING' WORDS

react(ion)	regret(ted)	requirement
reactionary(-ies)	regretful(ly)	research(es)
reactor	regretting	researched
reagent	rehearsal	researcher
real	rehearse(d)	resemblance
realise(d)	reject(ion)	resemble(d)
ze	rejoice(d)	resembling
realism	rejoin(ed)	resent
realistic(ally)	relate(d)	resentful(ly)
reality(-ies)	relation(ship)	resentment
really	relax(es)	reserve(d)
rearm(ed)	relaxed	resign(ed)
rebel(led)	relent(less)	resist(ance)
rebelling	reliable	resistor
rebellion	reliability(-ies)	resolve(d)
rebellious	reliance	resort
rebound	religion	resource(d)
recall(ed)	religious	resources
receptacle	reluctant(ly)	respect(able)
reception	rely(-ies)	respectful(ly)
receptive	(relied)	respective(ly)
recess(es)	remain(ed)	respire(d)
recessed	remainder	respond
recession	remaining	response
recessive	remark(ed)	responsibility(-ies)
reciprocal(ly)	remarkable	responsible
reciprocate	remember(ed)	responsive
recital	remembering	restore(d)
recite	remembrance	restrain(ed)
reclaim(ed)	remind(ed)	restrict(ion)
recoil(ed)	reminder	result(ed)
record(ed)	remote	resultant
recorder	removal	resulting
recording	remove(d)	resume(d)
recover(ed)	removing	resuscitate
recovery(-ies)	Renaissance	resuscitation
recruit	renew(ed)	retain(ed)
reduce(d)	renown(ed)	retard(ed)
reduction	repair(ed)	retire(d)
refer(red)	repay	retirement
referral	[repaid]	retort
referring	repeal(ed)	retreat
refine(d)	repeater	return(ed)
refinery(-ies)	repel(led)	returnable
reflect(ed)	repellent	returning
reflection	repelling	reveal(ed)
reflector	repentance	revenge(d)
reflexive	repetitive	reverberate
reform(ed)	replace(d)	reverse(d)
refract(ion)	replacement	reversal
refrain(ed)	reply(-ies)	reversible
refresh(es)	(replied)	review(ed)
refreshed	report(ed)	revise(d)
refreshment	reporter	revision
refrigerator	repose(d)	revive(d)
refund	reproach(es)	revolt
refuse(d)	reproached	revolve(d)
refusal	republic(an)	revolver
regain(ed)	repudiate	revue
regard(ed)	repulsive	reward
regardless	request	
regatta	require(d)	

In these words you can hear the vowel sound **ee** as in **eagle**

*

cease(d)
*cede (give up)

*scene (part of
   play / display /
   place / view)
scheme(d)
scream(ed)
screech(es)
screeched
screen(ed)

*sea (ocean)
*seas (oceans)
seal(ed)
*seam(ed) (join)
seat
*see (register by
   eye / understand)
[saw]
[seen]
*seed (part of a
   plant from which
   a new one can
   grow / selected
   player in a
   tournament draw)
seek
[sought]
*seem(ed) (appear)
*seen (registered by
   eye / understood)
seep(ed)
seer
*sees (does see)
seethe(d)
*seize (grab)
seize(d)
-see next page

* *

cedar
*ceiling (inner roof of room)

scenic(ally)

*sealing (fastening)
sealskin
*seaman (sailor)
*seamen (sailors)
seaport
seashore
seaside
season(ed)
seated
seaweed
*secret (kept hidden)
*secrete (produce
   liquid in body /
   hide)
seedling
seeing
seeking
seesaw
seething
seizure
*semen (sperm-
   carrying liquid)
sepal
sequence
sequel
sequin(ned)
series
settee
severe

sheepskin

*Signor (Italian for
   'Mr.')
sincere

skier
skiing

sleeper
sleeping

speaker
speaking
species
-see next page

* * *

*cereal (food from grain /
   plant producing grain)

scenery
scenically

seasoning
secrecy
secretion
*senior (older / more
   important)
*serial(ly) (parts in
   order)
serious
severely

Signora
sincerely

sleepily

strategic(ally)

* * * * [*]

scenically

seniority(-ies)
serially
seriously

Signorina

speedometer

strategically

In these words you can hear the vowel sound ee as in eagle

*

* *

she
sheaf(-ves)
*shear(ed) (cut off
   wool or hair)
[shorn]
shears
sheath(ed)
she'd
sheen
sheep(sheep)
*sheer (pure / very
   steep / very
   thin / go off at
   an angle)
sheered
sheet
she'll
she's
shield
shriek(ed)

siege

ski(ed)

sleek
sleep
[slept]
sleet
sleeve(d)

smear(ed)

sneak(ed)
sneer(ed)
sneeze(d)

speak
[spoke]
[spoken]
spear(ed)
speech(es)
speed
[sped]
sphere
spree
-see next page

steamer
steeple
steering
streaky(-ier,-iest)
streamer
streamlined

succeed

sweeper
sweeping
sweetheart
Sweden

In these words you can hear the vowel sound **ee** as in **eagle**

*

squeak(ed)
squeal(ed)
squeeze(d)

*steal (thieve /
    move quietly)
[stole]
[stolen]
steam(ed)
steed
*steel (metal)
steeled
steep
steer(ed)
streak(ed)
stream(ed)
street

*suite (pieces that
    go together)

Swede
swede
sweep
[swept]
*sweet (of sugary
    taste / nice)

> **In these words the first letter
> 'e' sounds like the 'i' in 'pig'.**
>
> 'SELECTED' WORDS
>
> | | |
> |---|---|
> | secession | selecting |
> | seclude(d) | selection |
> | secrete | selective |
> | secretion | selector |
> | secure(d) | sequoia |
> | security(-ies) | severity(-ies) |
> | select(ed) | specific(ally) |

*

* *

* * *

* * * * [* *]

*tea (drink / meal)
teach(es)
[taught]
teak
*team (working
   group/ playing
   side)
teamed
*tear (sign of
   distress)
*teas (drinks /
   meals)
*tease(d) (mock in
   fun / comb)
teat
*tee (support for
   golf ball)
*teem (swarm)
teemed
teens
teeth

thee
theme
these
thief
three

*tier (one of a
   number of levels)
tiered

treat
tree

tweed
tweet

teacher
teaching
teamwork
teapot
teaspoon
teeming
teepee/tepee
teething

theatre
theorem
theory(-ies)
thesis(-es)

trapeze
treacle
treason
treatment
treaty(-ies)
treetops
trio

tweezers

tedious
tedium
teenager

trachea

theatrical(ly)
theodolite
theological(ly)
theology(-ies)
theoretical(ly)

trapezium

In these words the first letter
'e' sounds like the 'i' in 'pig'.

'TERRIFIC' WORDS

telegraphy
telephonist
tepee
terrestrial(ly)
terrific(ally)
theatrical(ly)

theodolite
theological(ly)
theology(-ies)
theoretical(ly)
tremendous

In these words you can hear the vowel sound ee as in eagle

*

veal

via

* *

vehicle
veneer(ed)
Venus
veto(es)
vetoed

via

* * *

vehement
vehicle

viola

* * * *

In this word the letter 'e'
sounds like the 'i' in 'pig'.

velocity(-ies)

*	**	***	****

*we (people speaking)   weakling   wearily
*weak (feeble)   weakness(es)   weariness
*weal (mark left on   weary(-ier,-iest)
   skin by whip)   weasel   wheelbarrow
*weald (open or   weaver
   wooded country) weaving
*weave (interlace   weekend
   threads)   weekly
 [wove]   weevil
 [woven]
*we'd (we had / we wheelie
   would)
*wee (small / pass
   water)
*weed (passed water)
*weed (unwanted
   wild plant)
*week (seven days)
 weep
 [wept]
*weir (dam across
   river)
 weird
*we'll (we will)
*we're (we are)
*we've (we have)

 wheat
*wheel (round
   rotating frame
   or disc)
*wheeled (did wheel)
 wheeze(d)

*wield (have and use)

*wreak(ed) (bring
   about)
 wreath(ed)

In these words you can hear the vowel sound ee as in eagle

Y

*

ye
year
yeast

yield

* *

yielding

* * *

* * * *

Z

*

zeal

* *

zebra
zero(es/s)

* * *

* * * *

*

*aisle (part of
    church / gangway)

*aye (yes)

* *

abide
[abode]

acquire(d)

admire(d)
advice
advise(d)

alight
alike
alive
ally(-ies)
    (allied)
apply(-ies)
    (applied)

arise
[arose]
[arisen]
arrive(d)

aside
assign(ed)

awhile
awry

for H ...
see page 182

* * *

abided

adviser

alignment
alliance
almighty

appliance

arrival

assignment
asylum

* * * *

advisable
advisory

annihilate

In these words you can hear the vowel sound ie as in lion

*

bide(d)
[bode]
bike(d)
bile
bind
[bound]
*bite (tear with
  teeth)
[bit]
[bitten]

blight
blind

bribe
bride
bright
brine

*buy (purchase)
[bought]
*buyer (purchaser)

*by (beside / not
  after / past /
  through / etc.)
*byre (cow-house)
*byte (unit of
  information)

* *

behind
beside
besides

bias(ed/sed)
bible
biceps
binding
biped
bisect
bison

blindfold

*bridal (of the bride)
bridegroom
bridesmaid
*bridle (gear for
  controlling a
  horse)
bridled
bridling
brighten(ed)
brighter
brightest
brightly

buyer
buying

bye-bye
bypass(ed)
byway

* * *

biasing/biassing
bicycle(d)
binary

bribery

by-product

* * * * [* *]

biennial(ly)
bifurcated
bilateral(ly)
binomial
biographical(ly)
biography(-ies)
biological(ly)
biology

*

chide(d)
[chid/chidden]
child
chime(d)
*choir (singing
  group / part of
  church)
Christ

*cite (give as
  example / quote)

climb(ed)

cried
cries
crime
cry(-ies)
  (cried)

kind
kite

for Qu ...
see page 189

* *

childhood
china
China
Chinese

cider
cipher(ed)

client
climate
climax(es)
climaxed
climber
climbing

collide
combine(d)
compile(d)
comprise(d)
confide
confine(d)
conspire(d)

crisis(-es)
crying

cycle(d)
cyclist
cyclone
cypress(es)

Cyprus

kindly
kindness

* * *

climatic

combining
comprising

* * * *

criterion(-ia)

cytoplasm

kaleidoscope

D

*

dial(led)
dice
-see next page

* *

decide
decline(d)
decry(-ies)
  (decried)
-see next page

* * *

decipher(ed)
decisive
defiance
defiant
-see next page

* * * *

delightfully
desirable
-see next page

In these words you can hear the vowel sound **ie** as in **lion**

*	* *	* * *	* * * * [* * *]
*die (cease living / small cube / tool for stamping or shaping)	define(d)	delighted	diabetes
died	defy(-ies) (defied)	delightful(ly)	diagnosis(-es)
dike/dyke	delight	denial	diagonal(ly)
*dine (have dinner)	deny(-ies) (denied)	describing	diagrammatic(ally)
dined	deprive(d)	designer	dialectical(ly)
*dire (desperate)	derive(d)		diameter
dive(d)	describe(d)	diagnose(d)	digestible
	design(ed)	diagram	dimensional
dried	desire(d)	dialect	directory(-ies)
drive	despise(d)	dialling	diversity
[drove]	despite	dialogue	
[driven]	*device (gadget / plan)	diamond	dynamically
dry(-ies) (dried)	*devise(d) (invent / work out)	diaphragm	dynamometer
		diarrhoea	
*dye(d) (stain)	dial(led)	diatom	
*dyer (person using dyes)	dialling	digestion	
dyke/dike	diamond	dilemma	
*dyne (unit of force)	diary(-ies)	diluted	
	diecast	dimension	
	diet	dinosaur	
	digest	dioxide	
	dilute	directed	
	dining	direction	
	direct	directive	
	disguise(d)	directly	
	dislike(d)	director	
	diver	disciple	
	diverge(d)	diversion	
	diverse	divided	
	divert	dividers	
	divide	dividing	
	divine(d)	divisor	
	diving		
		dynamic(ally)	
		dynamite	
		dynamo(s)	
	*drier (more dry)		
	driest		
	drily/dryly		
	driver		
	driveway		
	driving		
	*dryer/drier (person, substance or machine that dries)		
	drying		
	dryly/drily		
	*dyeing (using dye)		
	*dying (ceasing to live)		

179

In these words you can hear the vowel sound ie as in lion

*

*eye (visual organ)
*eyed (looked at
   with interest)

* *

eider
either

enquire/inquire(d)
entire

en- or in- ?

esquire

excite

eyeball
eyebrow
eyeing
eyelash(es)
*eyelet (small hole)
eyelid
eyesight

* * *

eisteddfod

enlighten(ed)
enquiry/inquiry(-ies)
entirely
entitle(d)

en- or in- ?

excited
excitement
exciting

* * * * [* *]

encyclopedia
environment
environmental(ly)

excitedly

en- or in- ?

for H . . .
see page 182

for I . . .
see page 183

In these words you can hear the vowel sound **ie** as in **lion**

*	**	***	****
fight	fibre	fibreglass	financially
[fought]	fibrous	finally	
*file (tool /	fiery	financial(ly)	
information	fighter	fire-engine	
system / line of	fighting		
people)	final	frightening	
filed	finance(d)	frightfully	
*find (discover)	finding		
[found]	finest		
fine	finite		
*fined (made to pay	firearm		
a fine)	firefly(-ies)		
fire(d)	firelight		
five	fireman		
	fireplace		
flies	firewood		
flight	firework		
fly(-ies)	firing		
[flew]	fiver		
[flown]			
	flier		
	flying		
*friar (religious	flywheel		
man who lived by			
begging)	*friar (religious		
fried	man who lived by		
*frier (person who	begging)		
fries)	*frier (person who		
fright	fries)		
fry(-ies)	Friday		
(fried)	frighten(ed)		
	frightening		
*phial (small vessel or	frightful(ly)		
bottle)			

for th ...
see page 192

*	* *	* * *	* * * *
jive(d)	jiving	gigantic	
*gibe/jibe (taunt)	Geiger	Guyana	
glide	giant	gyroscope	
*gneiss (rock)	glider		
grime	goodbye		
grind	goodnight		
[ground]			
	grimy(-ier,-iest)		
*guide (show the way)	guidance		
*guise (appearance)			
guy	gyrate		
*guyed (ridiculed)			
*guys (more than one guy / does guy)			
*gybe/gibe/jibe (alter course by swinging sail)			

H

*	* *	* * *	* * * * [* * *]
height	haiku	hibernate	hibernation
		highwayman	hieroglyphics
*hi (!)	hiding		
hide	hi-fi	horizon	hydraulically
[hid]	higher		hydrocarbon
[hidden]	highest	hyacinth	hydrochloric
*high (tall / great)	highlands	hydraulic(ally)	hydroelectric(ally)
*higher (taller / greater)	highlight	hydrofoil	hydrometer
hike(d)	highly	hydrogen	hygienically
hind	Highness	hygienic(ally)	*hyperbola (form of curve)
*hire(d) (grant use if paid / employ)	highway	hyphenate	*hyperbole (exaggeration)
hive(d)	hybrid		hyphenated
	hygiene		hypotenuse
	hyphen		hypothesis(-es)
			hypothetical(ly)

In these words you can hear the vowel sound ie as in lion

*

*aisle (part of church / gangway)

*aye (yes)

*eye (visual organ)
*eyed (looked at with interest)

*I (the person speaking)

*I'd (I would / I had)

*I'll (I will)

I'm

*ion (charged particle)

*iron (metal)
ironed

*isle (island)

I've

for E ...
see page 180

* *

eider
either

*eyelet (small hole)

iceberg
ice-cream
ice-floe
Iceland
icing
icon
icy(-ier,-iest)

idea
ideal(ly)
*idle (lazy)
*idol (image for worship)

ignite

imply(-ies)
(implied)

*incite (urge)
incline(d)
inquire/enquire(d)
inscribe(d)
inside
*insight
(understanding)
inspire(d)
invite

in- or en- ?

*ion (charged particle)

Ireland
iris(es)
Irish
*iron (metal)
ironed
ironing

island
*islet (small island)

item

ivy

ix- or ex- ?

* * *

eisteddfod

icicle

idea
ideal(ly)
idolise(d)
ze

incisor
inquiry/enquiry(-ies)
invited

in- or en- ?

iodine

Irishman
ironic(ally)
ironmonger

isolate
isotope

ivory(-ies)

ix- or ex- ?

* * * * [* * *]

ideally
identical(ly)
identification
identified
identify(-ies)
(identified)
identity(-ies)
ideological(ly)

in- or en- ?

ironical(ly)
ironmonger

isometric(ally)
isomorphic
isosceles
isotopic
isolation

itinerant
itinerary(-ies)

183

In these words you can hear the vowel sound ie as in lion

J

*

*gybe/gibe/jibe (alter
  course by swinging sail)

*jibe/gibe (taunt)
jive(d)

* *

giant

gyrate

jiving

* * *

gigantic

gyroscope

* * * *

K

*

kind
kite

knife(-ves)
knifed
*knight (Sir --- /
  chess piece)

* *

kindly
kindness

* * *

* * * *

kaleidoscope

for C ...
see page 178

for Qu ...
see page 189

In these words you can hear the vowel sound ie as in lion

*

* *

* * *

* * * *

*liar (person who
  tells lies)
lice
lie(d)
lie
[lay]
[lain]
life(-ves)
light
[lit]
like(d)
lime(d)
line(d)
lion

*lyre (musical
  instrument)

*liar (person who
  tells lies)
*licence (official
  permission)
*license(d) (give
  official
  permission)
*lichen (plant)
lido
lighted
lighter
lighthouse
lighting
*lightning (electric
  flash in the sky)
lightweight
likely
*liken(ed) (thought of
  as similar)
likewise
lilac
limelight
limestone
liner
lining
lino
lion
lively(-ier,-iest)
livestock

lying

liable
library(-ies)
*lightening (making
  lighter)
likelihood
livelihood

librarian

*

mice
*might (would
　　perhaps / power)
mild
mile
mime(d)
*mind (system of
　　thought and
　　feeling / look
　　after / watch /
　　object)
mine
*mined (did mine)
*mite (tiny thing)

my

* *

mica
microbe
mighty
migrate
mileage
milestone
*miner (worker in
　　mine)
mining
*minor (less
　　important)
minus
miser
missile
minute
mitre(d)

myself

* * *

microchip
microphone
microscope
microwave
migration

* * * * [*]

microcomputer
micrometer
microprocessor
microscopic
minority(-ies)

In these words you can hear the vowel sound ie as in lion

*

* *

* * *

* * * *

*gneiss (rock)

neither

nightingale
ninetieth
nitrogen

Nigeria

knife(-ves)
knifed
*knight (Sir —- / chess
    piece)

nightdress(es)
nightfall
nightie
nightmare
nighttime
nineteen(th)
ninety(-ies)
nitrate
nitric

*nice (pleasant)
nigh
*night (hours of
    darkness)
nine
ninth

nylon

O

*

* *

* * *

* * * *

alright

almighty

oblige(d)

In these words you can hear the vowel sound ie as in lion

*

*phial (small vessel
  or bottle)

*pi (3.142 / Greek
  letter)
*pie (meat or fruit
  baked in pastry)
pike
pile(d)
pine(d)
pint
pipe(d)

pliers
plight
ply(-ies)
   (plied)

price(d)
*pride (high opinion
  of oneself)
*pried (did pry)
*pries (does pry or
  prise)
prime(d)
prior
*prise/prize (lever
  with a metal bar)
*prised (did prise)
*prize (reward /
  value / prise)
*prized (did prize)
*pry(-ies) (inquire
  into private
  matters / lever
  with a metal bar)
  (pried)

pyre

* *

perspire(d)

pilot
pious
pipeline
piper
piping
pirate

pliers
plywood

polite

precise
prescribe(d)
preside
prior
private
provide

psychic(ally)

pylon
python

* * *

piety
pineapple
pioneer

politely

precisely
primary(-ies)
primeval
privacy
provided
providing

psychical(ly)
psychosis(-es)
psychotic(ally)

pyrites

* * * * [* *]

primarily
priority(-ies)
proprietor

psychiatric(ally)
psychiatrist
psychiatry
psychically
psychoanalyse(d)
psychoanalysis
psychoanalyst
psychological(ly)
psychologist
psychology(-ies)
psychotherapist
psychotherapy
psychotically

In these words you can hear the vowel sound ie as in lion

*

*choir (singing group /
   part of church)

quiet
*quire (24 sheets of
   writing paper)
quite

* *

quiet

* * *

quietly

R

*

*rhyme/rime (to
   end with the
   same sound)
rhymed

rice
ride
[rode]
[ridden]
*right (correct /
   direction)
*rime (hoar-frost)
rind
ripe
rise
[rose]
[risen]
*rite (ceremony)

*rye (grain)

*write (set down on paper)
[wrote]
[written]
writhe(d)
*wry (twisted)

* *

recite
refine(d)
rely(-ies)
   (relied)
remind
reply(-ies)
   (replied)
require(d)
resign(ed)
respire(d)
retire(d)
revise(d)
revive(d)
rewrite
[rewrote]
[rewritten]

rider
riding
rifle(d)
rightful(ly)
riot(ed)
ripen(ed)
rising
rival(led)

writer
writing
wryly

* * *

recital
reliance
reminded
reminder
requirement
retirement

rightfully
rioted
rioting
rivalling

* * * * [* *]

refinery(-ies)
reliability(-ies)
reliable

rhinoceros(es/-i)

riboflavin

In these words you can hear the vowel sound **ie** as in **lion**

*	* *	* * *	* * * * [* *]
*cite (quote)	cider	psychical(ly)	cytoplasm
	cipher(ed)	psychosis(-es)	
scythe(d)		psychotic(ally)	psychiatric(ally)
scribe	cycle(d)		psychiatrist
	cycling	saliva	psychiatry
shine	cyclist		psychically
[shone]	cypress(es)	scientist	psychoanalyse(d)
*shire (county)			psychoanalysis
shrine	psychic(ally)	Siamese	psychoanalyst
shy(-ies)		silently	psychological(ly)
(shied)	science	sizable/sizeable	psychologist
*shyer (more shy)	scientist		psychology(-ies)
	scriber	skyscraper	psychotherapist
*side (edge /	scribing		psychotherapy
surface /		society(-ies)	psychotically
aspect / team)	shining		
sigh	shiny(-ier,-iest)	spiralling	scientific(ally)
*sighed (did sigh)	shyer	spirally	
*sighs (more than	shyly/shily		seismology
one sigh)		surprising	
*sight (vision)	Siam	survival	Siberia
*sign(ed) (mark with	sideboard	survivor	
a meaning)	sidelight		society(-ies)
*sine (function of	sideline		
an angle)	siding		
sire(d)	signing		
*site (place)	signpost		
*size (spatial	silence(d)		
extent / a weak	silent		
glue)	siphon		
sized	siren		
	sisal		
sky(-ies)			
	skyline		
*sleight (quickness)			
slice(d)	slightly		
slide	slimy(-ier,-iest)		
[slid]	slyly/slily		
*slight (small /			
thin and	smiling		
delicate / treat			
without respect)	spicy(-ier,-iest)		
slime	spider		
sly	spinal		
	spiral(led)		
smile(d)	spiral(ly)		
smite	sprightly(-ier,-iest)		
[smote]	-see next page		
[smitten]			
-see next page			

In these words you can hear the vowel sound **ie** as in **lion**

*

snipe(d)

spice(d)
spike(d)
spine
spire
spite
spline(d)
spy(-ies)
  (spied)

squire

*stile (barrier
  with steps)
stride
[strode]
[stridden]
strife
strike
[struck]
[stricken]
stripe(d)
strive
[strove]
[striven]
sty(-ies)
*style (manner)
styled

swipe(d)

**

stifle(d)
stifling
stipend
striking
stylus(es/-i)

subscribe(d)
subside
supply(-ies)
  (supplied)
surprise(d)
survive(d)

*	* *	* * *	* * * * [*]
*thigh (upper part of leg)	Taiwan	thiamine	titanium
thine	Thailand	timetable(d)	triangular
thrice	thyroid	tinier	triangulation
thrive(d)		tiniest	triceratops
[throve]	tidal		triumphally
[thriven]	tidings	trialling	
*thy (your)	tidy(-ier,-iest)	triangle	
*thyme (herb)	tiger	triumphal(ly)	
	tighten(ed)	triumphant	
*tide (ebb and flow)	tightly		
tie	tiling	typewriter	
*tied (fastened with knot)	timing		
tight	tiny(-ier,-iest)		
tights	tiresome		
tile(d)	title(d)		
*time (period)			
timed	tonight		
*tire (make weary / ring fitted to wheel)			
tired	trial(led)		
	trialling		
trial(led)	tribesman		
tribe	trifle(d)		
tripe	tripod		
try(-ies) (tried)	triumph(ed)		
	trying		
twice			
twine(d)	twilight		
type(d)	tying		
*tyre (ring fitted to wheel)	typhoon		
	typist		
	tyrant		

In these words you can hear the vowel sound ie as in lion

*

via
*vial (small vessel
   or bottle)
vice
vie(d)
*vile (disgusting)
vine
*viol (stringed
   instrument)

* *

via
*vial (small vessel
   or bottle)
vibrate
Viking
*viol (stringed
   instrument)
violence
violent
violet
viper
virus
viscount
visor
vital(ly)

* * *

viaduct
vibrating
vibration
violate
violence
violent
violet
violin
vitally
vitamin

* * * *

variety(-ies)

vice-versa
violation
vitality
vivarium

W

*

*while (time / during
   the time that)
*whiled (did while)
whilst
*whine(d) (complain)
white
why

wide
wife(-ves)
*wild (untamed)
*wile (trick)
*wind(ed) (move by
   turning)
[wound]
*wine (drink)
*wined (supplied
   with wine)
wipe(d)
wire(d)
wise

*write (set down on
   paper)
[wrote]
[written]
writhe(d)
*wry (twisted)

* *

whitewash(es)
whitewashed
whiting
whitish

widely
widen(ed)
wider
widespread
wildlife
wildly
wily(-ier,-iest)
winding
wiper
wireless(es)
wiry(-ier,-iest)

writer
writing
wryly

In these words you can hear the vowel sound **ie** as in **lion**

X

*   * *   * * *   * * * *

xylophone

Z

*   * *   * * *   * * * *

xylophone

In these words you can hear the vowel sound **ie** as in **lion**

*

* *

abode
afloat

ago

alone

approach(es)
approached

arose

atone(d)

awoke

* * *

approaching

aroma

atonement
atrocious

awoken

* * * * [*]

ammonia
ammonium

appropriate

associate
association
associative

for oe-r
see page 256

B

*

*beau (dandy)

blow
[blew]
[blown]

boat
boast
*bode (did bide)
*bold (brave)
*bole (tree-trunk)
bolt
bone(d)
both
*bow (wood and
   string / knot /
   bend)
*bowed (curved like
   a bow)
*bowl (container /
   send a ball)
*bowled (rolled /
   bowled out)
bowls

*broach(es) (open up)
broached
broke
*brooch(es) (ornament)

* *

behold
[beheld]
below
bestow(ed)

blowing
blowlamp

boatman
bolster(ed)
bonus(es)
boulder
bouquet
bowler

brocade
broken
broker

* * *

* * * *

In these words 'o' is a neutral vowel.
It sounds like the 'a' in 'astonish'.

Bolivia   botanical   brocade

for oe-r
see page 257

In these words you can hear the vowel sound oe as in goat

*	* *	* * *	* * * * [*]
choke(d)	chauffeur(ed)	chromium	coagulate
chose		chromosome	coefficient
chrome(d)	-choral		coincidence
	-chorus(es)	coconut	collinear
cloak(ed)	-chorused	coincide	colonial(ly)
close	chosen	commotion	cooperate
closed		component	cooperation
*clothe(d) (provide	cloakroom	composer	cooperative
with clothes)	closing	controller	coordinate
*clothes (garments)	clothesline	controlling	coordination
*clove (spice / did	closure	corrosion	
cleave)	clothing	cotangent	
*cloves (spice)	cloven		
	clover	kimono(s)	
coach(es)			
coached	coastal		
coal	coastline		
coast	coating		
coat	cobalt		
coax(es)	cobra		
coaxed	cocoa		
code	colder		
coke(d)	coleslaw		
cold	cologne		
colt	colon		
comb(ed)	compose(d)		
cone	console(d)		
cope(d)	control(led)		
cove	corrode		
	cosine		
croak(ed)	cosy/cozy(-ier,-iest)		
crow(ed)	crochet(ed)		
[crew]	crocus(es/-i)	for Qu ...	for oe-r
[crown]	croquet	see page 206	see page 258
	crowbar		

In these words the first letter 'o' is a neutral vowel.
It... er.... er.... er.... sounds like the 'a' in 'astonish'.

'COMMUNICATING' WORDS

cholesterol	collector	commandment	commitment	communion
chorale	collide	commemorate	committee	community(-ies)
cocoon(ed)	collision	commemoration	committing	commutative
collapse(d)	cologne	commence(d)	commotion	commuter
collapsible	colonial(ly)	commercial(ly)	communal(ly)	corrode
collect(ing)	comedian	commission(ed)	commune(d)	corrosion
collection	comedienne	commissioner	communicate	corrupt(ion)
collective	commander	commit(ted)	communication	

In these words you can hear the vowel sound oe as in goat

*

* *

* * *

* * * * [*]

*doe (female deer)	decode	decoding	diplomacy
dole(d)	denote	devoted	
dome(d)	devote	devotion	domestically
don't			domesticate
dose(d)	disclose(d)	diploma	
*dough (flour and	disown(ed)	disposal	
water)	dispose(d)		
doze(d)		domestic(ally)	
	docile	donated	
droll	domain	donation	
drone(d)	donor		
drove	doughnut		

for oe-r
see page 259

In these words the letter
'o' may be a neutral vowel.

domain   domestic(ally)   domesticate

*

* *

* * *

* * * * [*]

	elope(d)	emotion	eau-de-cologne
		emotive	
	em- or im- ?		emotional(ly)
		em- or im- ?	
	enclose(d)		
	enfold	enclosure	
	enrol(led)	enrolling	
		enrolment	
	erode		
		erosion	
for H ...	explode		
see page 200	expose(d)	explosion	for oe-r
		explosive	see page 259
for I ...		exponent	
see page 201		exposure	

*

float
*floe (floating ice-sheet)
*flow(ed) (run)

foal
*foaled (given birth to a foal)
foam(ed)
foe
*fold (bend double / crease / sheep enclosure)
folk

fro
froze

phone(d)

* *

floated
floating
flowchart
flowing

focal
focus(es)/foci
focus(es/ses)
focused/focussed
folded
folding
folklore
foretold
forgo/forego
[forwent/forewent]
[forgone/foregone]

frozen

phobic
phoneme
photo

* * *

ferocious

focusing/focussing
foliage
folio

phobia
photograph(ed)

* * * * [*]

photocopier
photocopy(-ies)
(photocopied)
photo-electric
photofinish
photographic(ally)
photosynthesis

for th ...
see page 208

for oe-r
see page 260

In these words you can hear the vowel sound oe as in goat

*

ghost

gloat
globe
glow(ed)

gnome

go
[went]
[gone]
goal
goat
goes
gold

*groan (deep moan)
groaned
grope(d)
gross(ed)
grove
grow
[grew]
*[grown] (developed)
growth

* *

global(ly)
glowing

goatskin
going
golden
goldfish
gopher

*grocer (shopkeeper
   selling food and
   other goods)
*grosser (fatter /
   more disgusting)
grotesque
growing
grownup

* * *

globally

grocery(-ies)

for oe-r
see page 261

* * * *

hoax(es)
hoaxed
hoe(d)
*hoes (more than
    one hoe)
*hold (grip /
    support /
    continue)
[held]
*hole (opening)
*holed (hit ball
    into hole)
home(d)
hope(d)
*hose (flexible
    water-pipe /
    stockings)
hosed
host
hove

*whole (total / complete)

holding
*holy(-ier,-iest)
    (sacred / full of
    holes)
homeland
homesick
homeward
homework
hopeful(ly)
hopeless
hoping
hosepipe
hostess(es)
hotel

wholemeal
wholesale
wholesome
*wholly (totally /
    completely)

heroic(ally)

hopefully

hypnosis

heroically

homeopathic(ally)
homosexual(ly)

for oe-r
see page 261

I

for E . . .
see page 197

il- or el- ?

impose(d)

in- or en- ?

ir- or er- ?

ix- or ex- ?

immobile

im- or em-?

in- or en- ?

ir- or er- ?

ix- or ex- ?

im- or em- ?

for oe-r
see page 262

In these words you can hear the vowel sound oe as in goat

joke(d)

joker

jovial(ly)

jovially

K

knoll
*know (understand)
 [knew]
 [known]
*knows (does know)

knowing

kosher

kimono(s)

koala

for C ...
see page 196

In this word 'o' is a neutral vowel.
It sounds like the 'a' in 'astonish'.

Korea(n)

for Qu ...
see page 206

L

*lo (behold)
*load (amount carried)
 loaf(-ves)
 loafed
 loam
*loan(ed) (lend /
    amount lent)
 loathe(d)
*lode (vein of metal
    ore / ditch)
*lone (single)
*low (not high / moo)
*lowed (mooed)

loaded
local(ly)
locate
locust
lodestone
logo(s)
lonely
lonesome
lotion
lower(ed)
lowest
lowlands
lowly

locally
located
location
loneliness

locality(-ies)
locomotion
locomotive
loganberry(-ies)

for oe-r
see page 263

In these words you can hear the vowel sound oe as in goat

*

mauve

*moan(ed) (complain)
moat
*mode (way /
    fashion)
mole
mope(d)
most
mould
moult
mow
*[mowed] (cut)
*[mown] (cut)

* *

mobile
molten
moment
mostly
motel
*motif/motive (theme /
    figure)
motion(ed)
*motive (cause of
    action)
motor(ed)
mouldy(-ier,-iest)
mower

* * *

Mohammed
molasses
momentary
momentum
mosaic
motionless
motorbike
motorist
motorway

* * * * [*]

melodious

mobility
molecular
momentarily
momentary
motorcycle

 for oe-r
see page 263

> In these words the letter
> 'o' may be a neutral vowel.
>
> | Mohammed | molecular | morale |
> |---|---|---|
> | molasses | momentum | |

N

*

gnome

knoll
*know (understand)
[knew]
[known]
*knows (does know)

*no (not any)
node
*nose (part of face)
nosed
note

* *

noble
nomad
no-one
nosy(-ier,-iest)
notebook
noted
notice(d)
notion
nowhere
nova

* * *

neurosis(-es)

noblemen
nobody
nomadic
notable
notation
notify(-ies)
    (notified)
November

* * * * [*]

negotiate

nobility
noticeable
notification
notoriety
notorious

> In these words the letter
> 'o' may be a neutral vowel.
>
> | nobility | notation |
> |---|---|
> | nomadic | November |

In these words you can hear the vowel sound   oe   as in   goat

<table>
<tr><td>*</td><td>* *</td><td>* * *</td><td>* * * * [*]</td></tr>
</table>

*	* *	* * *	* * * * [*]
oak	although	oasis(-es)	eau-de-cologne
oath			
oats	oatmeal	odious	obedience
			obedient
*ode (long poem)	obey(ed)	omission	
	oblique	omitted	oceanography
*oh (!)	oboe	omitting	
			overlapping
old	ocean	opening	overlooking
	ochre	opium	overwhelming
*owe (must pay)		opponent	
*owed (did owe)	odour		
own(ed)		-orally	
	ogre		
	ogress(es)	osier	
	older	ovary(-ies)	
	oldest	overalls	
		overboard	
	omen	overcast	
	omit(ted)	[overcast]	
		overcoat	
	only	overcome	
		[overcame]	
	opal	[overcome]	
	opaque	overdo	
	open(ed)	[overdid]	
	opening	[overdone]	
	oppose(d)	overeat	
		[overate]	
	-oral(ly)	[overeaten]	
		overfeed	
	osier	[overfed]	
		overflow(ed)	
	*ova (eggs)	overgrow	
	oval	[overgrew]	
	*over (above)	[overgrown]	
	ovum(-a)	overhang	
		[overhung]	
	owing	overhead	
	owner	overhear	
		[overheard]	
	ozone	overjoyed	
		overlap(ped)	
		overlay	
		[overlaid]	
		overload	
		overlook(ed)	
		-see next page	

for H ...
see page 200

for oe-r
see page 264

* * *

overpower(ed)
override
[overrode]
[overridden]
overrun
[overran]
[overrun]
overseas
oversee
[oversaw]
[overseen]
overshoot
[overshot]
oversize
oversleep
[overslept]
overtake
[overtook]
[overtaken]
overthrow
[overthrew]
[overthrown]
overtime
overtone
overture
overturn(ed)
overwhelm(ed)
overwork(ed)

ownership

> In these words the first letter 'o' is a neutral vowel. It.. er... er... sounds like the 'a' in 'astonish'.
>
> 'OBLIGING' WORDS
>
> | | |
> |---|---|
> | obedience | offensive |
> | obedient | official(ly) |
> | obey(ed) | omission |
> | oblige(d) | omit(ted) |
> | oblique | omitting |
> | obliterate | opinion |
> | oblivion | opossum |
> | oblivious | opponent |
> | occasion(al) | oppose(d) |
> | occasionally | oppression |
> | occurr(ed) | oppressive |
> | occurrence | oppressor |
> | occurring | original(ly) |
> | o'clock | originality |
> | offence | originate |
> | offend | |

for oe-r
see page 264

P

*

phone(d)

poach(es)
poached
poke(d)
*pole (long rod)
*poll (number of
    voters / head /
    cut off top)
polled
pope
pose(d)

probe(d)
prose

* *

patrol(led)

phobic
phoneme
photo(s)
-see next page

for oe-r
see page 265

* * *

patrolling

phobia
photograph(ed)

poetic(ally)
poetry
polio
postmaster
potency
potential(ly)
-see next page

* * * * [* *]

petroleum

photocopier
photocopy(-ies)
    (photocopied)
photographic(ally)
photosynthesis
-see next page

In these words you can hear the vowel sound oe as in goat

** **

** ** **

** ** ** ** [**]

poacher
poem
poet
poetry
poker
Poland
polar
Polish
polo
pony(-ies)
postage
postal
poster
postman
postpone(d)
posy(-ies)
potent
potion
poultice(d)
poultry

proceed
process(es)
processed
proclaim(ed)
profile(d)
profuse
*program (instructions
    for computer)
programmed
*programme (plan of
    performance /
    broadcast)
progress(es)
progressed
project
prologue
prolong(ed)
promote
pronoun
propose(d)
protein
protest
proton
proven
provoke(d)

precocious
probation
procedure
proceeding
programmer
programming
progression
progressive
prohibit(ed)
projectile
projection
projector
prolific(ally)
promotion
proposal
prototype

poetically
potentially

prohibited
prohibiting
prohibitive
prolifically
protoplasm
protozoa

for oe-r
see page 265

In these words the first letter 'o'
is a neutral vowel. It.. er... er...
sounds like the 'a' in 'astonish'.

'PROGRESSIVE' WORDS

phonetic(ally)	profane	pronouncing
photographer	profess(es)	pronunciation
photography	professed	propel(led)
police(man)	professing	propelling
polite(ly)	professional(ly)	propeller
political(ly)	professor	proportional(ly)
pollute	proficiency	proposal
pollution	proficient	propose(d)
position(ed)	profound	proprietor
possess(es)	profuse	propulsion
possessed	profusion	prospect(ive)
possession	progression	prospector
possessive	progressive	prospectus(es)
potato(es)	prohibit(ed)	protect(ed)
potential(ly)	prohibiting	protection
probation	prohibitive	protective
procedure	project(ion)	protector
proceed(ing)	projectile	protest
procession	projector	protractor
proclaim(ed)	proliferate	protrude
procure(d)	proliferation	provide(d)
prodigious	prolific(ally)	providing
produce(d)	prolong(ed)	provincial
producer	promote	provision(s)
producing	promotion	provisional(ly)
production	pronounce(d)	provocative
productive	pronouncement	

*

quote
quoth

* *

quota
quotient

* * *

quotation

* * * *

R

*

roach(roach)
*road (track)
*roam(ed) (wander)
roan
roast
robe(d)
*rode (travelled on/by)
*roe (fish eggs or sperm / small deer)
rogue
*role (actor's part)
*roll(ed) (turn over and over)
*Rome (city)
rope(d)
*rose (flower / did rise)
*rote (repetition)
rove
*row (line / move with oars)
*rowed (moved with oars)
*rows (lines / moves with oars)

*wrote (set down on paper)

* *

remote
repose(d)
reproach(es)
reproached
rewrote

robot
robust
rodent
roller
rolling
Roman
romance(d)
rosette
rotate
rotor
roving

* * *

rodeo
rolling-pin
romantic(ally)
rotary
rotation

* * * * [*]

rhododendron

romantically

> In these words the first 'o' may be pronounced like the 'a' in 'astonish'.
>
> romance   rosette
> romantic(ally)   rotation

for oe-r
see page 266

In these words you can hear the vowel sound oe as in goat

*	* *	* * *	* * * * [*]
scold	chauffeur	chauvinist	sociology
scone			socialism
scope	scrolling	samosa	Somalia
scroll(ed)			
	sewing	sociable	supposedly
*sew(ed) (stitch)		socialist	
[sewn]	shoulder(ed)	socially	
		sodium	
shoal	slogan	soldering	
show(ed)	slower	soprano(s)	
[shown]	slowly	soviet	
*sloe (blackthorn	smoking	stowaway	
fruit or bush)	smoky(-ier,-iest)		
slope(d)	smoulder(ed)		
*slow (at a low			
speed)	snowball(ed)		
slowed	snowdrop		
	snowfall		
smoke(d)	snowflake		
smote	snowman		
	snowshoes		
snow(ed)	snowstorm		

In these words the first 'o' is neutral.

society(-ies) sophisticated
solicitor soprano(s)
solution

*	* *
*so (therefore / to	sober(ed)
such a degree /	social(ly)
in that way)	soda
soak(ed)	sofa
soap(ed)	solar
*sold (given for	solder(ed)
money)	soldier(ed)
*sole (only / part	solely
of foot and	solo(s)
shoe / fish)	sonar
*soled (fitted with	
new sole)	spoken
*soul (spirit)	spokeshave
*sow(ed) (plant)	spokesman
[sown]	
	stolen
spoke	stony(-ier,-iest)
	-storey (floor)
stoat	-story(-ies) (tale)
stoke(d)	
stole	suppose(d)
stone(d)	
stove	swollen
stow(ed)	
strobe	
strode	
stroke(d)	
stroll(ed)	
strove	

for oe-r
see page 267

*

those
though
throat
*throe (sharp pain)
*throne (state chair)
throned
throve
*throw (hurl)
[threw]
*[thrown] (hurled)

*toad (animal)
toast
*toe (part of foot)
*toed (placed toes
   against / fitted
   with a toe)
*told (did tell)
toll
*tolled (did toll)
tone(d)
tote
*tow (pull behind)
*towed (pulled
   behind)

troll

* *

throwing

toadstool
toasted
toastie
token
tonal(ly)
topaz
-Tory(-ies)
total(led)
totem

trophy(-ies)

* * *

tonally
totalling
totally

In these words the first 'o' is neutral.
It sounds like the 'a' in 'astonish'.

tobacco(s)	tomato(es)	topology
tobacconist	topography	torrential(ly)

for oe-r
see page 268

V

*

vole
*volt (unit of
   electrical force)
vote

* *

vocal(ly)
voltage
voted

* * *

viola

vocally
vocation
voltmeter

* * * * [*]

vocabulary(-ies)
vocational(ly)

In these words the first 'o' may be
pronounced like the 'a' in 'astonish'.

vocabulary(-ies)   vocation(ally)

In these words you can hear the vowel sound **oe** as in goat

W

* | * * | * * * | * * * *

*whoa! (stop!)
*whole (total /
    complete)

*woe (distress)
woke
won't
wove

*wrote (set down on
    paper)

wholemeal
wholesale
wholesome
*wholly (totally /
    completely)

woeful(ly)
woken
woven

woefully

> for oe-r
> see page 269

Y

* | * * | * * * | * * * *

*yoke (neck-piece)
yoked
*yolk (yellow part
    of egg)

yoga
yoghourt/
yoghurt/yogurt
yogi
yokel

> for oe-r
> see page 269

Z

* | * * | * * * | * * * * [* *]

zone(d)

zodiac

zoological(ly)
zoology

In these words you can hear the vowel sound **oe** as in **goat**

*
    * *
       * * *
         * * * * [*]

-about
abuse(d)

amusement

accumulate
accumulation
accumulator

assurance

accrue(d)
accuse(d)
acute

alluvial
alluvium

adieu

-afoot

aloof

amuse(d)

approve(d)

for H ...
see page 215

assume(d)
assure(d)

In these words you can hear oo as in goose   or ue as in newt

B

*

balloon(ed)

*blew (puffed)
 bloom(ed)
*blue (colour)

-book(ed)
 boom(ed)
-boor
 boost
 boot
 booth

 brew
*brewed (fermented)
*brews (does brew)
*brood (offspring)
-brook(ed)
 broom
*bruise (injury)
 bruised
 brute

-bull
-bush(es)
-bushed

* *

baboon
balloon(ed)

beauty(-ies)

bluebell
bluetit

booby(-ies)
-bookcase
-booklet
-bookshelf(-ves)
 booster
-bosom

brewer
brunette
brutal(ly)

-Buddha
-Buddhist
 bugle
-bulldog
-bullet
-bullfrog
-bullock
-bully(-ies)
-   (bullied)
 bureau
-bushel
-butcher(ed)

* * *

bazooka

beautiful(ly)
Bermuda

boulevard

brewery(-ies)
brutally

-Buddhism
-bulletin
-bulldozer(ed)

* * * *

beautifully

✳

chew(ed)
*chews (does chew)
*choose (select)
 [chose]
 [chosen]
*chute (slope for
   things to slide
   down)

 clue(d)

-cook(ed)
 cool(ed)
*coop (cage)
-could
*coup (stroke /
   successful
   action)
-course(d)
-court

 crew
 crewed (acted as a
   crew member)
*crews (more than
   one crew)
-crook
 croon(ed)
*crude (untreated /
   done without
   skill)
 cruel(ly)
*cruise (voyage)
 cruised

 cube(d)
*cue (rod / signal)
 cued
 cure(d)
 cute

*queue (waiting line)
 queued

:.............................:
: for Qu ...   :
: see page 219   :
:.............................:

✳ ✳

canoe(d)
cashew

chewing
choosing

cocoon(ed)
commute
compute
conclude
confuse(d)
consume(d)
-cooker
-cooking
cooler
-couldn't
coupe
coupon

-crooked
crucial(ly)
cruel(ly)
cruelty(-ies)
cruet
cruiser
crusade

cubic
cuboid
-cuckoo
curate
-cushion(ed)

✳ ✳ ✳

communal(ly)
communion
commuter
computer
conclusion
confusion
consumer

crucially
crucible
crucifix(es)
cruciform
crucify(-ies)
  (crucified)
cruelly
cruelty(-ies)

cubicle
cucumber
cumulus
curator
curio(s)
curious

Kuwait

✳ ✳ ✳ ✳ [✳]

communally
communicate
communication
communion
community(-ies)
commutative
computerise(d)
                ze

crucifixion

cumulative
curiosity(-ies)

In these words you can hear oo as in goose   or ue as in newt

*

*dew (moisture)

do
[did]
[done]
*doer (active person)
doom(ed)
*dour (unsmiling)

drew
droop(ed)

*due (owing)
duke
dune

* *

deduce(d)

diffuse(d)
disprove(d)
dispute
disused

doer
doing
doodle(d)
doodling

*dual (double)
ducal
*duel(led) (fight)
duelling
duet
duly
during
duty(-ies)

* * *

diffusion
disproven

duelling
duplicate
dutiful(ly)

* * * *

dutifully

E

*

*ewe (female sheep)
*ewes (more than
    one ewe)

for H ...
see page 215

for I ...
see page 215

* *

em- or im- ?

endure(d)
*ensure(d) (make
    certain)

en- or in- ?

Europe

exclude
excuse(d)

* * *

*elusive (hard to find)

el- or il- ?

em- or im- ?

endurance

en- or in- ?

eureka!

exclusion
exclusive
extrusion

* * * * [* * *]

enthusiasm
enthusiastic(ally)

eucalyptus(es)
euphonium
European
euthanasia

exclusively
exuberance
exuberant

In these words you can hear oo as in goose or ue as in newt

*

feud
*few (not many)

*flew (passed in flight)
*'flu (influenza)
*flue (pipe)
fluke
flute

food
fool(ed)
-foot
-fourth

fruit

fuel
-full
fume(d)
fuse(d)

*phew/whew (!)

for th ...
see page 222

**

feudal(ly)
fewer

fluent
fluid
fluoride
fluorine

foodstuff
foolish
-football
-foothill
-foothold
-footpath
-footstep
-forsook

fuel(led)
fuelling
-fulcrum
-fulfil(led)
-fully
fury(-ies)
fusion
futile
future

***

feudally

fluorescent

foolhardy

fruiterer

fuelling
fugitive
-fulfilling
fumigate
funeral
furious
fuselage

****

fluorescent

foolhardiness

G

*

gloom
glue(d)

*gnu (animal)

-good
-goods
goose(geese)
gourd

grew
groom(ed)
group(ed)
groove(d)

**

gloomy(-ier,-iest)
glucose

-goodbye
-goodness
-goodnight
-gooseberry(-ies)
grouping
gruelling

***

-gooseberry(-ies)

gruelling

****

In these words you can hear oo as in goose   or ue as in newt

H

*

*hew(ed) (cut down)
  [hewn]

-hood
 hoof(-ves)
 hoofed
-hook(ed)
*hoop (large ring or
    band)
 hoop(ed)
 hoot
 hooves
-house

*hue (colour)
 huge

who
whom
*whoop(ed) (cry out with joy)
whose

* *

hoover(ed)

hula
human
humid
humour(ed)
humus
-hurrah!
-hurray!

* * *

hooligan

*humerus (bone in
    upper arm)
*humorous (funny)

whoever
whooping-cough

* * * * [* *]

humanitarian
humanities
humanity
humidity
humiliate
humiliation

I

*

* *

immune
improve(d)
impure

include
induce(d)
*insure(d) (protect
    against loss)
intrude

in- or en- ?

ix- or ex- ?

* * *

illusion
*illusive (deceptive)

improvement
improving

included
including
inclusion
inclusive
inhuman
insurance
intruder
intrusion

in- or en- ?

* * * * [*]

illuminate
illumination

immovable
immunity
impunity
impurity(-ies)

incurable
infuriate
injurious
innumerable

in- or en-?

for E . . .
see page 213

In these words you can hear oo as in goose   or ue as in newt

J

*	* *	* * *	* * * *
Jew	jewel(led)	Jacuzzi	jubilation
jewel(led)	jeweller		judicially
	jewellry/jewelry	jeweller	jurisdiction
juice	Jewess(es)	jewellry/jewelry	jurisprudence
June	Jewish		
		jubilant	
	judo	jubilee	
	juicy(-ier,-iest)	judicial(ly)	
	July	juicier	
	juror	juiciest	
	jury(-ies)	junior	
		Jupiter	
		juvenile	

K

*	* *	* * *	* * * *
*knew (understood)	Kuwait		

for C ...
see page 212

for Qu ...
see page 219

L

*	* *	* * *	* * * *
*lieu (place)	lagoon	lubricant	lubrication
		lubricate	
*loo (toilet)	-lookout	luminous	
*loos (toilets)	loosely		
-look(ed)	loosen(ed)		
loom	loser		
loop(ed)	losing		
loose(d)			
*loot (stolen goods)	ludo		
*lose (have no	lukewarm		
longer / fail to	lunar		
win)	lupin		
[lost]			
lure(d)			
*lute (musical			
instrument)			

In these words you can hear oo as in goose   or ue as in newt

*

mew(ed)
*mewl(ed) (mew)
*mews (houses
    converted from
    stables)

moo
*mooed (went 'moo')
*mood (state of
    feeling)
moon(ed)
moor(ed)
*moose (animal)
-mourn(ed)
move(d)
*-mouse (animal)
*mousse (sweet dish)

*mule (animal)
*muse (think deeply)
mute

* *

manure(d)
maroon(ed)
mature(d)

-mistook
misuse(d)

moonlight
mooring
-Moslem
-mournful
-mourning
movement
movie
moving

*mucous (of/covered
    with mucus)
*mucus (slimy liquid)
muesli
mural
music(ally)
-Muslim
mutual(ly)

* * *

manoeuvre(d)

movable/moveable

museum
musical(ly)
musician
mutation
mutiny(-ies)
    (mutinied)
mutineer
mutually

* * * * [*]

maturity

municipal(ly)
musically

*

*gnu (animal)

*knew (understood)

*new (unused)
news
newt

-nook
noon
noose
-now

nude

* *

neuron
neutral(ly)
neutron
newly
newton

nougat

nuisance

* * *

neurosis(-es)
neurotic(ally)
neutralise(d)
        ze
neutrally
newcomer
newsagent
newspaper
New Zealand

nuclear
nucleus(nuclei)
nudity
numeral
numerous
nutrient
nutrition
nutritious

pneumatic

* * * * [*]

neurotically
neutrality

numeration
numerator
numerical(ly)

pneumonia

O

*

ooze(d)

-out

* *

obscure(d)
obtuse

* * *

* * * *

obscurity(-ies)

for H . . .
see page 215

In these words you can hear oo as in goose   or ue as in newt

P

*

pew
*phew/whew (!)

plume(d)

pool(ed)
*poor (badly off)
*-pour(ed) (flow out)

proof
prove(d)
[proven]
prune(d)

-pull(ed)
*pure (unmixed)
-push(es)
-pushed
-puss(es)
-put
-[put]

* *

perfume(d)
Peru
pewter

plumage
plural(ly)
Pluto

pollute
poodle
poorly
-pouring

presume(d)
procure(d)
produce(d)
proofread
profuse
protrude
proven
prudence
prudent
pruning

-pudding
-pulley
-pulpit
puma
puny(-ier,-iest)
pupa(e)
pupil
purely
pursue(d)
pursuit
-pushchair
-pussy(-ies)
putrid
-putting

* * *

peculiar

plurally

pneumatic

pollution

producer
producing
profusion

-pullover
purify(-ies)
  (purified)
purity
pursuant
pursuer
putrify(-ies)
  (putrified)

* * * * [*]

peculiar

pneumonia

presumably

purification

Q

*

*queue (waiting
    line)
queued

* *

* * *

quintuplet

* * * *

In these words you can hear oo as in goose   or ue as in newt

219

*

**

***

****

*rood (crucifix /
  ½ of an acre)
roof(ed)
-rook
room(ed)
roost
*root (part of
  plant / origin)
rouge
*route (way)

ruche(d)
*rude (impolite)
rule(d)
rue(d)
*rued (regretted)

racoon

recruit
reduce(d)
refuse(d)
remove(d)
renew(ed)
-resource(d)
resume(d)
*review (survey)
reviewed
*revue (theatrical
  entertainment)

rhubarb

rooftops
roommate
rooster
routine

ruby(-ies)
ruin(ed)
ruler
rumour(ed)
rural(ly)
ruthless

refusal
removal
removing
-resources
reunion

rheumatic

-rookery(-ies)

ruinous
rurally

repudiate
reunion

rheumatism

-Romania/Roumania/
  Rumania

In these words you can hear oo as in goose or ue as in newt

*

*chute (slope for things
   to slide down)

school(ed)
scoop(ed)
screw(ed)

*shoe (footwear)
 [shod]
*shoo(ed) (scare
   away)
-shook
*shoot (fire / hit
   with bullet /
   move very fast /
   new growth from
   plant)
 [shot]
-should
shrewd

skew(ed)

sleuth(ed)
slew
sluice

smooth(ed)

soon
-soot
soothe(d)
soup

spool(ed)
spoon(ed)
spruce

stew(ed)
-stood
stool
*stoop (bend down)
stooped
*stoup (basin for
   holy water)
strew(ed)
[strewn]

suit
sure

swoop(ed)

* *

saloon
salute

schoolboy
schoolgirl
schooner
scooter
scuba

seclude
secure(d)
sewage
sewer

shooting
-shouldn't

skewer(ed)

smoothly

snooker(ed)

sooner

spoonful
-sputnik

steward
Stuart
student
stupid

subdue(d)
Sudan
suet
-sugar(ed)
suitcase
suited
suitor
super
superb
supreme
surely

* * *

schoolteacher
screwdriver

secluded

solution
souvenir

stewardess(es)
studio
studious
stupendous
stupify(-ies)
   (stupified)

Sudanese
suicide
suitable
supervise(d)

* * * * [* *]

security(-ies)

stupidity(-ies)

suicidal(ly)
superconductor
superficial
superimpose(d)
superintendent
superior
superlative
supermarket
supernatural(ly)
supersonic(ally)
superstition
superstitious
supervision
supervisor
supremacy

* ** *** **** [*]

*threw (hurled)
*through (by way
   of / because of)

*to (towards)
 tomb
*too (also)
-took
 tool(ed)
 toot
 tooth(ed)
 tour(ed)

*troop(ed) (move as
   a group)
*troupe (group of
   entertainers)
 truce
 true(d)
 truth

 tube(d)
 tune(d)

*two (2)

tattoo(ed)

throughout

today
tonight
toothbrush(es)
toothcomb
toothpaste
toothpick
tourist
toward
towards

trousseau
truly
truthful(ly)

tuba
Tuesday
Tudor
tulip
tumour
tumult
*tuna (fish)
*tuner (person who
   tunes)
tunic
tuning
tutor(ed)

together
tomorrow
tournament

truthfully

tubular
tuition

tubercular
tuberculin
tuberculosis
tumultuous

In these words you can hear oo as in goose   or ue as in newt

U

*

*ewe (female sheep)
*ewes (more than one ewe)

*use (employ)
 used

.·· for H ...
 see page 215 ·.

.·· for Y ...
 see page 224 ·.

* *

Europe

union
unique
unit
unite

urine

usage
useful(ly)
user
using
useless
usual(ly)
usurp(ed)

* * *

eureka!

uniform(ed)
unify(-ies)
  (unified)
union
unison
united
unity
universe

Uranus
urethane
urinate
Uruguay

usable
usefully
usefulness
usually

utensil
uterus(es/-i)
utile

* * * * [*]

eucalyptus
euphonium
European
euthanasia

ubiquitous

unicycle
unilateral(ly)
universal(ly)
university(-ies)

uranium

utility(-ies)
utopia

V

*

view(ed)

* *

viewpoint

* * *

* * * *

W

*

*whew/phew (!)
 who
 whom
*whoop(ed) (cry out
    with joy)
 whose

-wolf(-ves)
-wolfed
*-wood (timber / area
    with many trees)
-wool
*-would (was willing
    to / used to /
    was going to)
 wound

* *

-woman
-wooden
-woodland
-woodwork
-woollen
-woolly
-wouldn't
 wounded

* * *

whoever
whooping-cough
-woodcutter
-woodpecker

* * * *

*   * *   * * *   * * * * [*]

*ewe (female sheep)
*ewes (more than one ewe)

*yew (tree)
*yews (yew trees)

*you (person /
   people)
you'd
you'll
*your (belonging to
   you)
*you're (you are)
yours
youth
you've

yule

Europe

yourself
yourselves
youthful(ly)

eureka!

youthfully

eucalyptus
euphonium
European
euthanasia

Yugoslavia

....
: for U ...   :
: see page 223 :
....

Z

*   * *   * * *   * * * * [* *]

zoo
zoom(ed)

zoological(ly)
zoology

    In these words you can hear oo as in goose   or ue as in newt

A

☆	☆ ☆	☆ ☆ ☆	☆ ☆ ☆ ☆ [☆ ☆]
aft	aardvark	advancement	arbitrarily
		advancing	arbitrary
ah	advance(d)	advantage(d)	arbitration
			archeological
*alms (gifts to the	afar	afternoon	archeologist
poor)	after	afterwards	archeology
			architecture
*arc (curve)	aghast	answering	Argentina
arch(es)			argumentative
arched	alarm(ed)	apartheid	armadillo(s)
are	almond	apartment	arterial
*aren't (are not)			artesian
*ark (Noah's)	amen	arbitrate	articulate
arm(ed)		archaic	artificial(ly)
*arms (more than one	answer(ed)	architect	artillery
arm / weapons of		argument	
war)	apart	armada	
art		armament	
	*arbor (shaft)	armature	
ask(ed)	*arbour (garden or	armistice	
	part shaded by	armoury(-ies)	
*aunt (relative)	trees)	arsenal	
	arcade	arsenic	
	archer	artery(-ies)	
	arctic	arthropod	
	ardent	article	
	argon		
	argue(d)		
	armour(ed)		
	army(-ies)		
	artist		

for H . . .
see page 230

asking

Auntie/Aunty

*	* *	* * *	* * * *
*baa (lamb's cry)	*balmy (sweet-smelling, mad)	Bahamas	barbarian
balm	barbel	banana	
*bar(red) (prevent / barrier / rod)	barber	Barbados	
barb(ed)	bargain(ed)	barbecue(d)	
*bard (poet)	barley	barnacle	
barge(d)	barking	basketball	
bark(ed)	*barmy/balmy (mad)		
barn	barring		
*barred (prevented / fixed with bars)	barter(ed)		
bask(ed)	basket		
bath(ed)	basking		
	bastard		
	bathroom		
blast	*bazaar (Eastern market)		
bra			
branch(es)	behalf		
branched			
brass(es)	*bizarre (peculiar)		

In these words you can hear the vowel sound ar as in shark

C

LONG VOWEL ar

calf(-ves)
*calve(d) (produce
  a calf)
calm(ed)
can't
car
card
carp(ed)
cart
*carve(d) (cut)
cask
*cast (throw /
  mould / decide
  parts in a play /
  squint)
[cast]
*caste (social
  class)

*chance (lucky
  event / risk)
chanced
chant
*chants (does
  chant / more than
  one chant)
charge(d)
charm(ed)
char(red)
chart

clasp(ed)
class(es)
classed
clerk

craft

czar/tsar

* *

carbon
carcass(es)
cardboard
cargo(es)
carmine
carpet
carton
cartoon
cartridge
carving
*caster/castor
  (powdered sugar /
  swivelling wheel)
casting
castle
*castor (oil)
catarrh

chandler
charade
charcoal
charging
charter(ed)
charming
charring
*chorale (hymn tune)

cigar

classmate
classroom

command
contrast
*corral (enclosure
  for cattle and
  horses)

craftsman

khaki

Koran

* * *

cacao
carbonate
cardigan
cardinal
carnation
carnival
carnivore
carpenter
carpentry
cartilage
castaway

chancellor
chapati

commander
commandment
compartment

karate

* * * *

carbohydrate
carburetter
  or
carnivorous

In these words you can hear the vowel sound ar as in shark

227

*	* *	* * *	* * * *

daft
dance(d)
dark
darn(ed)
dart

*draft (rough plan /
 selected group)
*draught (current of
 air / depth of
 ship in water /
 piece in game)
draughts

dancer
dancing
darker
darkness
darling
data

demand
depart

disarm(ed)
discard
discharge(d)

drama
drastic(ally)
draughty(-ier,-iest)

demanded
department
departure

disaster
disastrous
dishearten(ed)

drastically

disarmament

drastically

E

*	* *	* * *	* * * *

embark(ed)

enchant
enlarge(d)
entrance(d)

er- or ir- ?

es- or is- ?

enchanting
entrancing

er- or ir- ?

escarpment

example

em- or im- ?

for H . . .
see page 230

for I . . .
see page 230

In these words you can hear the vowel sound ar as in shark

✻

far
farm(ed)
fast

flask

France

✻ ✻

farmer
farmhouse
farming
farmyard
*farther (greater
    distance)
farthered
farthest
fasten(ed)
faster
fastest
*father (male parent)
fathered

✻ ✻ ✻

faraway
fastener

*fiancé (man engaged
    to be married)
*fiancée (woman
    engaged to be
    married)

pharmacist
pharmacy(-ies)

✻ ✻ ✻ ✻ [✻]

father-in-law

pharmaceutical

G

✻

gasp(ed)

glance(d)
glass(es)

gnarled

grant
graph(ed)
grasp(ed)
grass(es)
grassed

guard

✻ ✻

garage(d)
garbage
garden(ed)
gardener
gargle(d)
gargling
garland
garlic
garment
garnet
garter(ed)

Ghana
ghastly(-ier,-iest)

giraffe

glasses

granted
grasslands

guitar

✻ ✻ ✻

gardener

Ghanaian

grasshopper

guardian

gymkhana

✻ ✻ ✻ ✻

*

half(-ves)
halve(d)
hard
hark(ed)
harm(ed)
harp(ed)
harsh
*hart (male deer)

*heart (organ that
    pumps blood /
    centre / inmost
    feelings)
hearth

* *

harbour(ed)
hardboard
harden(ed)
harder
hardest
hardly
hardship
hardware
hardwood
hardy(-ier,-iest)
harmful(ly)
harmless
harness(es)
harnessed
harpoon(ed)
harvest

hurrah!

* * *

harlequin
harmfully
harmonise(d)
    ze
harmonic(ally)
harmony(-ies)
harpsichord
Hawaii
Hawaiian

* * * * [*]

harmonica
harmonically
harmonium

I

*

* *

im- or em- ?

in- or en- ?

Iran
Iraq

Islam

* * *

in- or en- ?

Iraqi

is- or es- ?

ix- or ex- ?

* * * *

impassable

for E . . .
see page 228

J

*

jar(red)

* *

giraffe

jarring

* * *

gymkhana

* * * *

In these words you can hear the vowel sound **ar** as in shark

K

*   * *   * * *   * * * *

for C ...
see page 227

khaki   karate

Koran

L

*   * *   * * *   * * * *

lance(d)   lager   lasagne
larch(es)   larder
lard   larger
large   largest
lark(ed)   largely
last   largo
laugh(ed)   lasted
     lather(ed)
     laughter
     *lava (melted rock
       from volcano)
     *larva(e) (insect
       grub)

     llama

*

March
march(es)
marched
mark
marsh(es)
mask(ed)
mast

* *

mama
marble(d)
marching
margin
market(ed)
marking
*marshal (officer)
marshalled
*martial (warlike)
*marten (animal)
*martin (bird)
martyr(ed)
marvel(led)
massage(d)
master(ed)

morale
moustache(d)

* * *

macabre
margarine
marginal(ly)
marketed
marmalade
marshalling
marshmallow
marvelling
marvellous
masterpiece
mastery

* * * *

marginally
marsupial

N

*

gnarled

* *

nasty(-ier,-iest)

* * *

narcissus(es/-i)
narcotic
nastier
nastiest

* * * *

In these words you can hear the vowel sound ar as in shark

*	* *	* * *	* * * * [*]
palm(ed)	papa	Pakistan	Pakistani
par	parcel(led)	parcelling	parliamentary
parch(es)	pardon(ed)	parliament	participant
parched	parka	partialling	participate
park(ed)	parking	partially	participation
part	parlour	particle	pastorally
pass(es)	parsley	partisan	
*passed (went by)	parson	partition(ed)	pharmaceutical
*past (time that has	partake	partnership	
passed / beyond)	[partook]	passers-by	pianoforte
path	[partaken]	pasteurise(d)	
	partial(led)	ze	
plant	partly	pastoral(ly)	
	partner(ed)		
prance(d)	partridge	pharmacist	
	party(-ies)	pharmacy(-ies)	
psalm	passing		
	passport	pianist	
	password	piano(s)	
	pasture(d)	piranha	
	pianist	plantation	
	piano(s)		
		ptarmigan	
	planted		
	planting	pyjamas	
	plaster(ed)		
	plaza		

> In this word 'ar' is a neutral vowel.
>
> particular(ly)

R

*	* *	* * *	* * * *
raft	rafter	rascally	rechargeable
ranch(es)	rascal(ly)	raspberry(-ies)	remarkable
rasp(ed)	raspberry		
	rather	regarded	
		regardless	
	rearm(ed)	retarded	
	regard		
	remark(ed)		
	retard		

*	* *	* * *	* * * * [*]
psalm	charade	safari	sarcastically
		Sahara	
scar(red)	cigar	salami	Somalia
scarf(-ves)		sarcasm	
	sample(d)	sarcastic(ally)	
shaft	sampler		
shark	sampling	sharpening	
sharp	sardine		
		soprano(s)	
slant	scarlet		
	scarring	staccato	
smart		starvation	
	sergeant		
snarl(ed)		sultana	
	sharpen(ed)		
spar(red)	sharpening		
spark(ed)	sharply		
sparse			
	sparkle(d)		
staff(ed)	sparkling		
stance	sparring		
star(red)			
starch(es)	starboard		
starched	starfish		
stark	starlight		
start	starling		
starve(d)	starring		
	starry		
	started		
	starting		
	startle(d)		
	startling		
	starving		
	stratum(strata)		
	surpass(ed)		

In these words you can hear the vowel sound **ar** as in **shark**

T

*	* *	* * *	* * * *
tar(red)	target(ted)	ptarmigan	
tart	tarmac		
task	tarnish(es)	targetting	
	tarnished	tomato(es)	
trance	tarring		
	tartan		
tsar/czar			

V

*	* *	* * *	* * * *
vase	vantage	vibrato	
vast	varnish(es)		
	varnished		

Y

*	* *	* * *	* * * *
yard	yardstick		
yarn(ed)			

Z

*	* *	* * *	* * * *
czar/tsar		Zimbabwe	

In these words you can hear the vowel sound **ar** as in shark

*

*air (atmosphere /
   manner /
   feeling / tune)
aired

*heir (next owner)

```
for H ...
see page 238
```

* *

affair

aircraft
Airedale
airfield
airline
airmail
airport
airtight
airway

aware

Eire

heiress(es)
heirloom

* * *

aerial
aerobics
aerofoil
aerodrome
aeroplane
aerosol

airliner

area

* * * *

aeronautics

aquarium

B

*

*bare(d) (uncover)

*bear (animal)
*bear (carry)
 [bore]
 [born/borne]

 blare(d)

* *

barely

bearing
bearer
beware

* * *

barium

* * * *

Bulgaria

C

*

cairn
care(d)

chair(ed)

* *

careful(ly)
careless

chairman

compare(d)

* * *

canary(-ies)
carefully
carelessly

comparing
contrary

In these words you can hear the vowel sound air as in bear

D

LONG VOWEL **air**

*

dare(d)

* *

dairy(-ies)
daring

declare(d)
despair(ed)

* * *

* * * *

E

*

*air (atmosphere / manner /
   feeling / tune)
aired

*heir (next owner)

* *

aircraft
Airedale
airfield
airline
airmail
airport
airtight

éclair

Eire

heiress(es)
heirloom

* * *

aerial
aerobics
aerofoil
aerodrome
aeroplane
aerosol

airliner

area

* * * *

en- or in- ?

for H . . .
see page 238

for I . . .
see page 239

In these words you can hear the vowel sound **air** as in bear   237

*	* *	* * *	* * * *
*fair (just / funfair / market / fine weather / light in colour) *fare (charge for ride / food / get on) fared *flair (natural skill) *flare (burst into flame / get wider at the bottom) flared	fairground fairly fairy(-ies) farewell forbear [forbore] [forborne] forswear [forswore] [forsworn] pharaoh		

G

*	* *	* * *	* * * *
glare(d)			

H

*	* *	* * *	* * * *
*hair(ed) (thread- like growth) *hare (animal) hared *heir (next owner) *Herr (German for 'Mr.')	haircut hairy(-ier,-iest) heiress(es) heirloom	haircutting hairdresser hair-drier	hilarious Hungarian

In these words you can hear the vowel sound air as in bear

I

※

for E ...
see page 237

※ ※

ic- or ec- ?

※ ※ ※

※ ※ ※ ※

invariably

L

※

*lair (den)

※ ※

※ ※ ※

※ ※ ※ ※

M

※

*mare (female horse)
*mayor (head of town
    or city)

※ ※

mayoress(es)

※ ※ ※

※ ※ ※ ※

malaria

P

※

*pair (set of two)
paired
*pare(d) (trim /
    peel)

*pear (fruit)

prayer

※ ※

parent

pharaoh

prairie
prepare(d)

※ ※ ※

preparing

※ ※ ※ ※

*	* *	* * *	* * * *
rare	rarely		
	repair(ed)		

S

*	* *	* * *	* * * *
scarce	scarcely	scarcity	
scare(d)	scarecrow		
	scary(-ier,iest)	shareholder	
share(d)			
	sharing		
snare(d)			
	staircase		
spare(d)	staring		
square(d)			

*stair (step/s)
*stare(d) (look with
   fixed gaze)

swear
[swore]
[sworn]

In these words you can hear the vowel sound air as in bear

T

☆

tear
[tore]
[torn]

*their (belonging
    to them)
*theirs (something
    belonging to them)
*there (to/in that
    place / also used
    with 'is', 'are',
    'was', 'were' and
    other forms of
    'to be')
there'd
there'll
*there's (there is /
    there has)
*they're (they are)

☆ ☆

tearing

thereby
therefore
thereof
therewith

☆ ☆ ☆

thereafter
thereupon

☆ ☆ ☆ ☆

V

☆

☆ ☆

vary(-ies)
    (varied)

☆ ☆ ☆

variant
various
varying

☆ ☆ ☆ ☆

variable
variation

W

☆

*ware (products for
    sale / pottery)

*wear (carry on
    body / get worse
    with use)
[wore]
[worn]
*-were (form of verb
    'to be')
*where (to/in which
    place)

☆ ☆

warehouse
wary(-ier,-iest)

wearing

whereas
whereby
wherefore
wherein

☆ ☆ ☆

whereupon
wherever

☆ ☆ ☆ ☆

In these words you can hear the vowel sound air as in bear

*	* *	* * *	* * * *

*-air (atmosphere /
   manner /
   feeling / tune)
-aired
	absurd
	
	adjourn(ed)
		-aerial
		-aerobics
		-aerofoil
		-aerodrome
		-aeroplane
			adverbial(ly)
			advertisement
			
			-aeronautics

*-heir (next owner)	-affair affirm(ed)	-aerosol	alternative
	-aircraft -Airedale -airfield -airline -airmail -airport -airtight -airway	-airliner alternate -area assertion assertive	-aquarium
	alert		
	assert astern		
	-aware		
	-Eire		

for H ...
see page 247

-heiress(es)
-heirloom

In these words you can hear the vowel sound **er** as in **worm**

*	* *	* * *	* * * *
*-bare(ed) (uncover)	-barely	-barium	
*-bear (animal)	-bearing	burglary(-ies)	
*-bear (carry)	-bearer		
[bore]	-beware		
[born/borne]			
*berth (bunk / place	birthday		
for ship at quay)	birthplace		
berthed			
	blurring		
birch(es)			
birched	burden(ed)		
*bird (feathered	*burger (sandwich)		
animal)	*burgher (citizen)		
*birth (delivery of	burglar		
child / origin)	burlap		
	burly(-ier,-iest)		
-blare(d)	Burma		
blur(red)	burning		
blurt	burring		
burn(ed)			
[burnt]			
burr/bur			
*burred (murmured)			
burst			
[burst]			

In this word 'er' has a neutral sound.

Bermuda

*	* *	* * *	* * * * [*]
-cairn	-careful(ly)	-canary(-ies)	circulation
-care(d)	-careless	-carefully	circulatory
		-carelessly	circumference
-chair(ed)	certain		circumstances
chirp(ed)		certainly	
church(es)	-chairman	certify(-ies)	commercially
churn(ed)	churchyard	(certified)	conservative
			convertible
*curb(ed) (restrain)	circle(d)	circular	
curds	circling	circulate	
curl(ed)	circuit	circumscibe(d)	
curse(d)	circus	circumstance	
curt			
curve(d)	clergy	clergyman	
*kerb (edge of pavement)	*colonel (army	commercial(ly)	
	officer)	-comparing	
kirk	-compare(d)	-contrary	
	concern(ed)	concerning	
	confer(red)	conferring	
	confirm(ed)	convergent	
	conserve(d)	conversion	
	converge(d)	courteous	
	converse(d)	courtesy(-ies)	
	convert		
	courteous	curlier	
	curdle(d)		
	curdling		
	curfew		
	curly(-ier,-iest)		
	cursor		
	curtain(ed)		
	curtsey		
	y(-ies)		
	(curtsied)		
	curvy(-ier,-iest)		

for Qu ...
see page 251

*kernel (seed in nut)

> In these words 'er' and 'ir' have... er.... a neutral sound.
>
> certificate   circumference

In these words you can hear the vowel sound er as in worm

-dare(d)

dirt

-dairy(-ies)
-daring

-declare(d)
*desert (leave)
 deserve(d)
-despair(ed)
*dessert (sweet dish)
 deter(red)

dirty(-ies)
   (dirtied)
dirty(-ier,-iest)
discern(ed)
disperse(d)
disturb(ed)
diverge(d)
diverse
divert

deserted
detergent
determine(d)
deterring

dirtier
dirtiest
disturbance

determination
determining

diversity

E

*air (atmosphere / manner /
    feeling / tune)
aired

earl
*earn(ed) (get money
    by working)
earth(ed)

err(ed)

*-heir (next owner)

 urge(d)
*urn (vase / vessel)

-aircraft
-Airedale
-airfield
-airline
-airmail
-airport
-airtight

early(-ier,-iest)
earnest
earnings
earthquake
earthworm

-eclair

-Eire

emerge(d)

exert

-heirloom
-heiress(es)

urban
urchin
urgent

-aerial
-aerobics
-aerofoil
-aerodrome
-aeroplane
-aerosol

-airliner

-area

earlier
earliest
earthenware

emergence

encircle(d)

eternal(ly)

excursion
exertion
external(ly)

urgency

emergency(-ies)

en- or in- ?

eternally

exterminate
externally

for H ...
see page 247

for I ...
see page 247

In these words you can hear the vowel sound er as in worm

*	* *	* * *	* * * * [*]
*-fair (just / funfair / market / fine weather / light in colour)	-fairground -fairly -fairy(-ies) -farewell	fertilise(d) ze	fermentation fertilisation zation
*-fare (charge for ride / food / get on)	ferment fertile fervour	furniture furthermore	fertiliser zer fertility
-fared			
fern	firmly		
*fir (tree) firm(ed) first	-forbear [forbore] [forborne] -forswear [forswore] [forsworn]		
*-flair (natural skill) *-flare (burst into flame / get wider at the bottom)	furnace furnish(es) furnished furring furry further(ed) furtive		
-flared			
*fur (coat of animal) furred furl(ed) *furs (coats of animals) *furze (gorse)	pharaoh		

In this word 'er' has a neutral sound.

ferment

for th ...
see page 253

G

*	* *	* * *	* * * *
jerk(ed)	jerkin jersey Jersey	Germany germinate	germination
germ			
girl girth	journal journey(ed)		
-glare(d)	gerbil German		
	girder girdle(d) girdling		
	Guernsey gurgle(d) gurgling		

In these words you can hear the vowel sound er as in worm

| ✻ | ✻ ✻ | ✻ ✻ ✻ | ✻ ✻ ✻ ✻ |

*-hair(ed) (thread-
    like growth)
*-hare (animal)
 -hared

 *heard (did hear)
*-heir (next owner)
 her
 herb
 *herd (group of
    animals)
*-Herr (German for
   'Mr.')
 hers

 hurl(ed)
 hurt
 [hurt]

-haircut
-hairy(-ier,-iest)

-heiress(es)
-heirloom
herdsman
hermit

hurdle(d)
hurdling
hurtle(d)
hurtling

-haircutting
-hairdresser
-hair-drier

herbaceous
herbivore

> In this word 'er' has a neutral sound.
>
> herself

I

| ✻ | ✻ ✻ | ✻ ✻ ✻ | ✻ ✻ ✻ ✻ [✻] |

irk(ed)

ir- or ear- ?
ir- or er- ?
ir- or ur- ?

ic- or ec- ?

immerse(d)

im- or em- ?

inert
infer(red)
infirm
insert
invert

irksome

ir- or ear- ?
ir- or ur- ?

ix- or ex- ?

immersion
imperfect

inertia
inferring
internal(ly)
interpret(ed)
inversion

in- or en- ?

ir- or ur- ?

it- or et- ?

ix- or ex- ?

impersonal
impersonate
impersonation
impertinent

infirmary(-ies)
internally
interpolate
interpretation
interpreted
interpreter
interpreting
-invariably

it- or et- ?

ix- or ex- ?

for E ...
see page 245

*

germ

jerk(ed)

* *

gerbil
German

jerkin
jersey
Jersey
journal
journey(ed)

* * *

Germany
germinate

journalist

* * * *

germination

journalism

K

*

kerb(ed)

kirk

knurled

* *

*kernel (seed in nut)

* * *

* * * *

for C ...
see page 244

for Qu ...
see page 251

L

*

*-lair (den)

learn(ed)
[learnt]

lurch(es)
lurched
lurk(ed)

* *

learner
learning

* * *

* * * *

In these words you can hear the vowel sound er as in worm

M

*

*-mare (female horse)
*-mayor (head of town
   or city)

merge(d)

mirth

myrrh

* *

-mayoress(es)

merchant
mercy(-ies)
merger
merging

murder(ed)
murky(-ier,-iest)
murmur(ed)

* * *

mercenary(-ies)
merchandise
merciful(ly)
merciless
mercury
Mercury

murderer
murderous
murmuring

* * * *

-malaria

mercenary(-ies)
mercifully

N

*

knurled

nerve

nurse(d)

* *

nervous
nervy(-ier,-iest)

nursing

* * *

nasturtium

nursery(-ies)

* * * *

O

*

* *

observe(d)

occur(red)

* * *

alternate

observant
observer
observing

occurring

* * * * [*]

alternative

observatory(-ies)

*	* *	* * *	* * * * [*]
*-pair (set of two)	-parent	percolate	perforation
-paired		perfectly	perpendicular
*-pare(d) (trim /	perfect	perforate	persecution
peel)	perfume(d)	permanent	personality(-ies)
	person	permeable	personally
*-pear (fruit)	perspex	permeate	perspiration
*pearl (jewel)	perspire(d)	peroxide	
*per (for each)	perverse	persecute	purposefully
perch(es)		persevere(d)	
perched	-pharaoh	personal(ly)	
perm(ed)		personnel	
	-prairie	pertinent	
-prayer	prefer(red)	perversion	
	-prepare(d)		
purge(ed)	preserve(d)	preferring	
*purl (knitting		-preparing	
stitch)	purchase(d)		
*purr(ed) (sound of	purple	purposeful(ly)	
happy cat)	purpose	pursuer	
purse	purring		

In these words 'er' and 'ur' have... er.... a neutral sound.

'PERSISTENT' WORDS

perceive(d)	perfect(ion)	permissible	perplexing	persuasive
percentage	perform(ed)	permission	persist(ence)	pursue(d)
perception	performance	permit(ted)	persistent	pursuant
perceptive	performer	permitting	perspective	pursuit
perceptual(ly)	performing	perpetual(ly)	perspire(d)	
percussion	perfume(d)	perplex(es)	persuade	
percussive	perhaps	perplexed	persuasion	

for pre ...
see page 82

In these words you can hear the vowel sound er as in worm

Q

✼   ✼ ✼   ✼ ✼ ✼   ✼ ✼ ✼ ✼

quirk

R

✼	✼ ✼	✼ ✼ ✼	✼ ✼ ✼ ✼
-rare	-rarely	referral	returnable
		referring	reverberate
	refer(red)	rehearsal	reversible
	rehearse(d)	researcher	
	-repair(ed)	returning	
	research(es)	reversal	
	researched		
	reserve(d)		
	return(ed)		
	reverse(d)		

S

*	**	***	****
-scarce	certain	certainly	certificate
-scare(d)		certify(-ies)	
scourge(d)	circle(d)	(certified)	circulation
scurf	circuit		circumstances
	circus	circular	
search(es)		circulate	
searched	-scarcely	circumstance	surgically
*serf (slave)	-scarecrow		
*serge (woollen	-scary(-ier,-iest)	-scarcity	
cloth)	scurvy		
serve(d)		-shareholder	
	searching		
-share(d)	searchlight	suburban	
shirk(ed)	sermon	surgery(-ies)	
shirt	serpent	surgical(ly)	
	servant		
Sir	service(d)		
	serviette		
skirt	servile		
	serving		
slur(red)			
	-sharing		
-snare(d)	sherbet		
	shirty		
-spare(d)			
sperm	sirloin		
spur(red)			
spurn(ed)	slurring		
spurs			
spurt	spurring		
-square(d)	-staircase		
squirm(ed)	-staring		
squirt	sterling		
	stirring		
*-stair (step/s)	sturdy(-ier,-iest)		
*-stare(d) (look with			
fixed gaze)	submerge(d)		
stern	surface(d)		
stir(red)	surfer		
	surfing		
*surf (foaming sea)	surform		
surfed	surgeon		
*surge(d) (rush	surging		
forward)	surmount		
	surname		
-swear	surpass(ed)		
[swore]	*surplice (gown worn		
[sworn]	in church)		
swerve(d)	*surplus(es) (excess)		
swirl(ed)	survey(ed)		

In these words 'ur' has a neutral sound.

'SURPRISING' WORDS

surmount	surprising	survive(d)
surpass(ed)	surrender(ed)	survival
surprise(d)	surround(ings)	survivor

252

In these words you can hear the vowel sound er as in worm

*

-tear
[tore]
[torn]
term(ed)
*tern (bird)

*-their (belonging
to them)
*-theirs (something
belonging to
them)
*-there (to/in that
place / also
used with 'is',
'are', 'was',
'were' and other
forms of 'to be')
-there'd
-there'll
*-there's (there is /
there has)
*-they're (they are)
therm
third
thirst

turf(ed)
Turk
*turn(ed) (change
direction)

twirl(ed)

* *

-tearing

-thereby
-therefore
-thereof
-therewith
thermal(ly)
thermos
thirsty(-ier,-iest)
thirteen(th)
thirty(-ies)
Thursday

*turban (head-
covering)
*turbine (engine)
turbot
turmoil
turtle
Turkey
turkey
turning
turnip
turnpike
turnstile
turquoise

* * *

terminal(ly)
terminate
tertiary

-thereafter
-thereupon
thermally
thermostat
thirtieth

turbojet
turbulence
turbulent
turmeric
turpentine

* * * *

terminally

In this word 'er' has a neutral sound.

thermometer

U

*	* *	* * *	* * * *
earl	early	earliest	
*earn(ed) (get money by working)	earthquake		
earth(ed)	urban	urgency	
	urchin		
err(ed)	urgent		
urge(d)			
*urn (vase / vessel)			

for H ...
see page 247

V

*	* *	* * *	* * * * [*]
verb	–vary(–ies)	–variant	–variable
verge(d)	– (varied)	–various	–variation
verse(d)	verbal(ly)	–varying	
	verdict		vermiculite
	verger	verbally	vertically
	vermin	vermilion	
	version	vernier	virtually
	versus	vertebrate	virtuosity
	vertex(–ices)	vertical(ly)	virtuoso
		vertices	
	virgin		
	virtue	virginal	
	virtual(ly)	virtually	

In these words you can hear the vowel sound **er** as in **worm**

*	* *	* * *	* * * *

*-ware (products for
    sale / pottery)

*-wear (carry on
    body / get worse
    with use)
  [wore]
  [worn]
 *were (form of verb
    'to be')
  weren't

*-where (to/in which
    place)
 *whirl(ed) (spin
    around)
 *whirr(ed) (sound)
 *whorl (turn of
    spiral)
 *whorled (shaped in
    a spiral)

  word
  work(ed)
 *world (the earth)
  worm(ed)
  worse
  worst
  worth

-warehouse
-wary(-ier,-iest)

-wearing

-whereas
-whereby
-wherefore
-wherein
 whirlpool
 whirlwind
 whirring
 worker
 working
 workman
 workshop
 worldwide
 worship(ped)
 worsen(ed)
 worthless
 worthwhile
 worthy(-ies)

-whereupon
-wherever

 workable
 worshipper
 worshipping

Y

*	* *	* * *	* * * *

year
yearn(ed)

In these words you can hear the vowel sound **er** as in **worm**

*

*all (every one)

*awe (fear and
  wonder)
awed
*awl (boring tool)

*oar (rowing blade)

*or (marks choice)
*ore (mineral)

ought

* *

aboard
abroad
absorb(ed)

accord

adore(d)
adorn(ed)

afford

almost
alright
also
*altar (holy table)
*alter(ed) (change)
although
always

appal(led)
applaud
applause

ashore
assault
assure(d)

auburn
auction(ed)
*auger (tool)
*augur (suggest for
   the future)
August
august
*aural(ly) (by the ear)
austere
author
autumn

award
awesome/awsome
awful(ly)
awkward

*oral(ly) (by the mouth)
orbit(ed)
orchard
orchid
ordeal
order(ed)
organ
orgy(-ies)
orphan(ed)

* * *

abortion
absorber
absorption

accordance
according

adsorption

almighty
already
alternate

appalling

assorted
assortment
assurance

audible
audience
auditory
*aurally (by the ear)
aurora
Austria
authentic(ally)
authoress(es)
authorise(d)
           ze
autograph(ed)

awfully

*orally (by the mouth)
orbital
orbited
orbiting
orchestra
ordeal
orderly(-ies)
ordinary
organic(ally)
organise(d)
          ze
organist
orgasm
ornament

* * * * [* * * *]

accordingly
accordion

adorable

alternating
alternative
alternator
altogether

auditory
authentically
authority(-ies)
autobiography(-ies)
autobiographical(ly)
automatic(ally)
automation
automobile
autonomic
autonomous
auxiliary(-ies)

ordinarily
ordinary
organically
organisation
         zation
organism
oriental
ornithologist
ornithology

for H . . .
see page 261

In these words you can hear the vowel sound or as in horse

*   * *   * * *   * * * *

*bald (lacking hair)
balk/baulk(ed)
*ball (round
    object / dance)
*balled (made into a
    ball)
baulk/balk(ed)
*bawl (yell)
*bawled (did yell)

*boar (male pig)
*board (plank /
    daily meals /
    committee)
*boor (rough fellow)
*bore (drill /
    drilled hole /
    carried / fail to
    interest / tide-
    wave)
*bored (drilled /
    lacking an
    interest)
*born (delivered
    at birth)
*borne (carried)
bought

brawl(ed)
brawn
broad
brought

balsa
balsam
Baltic
ballroom
basalt
bauxite

because
befall
[befell]
[befallen]
before
besought

*boarder (person who
    pays for food and
    bed)
borax
*border (edge /
    frontier)
bordered
boring

brawny
broadcast
[broadcast]
broadside

befallen
beforehand

broadcasting

257

*   * *   * * *   * * * *

call(ed)	calling	caustically	caustically
*caught (got /	cauldron		
trapped)	causing	chloroform(ed)	conformity
*caulk(ed) (fill	caustic(ally)	chlorophyll	cordially
gaps with fibre	caution(ed)		corporation
and tar)	cautious	conformist	
*cause (bring about /		cordial(ly)	
reason)	chloride	corduroy	
caused	chlorine	cormorant	
*caw (harsh bird cry)	choral		
*cawed (did caw)	chorus(es)		
*caws (does caw)	chorused		

chalk(ed)   conform(ed)
*chord (notes   cordial(ly)
  sounded together /   corgi
  term in geometry)   corner(ed)
chore   cornet
                cornfield
*clause (words in   cornflakes
  sentence / part   courting
  of written   courtyard
  agreement)
claw(ed)   crawling
*claws (curved nails
  or limbs)

*coarse (rough)
*cord (string)
*core (central
  part / take out
  the core from)
*cored (did core)
*cork (bark of cork
  tree)
corked
corm
corn(ed)
*corps (group)
corpse
*course (track /
  direction /
  part of meal /
  of course)
coursed
*court (enclosed
  area / friends of
  sovereign / seek
  favour)

crawl(ed)

for Qu ...
see page 266

In these words you can hear the vowel sound or as in horse

*

daub(ed)
dawn(ed)

door

*draw (pull /
    sketch)
[drew]
[drawn]
*drawer (sliding
    container)
drawl(ed)

dwarf(ed)

* *

daughter
dawdle(d)
dawdling

deform(ed)
deport

distort
divorce(d)

doorway
dormant
dormouse(-mice)
dorsal

drawbridge
drawing

* * *

disorder(ed)

dormitory(-ies)

* * * *

dormitory(-ies)

E

*

* *

em- or im-. ?

endorse(d)
enforce(d)
*ensure(d) (make
    certain)

en- or in- ?

escort

exalt
exhaust
explore(d)
export

* * *

em- or im- ?

enforcement
enormous

en- or in- ?

exalted
exhausted
exhaustion
explorer
exploring

* * * * [* * *]

extraordinarily
extraordinary

for I ...
see page 262

In these words you can hear the vowel sound **or** as in horse

* | * * | * * * | * * * * [*]

fall
[fell]
[fallen]
false
fault
*faun (goat-God)
*fawn (young deer /
   colour / try to
   win favour)
fawned

fiord/fjord

flaunt
*flaw(ed) (fault)
*floor(ed) (levelled
   area)

*for (in place of /
   to belong to /
   because)
force(d)
ford
*fore (front /
   leading position)
forge(d)
fork(ed)
form(ed)
*fort (fortress)
*forth (forward)
*fought (contested)
*four (4)
*fourth (4th)

fraud

for th ...
see page 268

falcon
fallen
falling
fallout
falter(ed)
faulty

fiord/fjord

floral
fluoride
fluorine

forbear
[forbore]
[forborne]
forceful(ly)
forearm
forecast
[forecast]
forefoot
foreground
forehand
foreman
foremost
foresee
[foresaw]
[foreseen]
foresight
foretell
[foretold]
forewarn(ed)
forfeit
forgo/forego
[forwent/forewent]
[forgone/foregone]
forlorn
formal(ly)
format(ted)
former
forming
forswear
[forswore]
[forsworn]
*forte (loud / strength)
fortnight
fortress(es)
fortune
*forty (40)
fourteen(th)
forward

Fräulein

fluorescent

forcefully
forefather
forefinger
forgery
*formally (officially)
formation
formatted
formatting
*formerly (previously)
formula
formulate
fortieth
fortunate

fluorescent

fortification
fortunately

> In these words 'or' is a neutral vowel.
> It sounds like the 'a' in 'astonish'.
>
> 'FORGOTTEN' WORDS
>
> forbear | forgetful(ly)
> [forbore] | forgive
> [forborne] | [forgave]
> forbid | [forgiven]
> [forbad(e)] | forgiveness
> [forbidden] | forsake
> forbidding | [forsook]
> forgave | [forsaken]
> forget(ting)
> [forgot]
> [forgotten]

In these words you can hear the vowel sound **or** as in horse

G

✽

gaunt
gauze

*gnaw(ed) (keep
  biting)

gorge(d)
gorse

✽ ✽

gaudy(-ier,-iest)

glory(-ies)
  (gloried)

gorgeous

✽ ✽ ✽

Gibraltar

glorious

✽ ✽ ✽ ✽

H

✽

*hall (large room /
  passage)
halt
*haul (drag /
  amount gained)
hauled
haunt
hawk(ed)

*hoar (white)
*hoard (store)
*hoarse (rough and
  husky)
*horde (gang /
  tribe)
horn(ed)
*horse (animal)

*whore (prostitute)

✽ ✽

halter
haughty(-ier,-lest)
haunches

hoarding
hormone
hornblende
hornet
horseback
horsehair
horseman
horsepower
horseshoe

✽ ✽ ✽

haughtily

horsepower

✽ ✽ ✽ ✽

historian

I

*	* *	* * *	* * * * [*]
	ignore(d)	immortal(ly)	immortality
		importance	immortally
	implore(d)	important	
	import		inaugural
		informal(ly)	inauguration
	indoors	informant	incorporat(ed)
	inform(ed)	installing	informally
	instal(led)	instalment/	informative
	*insure(d) (protect	installment	
	against loss)	insurance	ix- or ex- ?

for E ...
see page 259

in- or en- ?   in- or en-?

ix- or ex-?

J

*	* *	* * *	* * * *
jaunt	jaunty(-ier,-iest)	Gibraltar	Jordanian
jaw(ed)			
	Jordan		

K

*	* *	* * *	* * * *
	Koran		

for C ...
see page 258

for Qu ...
see page 266

In these words the 'o' may be neutral.

Koran   Korea(n)

In these words you can hear the vowel sound **or** as in **horse**

*	* *	* * *	* * * *
launch(es)	launcher	launderette	
launched	launder(ed)		
*law (rules enforced in a country)	laundry(-ies)		
	laurel		
lawn	lawyer		
lord			
*lore (traditions and facts)			

M

*	* *	* * *	* * * *
*mall (public walk)	Malta	Majorca	memorial
malt			
*maul (batter)	*morning (before midday)	Minorca	mortality
mauled	morpheme	misfortune	
mauve	morsel		
	mortal(ly)	moreover	
*moor (open land / fasten to land or to buoy)	mortar	mortally	
	mortgage(d)		
*more (additional / a larger amount)	mortice(d) se		
*morn (morning)	mournful		
Morse	*mourning (showing sadness at loss or death)		
*mourn (show sadness at loss or death)			

N

*	* *	* * *	* * * *
*gnaw(ed) (keep biting)	naughty(-ier,-iest)	nautical(ly)	nautically
		naughtier	
naught/nought	normal(ly)	naughtiest	notorious
	Norman	naughtiness	
*nor (and not)	northern		
norm	northward	normally	
north	Norway	northernmost	
nought/naught		Norwegian	

* | * * | * * * | * * * * [* * * *]

*all (every one)

*awe (fear and wonder)
awed
*awl (boring tool)

*oar (rowing blade)

*or (marks choice)
*ore (mineral)

ought

---

almost
alright
also
*altar (holy table)
*alter(ed) (change)
although
always

auburn
auction(ed)
*auger (tool)
*augur
August
august
aural(ly) (by the ear)
austere
author
autumn

awesome/awsome
awful(ly)
awkward

*oral(ly) (by the mouth)
orbit(ed)
orchard
orchid
ordeal
order(ed)
organ
ornate
orgy(-ies)
orphan(ed)

---

almighty
already
alternate

audible
audience
auditory
*aurally (by the ear)
aurora
Austria
authentic(ally)
authoress(es)
authorise(d)
ze
autograph(ed)

awfully

*orally (by the mouth)
orbital
orbited
orbiting
orchestra
ordeal
ordering
orderly(-ies)
ordinal
ordinary
organic(ally)
organise(d)
ze
organist
orgasm
ornament

---

alternating
alternative
alternator
altogether

auditory
authentically
authority(-ies)
autobiography(-ies)
autobiographical(ly)
automatic(ally)
automation
automobile
autonomic
autonomous
auxiliary(-ies)

ordinarily
ordinary
organically
organisation
zation
organism
oriental
ornithologist
ornithology

---

for H ...
see page 261

264

In these words you can hear the vowel sound **or** as in **horse**

☀   ☀ ☀   ☀ ☀ ☀   ☀ ☀ ☀ ☀ [☀]

*pause (brief gap /   palfrey   performance   proportional(ly)
  hesitate)   performer
 paused   perform(ed)   performing
*paw (foot of
  animal)   poorly   porcelain
*pawed (examined by   porous   porcupine
  paw)   porpoise   portable
 pawn(ed)   porter   portcullis
*paws (feet of   porthole   Portugal
  animal)   portion   Portuguese
                         portrait
*poor (badly off)   portray(ed)   precaution
 porch(es)   pouring   proportion
*pore (tiny hole /
  study closely)
*pored (studied
  closely)
*pores (tiny holes)
 pork
 port
*pour (flow out)
*poured (did pour)

 prawn

Q

* | ** | *** | ****

quart
*quarts (more than
  one quart)
*quartz (mineral)

quarter
quartet

R

* | ** | *** | ****

*raw (untreated /
  sore / chilly)

*roar (loud noise)
roared

wrath
wrought

recall(ed)
record
reform(ed)
report
resort
resource(d)
restore(d)
retort
reward

roaring

recorded
recorder
recording
reported
reporter
resources

In these words you can hear the vowel sound **or** as in horse

✻

salt
*sauce (tasty
    liquid / rude
    talk)
*saw (looked at /
    cutting tool)
*sawed (did saw)
    [sawn]

scald
scorch(es)
scorched
score(d)
scorn(ed)
scrawl(ed)

shawl
*shore (coast)
shored
shorn
short
shorts

small

snore(d)

*soar (fly high)
*soared (flew high)
*sore (painful)
*sort (group)
*sought (looked for)
*source (origin)

spawn(ed)
spore
sport
sprawl(ed)

squawk(ed)

*stalk (stem /
    hunt / walk
    stiffly)
stalked
stall(ed)
staunch(es)
staunched
store(d)
*stork (bird)
storm
straw

-see next page

✻ ✻

salty(-ier,-iest)
saucer
saucepan
saucy(-ier,-iest)
sauna
saunter(ed)

scornful(ly)
scorpion

shortage
shortening
shorter
shortest
shorthand
shortly

slaughter(ed)

smaller
smallest
smallpox

snorkel

stalling
stalwart
storage
storehouse
*storey (floor)
stormy(-ier,-iest)
*story(-ies) (tale)
strawberry(-ies)

support
surely

swarthy(-ier,-iest)

✻ ✻ ✻

saucily

scornfully
scorpion

Signora

strawberry(-ies)

supported
supporter
supporting

✻ ✻ ✻ ✻

subordinate

✻

*sure (certain)

swarm(ed)
*sword (weapon)
swore
sworn

T

✻   ✻ ✻   ✻ ✻ ✻   ✻ ✻ ✻ ✻

*talk (speak)   talking   talkative
talked   taller
tall   tallest   thoughtfully
*taut (tight)
*taught (instructed)   thorax(es/-ces)   tornado(es)
taunt   thoughtful(ly)   torpedo(es)

thaw(ed)   torment
thorn   torsion
thought   torso(s)
thwart   tortoise
   torture(d)
*tor (hill)   Tory(-ies)
torch(es)   toward
*tore (did tear)   towards
torn
*torque (turning
   force / necklace)

V

✻   ✻ ✻   ✻ ✻ ✻   ✻ ✻ ✻ ✻

vase   Victorian
*vault (gymnastic   victorious
   leap /
   underground room /
   arched roof)

In these words you can hear the vowel sound **or** as in **horse**

*

walk(ed)
wall(ed)
waltz(es)
waltzed
*war (conflict)
*warred (waged war)
*ward (part of
    hospital / person
    under legal
    protection)
warm(ed)
warmth
*warn(ed) (caution)
warp(ed)
wart

wharf(-ves)
*whore (prostitute)

*wore (was dressed
    in)
*worn (carried on
    the body / worse
    for wear)

wrath
wrought

* *

walking
walnut
walrus
warble(d)
warbling
warden
wardrobe
warfare
warlike
warmer
warning
warpath
warring
warship
wartime
water(ed)

* * *

wallpaper(ed)
waterfall
waterfowl
watershed

* * * *

walkie-talkie

Y

*

yawn(ed)

*yore (ancient times)
*your (belonging to
    you)
*you're (you are)
yours

* *

Yorkshire
yourself
yourselves

* * *

* * * *

*	* *	* * *	* * * *
	ahoy!	adjoining	
	anoint	annoyance	
	annoy(ed)		
		appointment	
	appoint		
		avoided	
	avoid		

B

*	* *	* * *	* * * *
boil(ed)	boiler	boisterous	
*boy (lad)	boiling		
	boycott	buoyancy	
broil(ed)			
	buoyant		
*buoy (marker)			
buoyed			

C

*	* *	* * *	* * * *
choice	cloister(ed)		
coil(ed)			
*coin (money)			
coined			
coy			
quoit			

for Qu ...
see page 274

In these words you can hear the vowel sound oi as in oyster-catcher

✽

✽ ✽

destroy(ed)

disloyal(ly)

doily(-ies)/
doyley(s)

✽ ✽ ✽

destroyer

disloyally
disloyalty

✽ ✽ ✽ ✽

disloyally
disloyalty

E

✽

✽ ✽

embroil(ed)
employ(ed)

enjoy(ed)

exploit

✽ ✽ ✽

embroider(ed)
employee
employer
employment

enjoying
enjoyment

✽ ✽ ✽ ✽

embroidery

F

✽

foil(ed)

✽ ✽

foyer

Fräulein

✽ ✽ ✽

✽ ✽ ✽ ✽

*   * *   * * *   * * * *

*groin (part where
  legs join body)
*groyne (low
  structure built
  out into water)

H

*   * *   * * *   * * * *

hoist

J

*   * *   * * *   * * * *

join(ed)   joiner   joinery
joint   joining   joyfully
joist   joyful(ly)
joy   joyous

In these words you can hear the vowel sound **oi** as in **oyster-catcher**

L

.⋇.

loyal(ly)

⋇ ⋇

loyally
loyalty(-ies)

⋇ ⋇ ⋇

loyally
loyalty(-ies)

⋇ ⋇ ⋇ ⋇

M

.⋇.

moist

⋇ ⋇

moisture

⋇ ⋇ ⋇

⋇ ⋇ ⋇ ⋇

N

.⋇.

noise

⋇ ⋇

noisy(-ier,-iest)

⋇ ⋇ ⋇

noisier
noisiest
noisily

⋇ ⋇ ⋇ ⋇

O

.⋇.

oil(ed)

for H . . .
see page 272

⋇ ⋇

oilstone
ointment
oily

oyster

⋇ ⋇ ⋇

⋇ ⋇ ⋇ ⋇

*	* *	* * *	* * * *
point poise(d)	poignant pointed pointer pointing poison(ed)	poisoner poisonous	

Q

*	* *	* * *	* * * *
*quoin (corner- stone) quoit			

R

*	* *	* * *	* * * *
royal(ly)	recoil(ed) rejoice(d) rejoin(ed) royally royalty(-ies)	royally royalty(-ies)	

In these words you can hear the vowel sound oi as in oyster-catcher

*   * *   * * *   * * * *

soil(ed)   soya   sequoia

spoil(ed)
[spoilt]

T

*   * *   * * *   * * * *

toil(ed)   toilet
toy(ed)

V

*   * *   * * *   * * * *

voice(d)   voyage(d)
void

A

*

* *

abound
about

account

*aloud (loud enough
  to be heard)
allow
*allowed (permitted)

amount

announce(d)

around
arouse(d)

* * *

allowance

announcement
announcer
astounded
astounding

B

*

blouse

*bough (branch)
bounce(d)
bound
bout
*bow (bend / front
  of ship)

brow
brown(ed)
*brows (more than
  one brow)
*browse(d) (nibble /
  dip into books)

* *

bounty(-ies)

brownie

* * *

boundary(-ies)

In these words you can hear the vowel sound ou as in owl

＊

＊ ＊

＊ ＊ ＊

＊ ＊ ＊ ＊ [＊]

chow	cacao	*councillor (member of a council)	counterexample
cloud	cloudless	counselling	
clout	cloudy(-ier,-iest)	*counsellor (person who gives advice)	
clown(ed)		countenance	
	*council (group for directing affairs)	counterfoil	
couch(es)	*counsel (advice)	countersink	
couched	counselled	cowardice	
count	countdown		
cow(ed)	counted		
cower(ed)	counter		
	counting		
crouch(es)	countless		
crouched	county(-ies)		
crowd	*coward (person who lacks courage)		
crown(ed)	cowboy		
	cower		
	*cowered (did cower)		
	cowshed		
	cowslip		
	crowded		

*	* *	* * *	* * * *
doubt	denounce(d)	doubtfully	
*dour (unsmiling)	devour(ed)	dowelling	
*douse/dowse (put into water / put out)	discount		
doused/dowsed	dismount		
dowel(led)			
*dower (property of bride or widow)	doubtful(ly)		
	doubtless		
down(ed)	dowdy(-ier,-iest)		
*dowse (use divining rod)	dowel(led)		
	dowelling		
	downfall		
drought	downhill		
drown(ed)	downland		
	downright		
	downstairs		
	downstream		
	downward		
	dowry(-ies)		
	dowser		
	dowsing		
	drowsy(-ier,-iest)		

E

*	* *	* * *	* * * *
	endow(ed)	encounter(ed)	

In these words you can hear the vowel sound OU as in owl

flounce(d)
*flour (ground
    grain)
*flower (blossom)
flowered

*foul (dirty)
fouled
found
*fowl (bird)

Frau
frown(ed)

for th ...
see page 283

flounder(ed)

*founded (established)
founder
*foundered (sank /
    collapsed)
foundry(-ies)
fountain

foundation

G

gouge(d)
gown

ground
*grouse(grouse)
    (bird)
growl(ed)
*growse (grumble)

groundsel

H

hound
*hour (time)
house(d)
how
how'd
howl(ed)

hourglass(-es)
household
housing
housewife(-ves)
housework

however

In these words you can hear the vowel sound ou as in owl

* 　　　　　 * *　　　　　　 * * *　　　　　 * * * *

joust

L

* 　　　　　 * *　　　　　　 * * *　　　　　 * * * *

Laos　　　　　　louder　　　　　 loudspeaker
　　　　　　　　loudest
loud　　　　　　loudly
lounge(d)　　　 lousy(-ier,-iest)
louse
lout

M

* 　　　　　 * *　　　　　　 * * *　　　　　 * * * *

mound　　　　　miaow　　　　　 mountainous　　mountaineering
mount　　　　　　　　　　　　　 mountaineer
mouse　　　　　mountain　　　　 mountainside
mouth　　　　　mounted　　　　 mountaintop
mouthed　　　　mousy(-ier,-iest)
　　　　　　　　mouthful
　　　　　　　　mouthpiece

In these words you can hear the vowel sound **ou** as in **owl**

*

* *

* * *

* * * *

noun
now

nowadays

O

*

* *

* * *

* * * *

hour (time)

hourglass(es)

outbidding
outgoing
outlying
outnumber(ed)
outsider
outstanding
outwitted
outwitting

ounce
*our (belonging to
    us)
ours
out

owl

ourselves
outbid
[outbid]
outboard
outbreak
outburst
outcome
outdo
[outdid]
[outdone]
outdoors
outer
outfit
outing
outlaw(ed)
outlet
outline(d)
outlook
outpost
output
outrage(d)
outright
outrun
[outran]
outset
outshine
[outshone]
outside
outskirts
outstretched
outward
outwit(ted)

for H ...
see page 279

In these words you can hear the vowel sound OU as in owl

P

*

plough(ed)

pouch(es)
pouched
pounce(d)
pound
pout
power(ed)

proud
prow
prowl(ed)

* *

powder(ed)
power(ed)

profound
pronounce(d)
proudly
prowess

* * *

powerful(ly)

pronouncement
pronouncing

* * * *

powerfully

R

*

round
rouse(d)
rout

* *

rebound
renown(ed)

rounded
rounders
rounding
roundup
router
rowdy(-ier,-iest)

* * *

roundabout

* * * *

In these words you can hear the vowel sound ou as in owl

*

scour(ed)
scout
scowl(ed)
scrounge(d)

shout
shower(ed)
shroud

slouch(es)
slouched

snout

sound
sour(ed)
south
sow

spout
sprout

stout

* *

Saudi

scoundrel
scourer
scouring

shower(ed)
showery

sounded
sounding
southward

surmount
surround

* * *

showery

surrounded
surroundings

* * * *

T

*

thou

towel(led)
tower(ed)
town

trout
trowel(led)

* *

thousand
thousandth

tousle(d)

towel(led)
towelling
tower(ed)
towering

trousers
trowel(led)
trowelling

* * *

towelling
towering

trowelling

* * * *

V

*

* *

* * *

* * * *

vouch(es)
vouched
vow(ed)
vowel

voucher
*vouchers (more than
    one voucher)
*vouches (does vouch)
vowel

W

*

* *

* * *

* * * *

wound

In these words you can hear the vowel sound ou as in owl

Use these pages to make a note of words you find especially useful.

Useful Words

Useful Words

Useful Words

Useful Words

Useful Words

Useful Words

Useful Words

Useful Words

Useful Words

Useful Words

Useful Words

Useful Words

Useful Words